Trophy Trout Streams
of the Northeast

Trophy Trout Streams
of the Northeast

Edited by Jim Capossela

Northeast Sportsman's Press,
Tarrytown, New York

Stackpole Books,
Harrisburg, Pennsylvania

Library of Congress Cataloging-In-Publication Data

Trophy Trout Streams of the Northeast / edited by Jim Capossela.
    p.   cm.
ISBN 0-8117-4037-4 : $14.95
1. Trout fishing — Northeastern States. 2. Fly fishing -
-Northeastern States. I. Capossela, Jim.
SH688.N37T76 1990
799.1'755—dc20   90-28308
                                                                    CIP

Maps drawn by Jim Capossela
Photo on preceding pages by Ken Allen
Cover design by Jill Campbell
Sections edited by Bob Zajac

Published by Stackpole Books and Northeast Sportsman's Press

Distributed by Stackpole Books
Cameron & Kelker Streets
P.O. Box 1831
Harrisburg, Pennsylvania 17105

Printed in the United States of America
10-9-8-7-6-5-4-3-2-1

Warning!

Various State Departments of Health have determined that certain rivers in this book or portions of those rivers contain potentially harmful levels of toxic chemicals. Before you eat the fish from any of the waters discussed in this book, it is recommended that you find out what health advisories, if any, are in effect. Usually, the state's fisheries or conservation department will be helpful in providing such information

Table of Contents

Introduction

You hold in your hands somewhere between 300 and 400 years worth of knowledge about the best public-accessible trout streams in the northeast. Every author in this book was selected for his intimate, first-hand relationship with "his" river. To my knowledge, not a writer herein has fished his particular creek for a span of less than 10 years. Many have 20 to 40 years experience with their rivers. A few were born almost literally alongside theirs.

And what a four-star tour you are given! Start up north, with three of the best writers in Maine, and fish for wild brook trout and leaping landlocked salmon in the wildest part of the region. Work your way through Vermont and New Hampshire and fish big and small waters for brilliant rainbows, wild brookies and hook-jawed browns. Cross over into the Adirondacks and fish tumbling waters in a majestic setting. Work your way south to the "cradle," the Catskill Mountains with their trout rivers nonpareil. Make a quick detour to Connecticut to fish the legendary Housey. And if you're still not sated, cross the border into Pennsy and wander both spring creeks and freestone streams of national acclaim.

Do it all in one season, from early brown stones to autumn *Isonychias*? Ah, it's a compelling thought, a tempting odyssey, the very stuff of divorce.

An ordinary state road map or atlas of such maps should get you to the general vicinity. The stream maps in this book are intended to show as much local detail as possible, chiefly villages and cities, local highways and roads, interstates where they enter the picture, certain points of interest, and—in some instances—names of the famous pools. The maps are at varying scales (and their specific content varies somewhat too) but collectively, they serve to free the text from those interminable directions which dominate so many guide books. If you still feel disoriented, I highly recommend to you the fairly new 1:100,000 scale U.S.G.S. maps in their planimetric version.

For walk-in fishing, especially in the remoter areas, you'd be wise to purchase the standard topos of the areas: the 1:24,000 scale maps.

Each writer here is on his own. While I have fished about half of these streams, a big plus in keeping the troops honest, there was no practical way to police every sentence. The accuracy of each chapter was the direct responsibility of its author—and I stand behind the two I wrote.

But enough nattering. It's time for some hard information mixed in with a few stories of soft evenings and fleeting hatches. Start the journey in your armchair, if you will, but bring the book with you to help make those fireside fantasies come true. -

J.C.

Important Notes on the Text

Entomological terms are an editor's nightmare. As rich as the idiom of the fly fisher is, it is also that confusing. Some insects have common names and some don't. Some are called by their genus name and some by their species name. Many artificial flies are called by the same name as the fly itself. In many cases, the artificial fly, or the common name of the real thing has a proper noun.

Establishing a style sheet to deal with all this is not easy. Here's how we've done it in this book. It is at odds with what you'll see in a great many fly fishing books, but I believe it is the most sensible way.

All Latin names of organisms (except on these two pages) are italicized. The genus has a capital first letter and the species name has a lower case first letter. The species name always has a lower case first letter, even if that name begins a sentence.

All common names of organisms have lower case first letters, except those that are proper names. Hence: blue quill, brown trout, whitetail deer; but March brown, Atlantic salmon, American shad.

All established patterns have initial caps. Thus, in referring to specific artificial flies: Quill Gordon, Hendrickson, Muddler Minnow. In those instances when we are referring to a fly pattern that is not a distinct and established pattern, we use lower case first letters. Hence: blue winged olive, dark caddis, spider. What do you do, though, when it's not quite clear whether a pattern is distinct and established? Here, we feel common sense must prevail. For example, the popular salmon fly, the bomber, is tied so many different ways that we use a lower case first letter. But we give the Muddler Minnow initial caps since it is usually tied a certain way even though there are variations on that dressing.

We said that all Latin names are italicized. When a Latin name has been abridged and/or bastardized, though, we don't italicize it. A good example is tricos or trikes. These get lower case initial letters.

An interesting question arises when a fly pattern has been named after a person. Examples: White Wulff, Hendrickson, Light Cahill. We've already stated that we assign initial caps to established fly patterns. But what do you do when you are referring to an insect the pattern for which was named after a person? Do you make it (in reference to the insect) light Cahill, Hendrickson, quill Gordon? Or light cahill, hendrickson, and quill gordon? We choose to do the latter. The reasons are involved and we'll spare you that discussion. You're probably confused enough.

MAP LEGEND

River or stream. Arrows show direction of flow

Interstate highway

All other roads

Trail unless otherwise marked

Canoe carry or ferry

Railroad

Boundary

(12) Route number

Canoe Launch Or Take-Out Point

Point of interest

(P) Parking

Camping

Note: Only select parking areas and canoe launch areas are shown on the maps in this book. With few exceptions, only state (public) campgrounds are shown. Generally, county and local roads are not named. For map clarity, not all existing roads are shown.

One

The Allagash
by Bob Cram

It was one of those unusual sunsets, with everything, forest and grass, rocks and river, assuming a unique golden glow, like burnished brass in soft lamplight.

I was casting a Pink Lady Wulff, a bastardized fly created by a friend, toward the edges of the fast water. The high-floating fly bobbed and danced in eddies and cross currents before disappearing in a small swirl. Lifting the rod tip, I felt the solid tug of another Allagash River brookie, my ninth in 12 casts.

This fish used the current to good effect, but after a hectic few minutes of give and take, I slid the net under 15 inches of brilliantly hued eastern brook trout. I thought of my camera on the bank behind me, but the fish was tired. Easing the fly from its lip, I watched it fin slowly back into the depths of the pool.

From where I stood, in thigh deep water, angling upstream, the stolid wooden edifice of Churchill Dam a hundred yards away blocked the outlet of Heron Lake at the very head of Maine's Allagash River. Behind me, downstream, the river entered the turmoil of Chase Rapids, beginning a long, convoluted journey northward toward its junction with the St. John River near the Canadian border more than 60 miles away.

I never tire of fishing the Allagash River system. Its combination of remoteness, controlled access, and well balanced fishing regulations make it stand out among New England's trophy trout waters.

The Allagash is not just a river. It is an entire lake, stream, and river system, sprawling across more than a dozen townships in the wilderness area of northwestern Maine. The region's colorful history, varied ecosystem, and management practices combine to make fishing the Allagash as complex or as simple an experience as the angler desires.

The Allagash drainage is located in the nearly three million acres of forest land administered by the North Maine Woods organization, an agency representing the region's major landowners. Access is controlled by a system of strategically located gates and a fee is charged. Since gate and camping fees may change from year to year, sportsmen interested in up-to-date information should contact North Maine Woods, P.O. Box 382, Ashland, ME 04732.

In 1966 the people of Maine voted by referendum to create the Allagash Wilderness Waterway, preserving for all time the unique character of the lakes and river which make up this system. It was the first time in the history of the country that an entire river system was removed from the pressures of development and preserved for posterity. The Waterway is administered by the state Bureau of Parks & Recreation, which stations rangers at strategic locations throughout the region. Information concerning regulations and fees for Waterway use can be obtained from the Bureau of Parks & Recreation, Dept. of Conservation, Statehouse Station #22, Augusta, ME 04333.

The Allagash Chain begins with Allagash and Telos lakes and Round Pond which flow into Chamberlain, the largest lake in the system. The combined runoff of these waters empties through Lock Dam on Chamberlain into the adjoining lakes of Eagle and Churchill. North of Churchill, through a narrow opening called The Jaws, lies tiny Heron Lake, the backwater of Churchill Dam, which is at the head of the Allagash River itself.

The Allagash system contains a variety of fish, both game and non-game species, including brook trout, lake trout, hornpout (brown bullhead), lake whitefish, round whitefish, white sucker, and longnose sucker. Minnow species include the blacknose dace, blacknose shiner, pearl dace, redbelly dace, finescale dace, common shiner, and both creek and lake chub.

Fishermen usually concentrate on brook trout and lake trout in the lakes and brook trout in the river. Landlocked salmon can also be caught below Allagash Falls in the lower Allagash River.

Fishing the river is a major undertaking. Because of its remoteness, a trip involving several days is required. Camping facilities are very basic with each site along the Waterway containing simply a table, fire ring, and outhouse. A

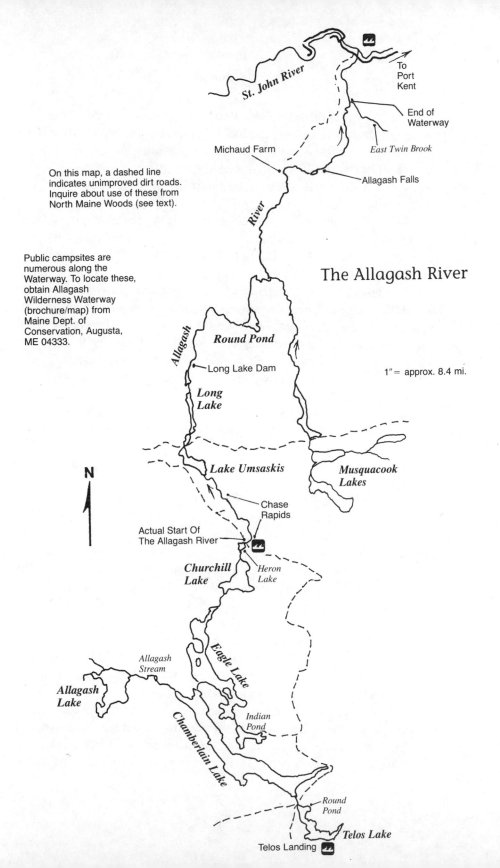

St. John River

To
Port
Kent

End of
Waterway

Michaud Farm

East Twin Brook

Allagash Falls

On this map, a dashed line
indicates unimproved dirt roads.
Inquire about use of these from
North Maine Woods (see text).

River

Public campsites are
numerous along the
Waterway. To locate these,
obtain Allagash
Wilderness Waterway
(brochure/map) from
Maine Dept. of
Conservation, Augusta,
ME 04333.

Allagash

Round Pond

Long Lake Dam

*Long
Lake*

1″ = approx. 8.4 mi.

The Allagash River

N

Lake Umsaskis

*Musquacook
Lakes*

Chase
Rapids

Actual Start Of
The Allagash River

*Churchill
Lake*

*Heron
Lake*

*Allagash
Stream*

Eagle Lake

*Allagash
Lake*

*Indian
Pond*

Chamberlain Lake

*Round
Pond*

Telos Lake

Telos Landing

good quality tent with a serviceable air mattress makes camping comfortable enough and most of the sites are located at spots combining high and dry elevations with scenic views and pleasant surroundings.

Since fishing the Allagash involves more than just throwing some gear into the car and driving to the river, detailed planning is the best way to ensure that your trip will be successful.

Most people fish the Allagash system while on canoe/camping expeditions, since direct vehicle access is limited to a few short sections of the river and lakes system. The individual or party that wants to experience the fishing and camping without all the bother of planning the entire trip might do well to hire a guide. Guides can plan each day's adventure, provide equipment (including canoes), cook the meals, and do the other mundane camp chores that free the sportsman for more fishing, sightseeing, or whatever.

Two types of guides operate on the Allagash: the recreational guide, who concentrates on the canoeing and camping experience, and the fishing guide whose principal aim is to show his clients the area's best fishing. Reputable Allagash guides are numerous, but the easiest way to select one is by checking the ads for such services in *The Maine Sportsman,* a monthly newspaper covering fishing and hunting in the Pine Tree State. The address is The Maine Sportsman, P.O. Box 910, Yarmouth, Maine 04096.

If you plan on doing the whole 100-mile trip, give yourself at least 10 days or, better yet, two weeks. The canoe trip can be easily completed in one week, but that doesn't allow for much fishing time.

The two principal put-in spots for an Allagash canoe trip are Chamberlain Thoroughfare Bridge, between Chamberlain Lake and Round Pond, and Churchill Dam at the head of the Allagash River itself. The first location is for those who want to explore the entire lake system as well as the river, while Churchill Dam is for sportsmen who want to concentrate on the river itself. The normal take-out point for both trips is at Allagash Village where the Allagash River empties into the St. John.

From Lock Dam on Chamberlain northward the only watercraft allowed on the Allagash Waterway are canoes with motors no larger than 10 horsepower. On Allagash Lake and Allagash Stream between Chamberlain and Allagash lakes, only canoes without motors are allowed.

It is entirely possible to do an Allagash canoe trip without a guide. Anyone with some experience at handling a canoe can make the trip. The worst stretch of whitewater on the river is at Chase Rapids just below Churchill Dam. This section is classified as a sharp Class II rapids and for those who don't wish to try it, the ranger at the dam will portage you, your canoe and your equipment around Chase Rapids for a small fee. Alternatively, he will portage just your gear so you can run the rapids in empty canoes.

The best fishing in the Allagash system is during the month after ice-out, which usually occurs on the big lakes about the first week of May. From mid-June to September, lower, warmer water makes the fish less active and the best action will take place near the mouths of cold water tributaries and in the deeper, colder levels of the lakes. Fly hatches appear sporadically throughout the summer, however, and for the fly fisherman, these times provide some of the best fishing of the year.

September's cooler waters again see an increase in fishing activity up through the season closing on September 30.

Good fishing spots abound on the river. Overfishing is not a problem since a majority of its visitors are canoe campers, most of whom fish casually

The edges of faster water harbor late season brookies on the Allagash. Churchill Dam is in the background.

or not at all. Like any angler, I have favorite spots on the river which have produced for me time after time.

The pool below Churchill Dam is a good spot. Beginning in mid to late April, high, cold, often roily water makes fishing slow, but when you catch a fish, it's usually a big one. Three and four pound brook trout aren't uncommon here in the early spring.

Fishing slow and deep at the tail end of the current with minnow imitating crank baits works very well. The fly fisherman should fish in the same fashion, with a sinking line and streamers such as Slaymaker's Little Brook Trout, Gray or Black Ghost, or a Warden's Worry. Anything which simulates a smelt, the trout's primary early spring forage fish, will bring results.

By mid-June, as the water drops and warms, spin fishermen switch to spoons like the Weeping Willow, Super Duper, or Swedish Pimple. Fly casters begin enjoying success with drys the likes of the Adams, Hornberg, Hendrickson, Quill Gordon, Grasshopper, and Elk Hair Caddis.

Below the pool, the first 1½ miles of Chase Rapids ends in the deep, tannin-stained waters of Big Eddy. The fast water sections contain many backwater areas and rock-lined pools which harbor brook trout. Fishing can be difficult in the strong current and a wading staff is a definite advantage. While a good path follows the high ground above the west bank, the best fishing access is along the eastern shore.

Big Eddy is deep and dark. In early spring it contains the same large, brightly speckled fish as the pool below the dam, and it can be fished in much the same fashion.

The problem is in finding adequate footing to cast. Alders overhang deep water along the sides. The only decent fishing position is from upstream in the last of the fast water. Footing is treacherous so care is advised.

Between Big Eddy and Umsaskis Lake lie more than seven miles of flat water interspersed with light rapids. Fishing access to this stretch and for most of the rest of the river is easiest by canoe.

Umsaskis Marsh, where Chase Rapids empties into Umsaskis Lake, can be very productive fishing by canoe, especially with a fly rod. This area of narrow channels and grassy islands is host to many late evening hatches and on especially still, hot afternoons, the surface is sometimes covered with the dimples of feeding trout.

Umsaskis Marsh is an interesting area to explore by canoe. Formed by a millennia of silt and debris washed down by Chase Rapids, it is home to a myriad of wildlife, including moose, whitetail deer, many species of ducks, and Canada geese. It's quite a thrill to paddle along one of these winding channels, only to find your way suddenly blocked by a giant bull moose. In such cases, discretion on your part is highly advisable.

Umsaskis Lake flows northward through a narrow channel into Long Lake, aptly named since it is really just a long wide spot in the river. Long Lake flows into Harvey Pond at the outlet of which is the remains of Long Lake Dam, a logging-related structure built in 1907. All that remains of the dam are the flooring timbers and rock piers of the sluiceways.

Canoeists should exercise care at Long Lake Dam. It is possible to run the sluiceways but old abutment spikes working up from the underwater timbers can damage canoes. A friend put a three foot gouge in the bottom of his ABS canoe and took an unwelcome spill at this spot. The more prudent course is to either line the canoe through the western side, or carry around.

I've experienced excellent fishing above and below this dam. Both morning and evening hatches are common occurrences in the still waters above the dam, and the deep pool below can be productive at any time of the day.

Between Long Lake Dam and Henderson Brook Bridge the river follows deep runs interspersed with short stretches of easy fast water. Again, fishing from your canoe is the best for this type of water.

Below Henderson Brook Bridge the character of the river begins to change. More hilly terrain borders the river, while from the bridge to Round Pond, a distance of less than two miles, the river itself widens into a broad delta, trickling across gravel shoals which invite a fisherman to wade and cast. Moose are frequent visitors to this area and their large, bucket-sized tracks litter the bottom in some places.

Round Pond (different from the one named earlier), with the delta above and its outlet rapids below, is one of my favorite places on the Allagash. The pond itself is beautiful in the evening, with the forested hills looking down and the trout rising in the dying light. The delta area is a joy to wade, especially in the early morning or late evening when the lower angle of the sun's rays makes the trout less spooky in the shallow water. The outlet rapids, called Round Pond Rips, holds decent trout well into the warmer times of early summer, as they prowl this more heavily oxygenated water.

After Round Pond Rips the river enters a long, flat water section called Musquacook Deadwater where Musquacook Stream enters the Allagash. In spring this slow moving section produces good trout action and even in early summer, evening hatches can bring on a feeding frenzy.

Shallower rapids extend downriver after Musquacook Deadwater. I find it easier to fish these sections using a canoe with a chain for an anchor. A four foot length of heavy chain with an anchor rope tied to one end makes a really effective anchor. The distribution of weight as the chain lays flat on the bottom allows it to hold in some pretty fast water and the beauty of it is, it seldom gets

Eye-popping Maine squaretails, such as this 4-pounder, still haunt the remoter sections of the Allagash Waterway.

hung up. After one section of fast water is fished, a long tug on the rope slides the chain across the bottom and sets the canoe a ways downstream where it again fetches up, allowing new water to be fished.

Fifteen miles below Round Pond is the ranger station at Michaud Farm. All river parties must check in here before continuing on. Below Michaud Farm is a three mile stretch of calm water threading its way through islands dotted with overhanging trees reminiscent of a southern river. It is a deceiving calm which leads up to Allagash Falls, a 40-foot drop with the mandatory carry on the east side.

Immediately below Allagash Falls are deep pools which extend about a quarter mile downstream and harbor some decent brook trout and the occasional landlocked salmon. Canoe fishermen should beware of the hydraulics created at the foot of the falls.

Downstream from the falls, the character of the river changes once again. It's almost as though it realizes the nearness of civilization. Here the river flattens out and becomes broader and shallower still. In the low water of summer it can become a chore to pick a canoe channel through the shoals, but a wading fisherman can have good luck along this section. Fourteen miles from Allagash Falls the river joins the St. John at Allagash Village.

The entire Allagash Wilderness Waterway is unique among eastern lake and river systems. No towns litter its shores, no ribbons of asphalt gleam darkly through the trees, no streetlights cast their artificial glow across the water. The fisherman may find other people along the river and lakes, but they will be, for the most part, kindred spirits, whose appreciation of the natural environment matches his own.

A river system far from any towns, in a wild setting, with plenty of scrappy trout. It seems almost too good to be true. But it isn't.

Bob Cram is Allagash Regional Columnist and Handguns columnist for *The Maine Sportsman*. He has published outdoor pieces in various state and local newspapers, including the *Bangor Daily News*, Maine's largest, and written articles for such magazines as *Fur-Fish-Game* and *New England Game & Fish*. He is a registered Maine Master Guide who regularly fishes Maine's Allagash River.

Two

The Penobscot
by Ken Allen

The mighty Penobscot River drains 8,765 square miles, making it the state's largest river system, and it is huge. Few fishermen live long enough to sample all of this river's varied fishing opportunities, which include everything from native brook trout to landlocked salmon to lunker smallmouth bass to the lordly Atlantic salmon to sea-run striped bass.

In the extreme upper reaches, brook trout attract anglers, but fishing success depends entirely upon water levels, which are typically good from late May to the end of June. As the river's flow dwindles under summer's glaring sun, chubs take over pools and runs where brook trout flourished during the spring. Then, it's a sport of fishing small feeder brooks and occasional spring holes in the river.

In the lower reaches, beginning around the town of Medway where the East Branch joins the West Branch of the Penobscot, smallmouth bass grow fat and sassy because of limited to nonexistent fishing pressure. In Maine, salmonids are king, and natives look at bass as trash fish.

In the 75-mile stretch of river between Medway and Veazie, bass are abundant, but occasional spring holes hold large brook trout. This isn't classic fly-fishing water for trout, however. It's a hit or miss affair in a setting that definitely looks like bass water, and development increases dramatically as you near Veazie and then the Queen City, Bangor.

The West Branch of the Penobscot between Seboomook Lake and Chesuncook Lake and between Ripogenus Dam and the Nesowadnehunk

Deadwater offers grand sport for folks interested in the occasional brook trout and abundant landlocked salmon. The latter species has made these stretches among the most storied waters in the Northeast. The East Branch of the Penobscot between Grand Lake Mattagamon and its confluence with the Seboeis River produces good brook trout and landlocked salmon fishing, but the landlocks run smaller than in the West Branch below Ripogenus. It's a wild setting, however, with spectacular rapids and mountain backdrops.

A landlocked salmon is taxonomically identical to its anadromous cousin, the Atlantic salmon. Atlantics spend the early part of their lives in streams and rivers, migrate as smolts to the ocean for its rich food resources, spend one or two years at sea, and then return to spawn. Landlocks do not migrate to the ocean, however, but live their life cycle in inland waters. Most strains of landlocks look identical to Atlantics, and pound for pound, these smaller versions fight just as hard with reel-screeching runs and twisting leaps.

Along these blue-ribbon stretches of river, development remains light to nonexistent, but paper-company roads offer easy access. Despite the roads paralleling these waters, though, it's a high-quality fishery because of strict regulations, which vary on different sections of the river and which furthermore, become more stringent in late summer and early fall when fish near spawning time. Artificial lures, fly fishing only, small bag limits, and longer minimum length limits all help maintain a quality fishery. (Always check Maine's Open Water Fishing Regulations before fishing these waters. The laws are complicated and subject to change.)

WEST BRANCH— RIPOGENUS DAM TO NESOWADNEHUNK DEADWATER

Through the years, a fisherman may have the great pleasure of learning one river intimately, or at least a chosen part of one, and this section between Ripogenus Dam and the Nesowadnehunk Deadwater (approximately six miles) is such a place for me.

Here, this river among rivers slides, rushes, tumbles, and churns between wooded hills. So many of its pools hold memories, memories stretching down through the years, but one thought always dominates my reveries—landlocked salmon.

Landlocks attract fly fishermen to this area southwest of Baxter Park, and the particular strain of landlocks in the river holds a special appeal.

In many watersheds, landlocked salmon spend the first stages of their young lives in flowing water, but at a certain time, they move to the still water of lakes or ponds to spend their adult years. They only return to rivers and streams to spawn, except during the limited spring periods when they might chase spawning rainbow smelts up or downstream, or when they are attracted by fresh, flowing water after a good rain.

In that famous stretch of the West Branch below Ripogenus Dam, wading almost always calls for caution—and felt soles.

The landlocks in this stretch of the Penobscot, however, do not have a lake or pond in which to spend their adult lives. They live from birth to death in the powerful currents of the river, and many anglers swear that because of this fact, landlocks below Ripogenus Dam fight harder than any other landlock that swims.

This stretch does have brook trout, though, and some of them grow to trophy sizes in the 5-pound class, and heavier. Brook trout do interest some anglers, but they are secondary to most folks on the West Branch below Ripogenus. Two things may contribute to this.

First, the West Branch's fame began with landlocks, and that's why anglers come, to catch a silver leaper. A brook trout is always a welcome bonus, but salmon remain the number one consideration.

Second, the big brookies have become exceptionally wary because of the intense fishing pressure. Anyone who claims brook trout are dumb has spent too much time on remote, lightly fished waters or on stocked streams or ponds, fishing for hatchery pets. These West Branch trout are intelligent with a capital I, so success begins with light tippets and exact imitations and ends with a definite commitment to catching brook trout. The latter thought is all important.

A number of years ago I fished the Steep Bank Pool below the Big Eddy nearly every evening through two summers. On the south shore at the tail end of the pool, near a lone pine, two or three submerged boulders always held a lunker brookie, but the lie presented a real obstacle to a decent presentation. Strong eddies and currents created a line drag that pulled the fly wildly.

Above this lie, salmon held on the edge of a drop-off near shore, farther out in the river behind boulders, and along a gravel bar formed by the converging currents of the river and a brook. During a typical evening hatch, landlocks offered a respectable chance of hooking into a decent-sized fish, even a trophy.

The brook trout behind the boulders, though, provided me with nothing but frustration. During one summer that I spent on this pool, a particular trout rose under my dry fly more than once. It would drift back with the current just an inch or two under my fly, and if the light was right, I could clearly see the vermiculations on its back. But it never took my dry fly, even when I used a long, slack tippet so the fly would drift well for six or eight feet.

Once, it hit a Gray Ghost Marabou with a short strike; another time, it took a Hare's Ear, but broke my tippet on the boulder.

Despite my tricks and techniques, the summer ended without my landing the lunker. Although I had cut my teeth on a river with big, wary browns, they didn't prepare me for these Penobscot trophy brook trout.

My commitment, I must say, did lack that 100 percent devotion. The landlocks kept me too interested to spend the needed time and energy for a trophy brookie.

Below the Steep Bank Pool on the north shore, a brook from Fowler Pond comes into the river. Here, a cove at the brook's mouth holds trout, and the chances of catching fish in the 8- to 15-inch range are better, much better. Even here, though, the brookies are selective and wary.

This stretch of the West Branch has become the most storied on the river, and anyone who reads outdoor magazines probably has seen at least one article about it. Interestingly enough, Ripogenus Dam is directly responsible for this wonderful landlocked salmon and brook trout fishery.

This 96-foot-high dam holds back the waters of Chesuncook, Maine's third largest lake. Because the river flows from a huge pipe near the dam's bottom, the water remains cold throughout the summer, creating ideal habitat for salmonids, smelts, and aquatic insect life.

Also, rivers and streams below impoundments tend to be exceptionally fertile because of the nutrients that still water accumulates. Maine salmonid waters are generally sterile, but these blue-ribbon sections of the West and East Branch lie below dams. It makes all the difference in the fertility of these waters.

This fecundity is apparent to anyone who has fished the West Branch. Insect hatches are heavy and the trout and salmon are butterballs. For instance, I have caught 20-inch landlocked salmon that weighed four pounds. In many Maine waters, a fish may have to be 23 to 24 inches long before reaching the four-pound mark. The Penobscot salmon look like footballs.

The most popular pool on this section is the Big Eddy. It can be fished from shore, or more appropriately, from a canoe. Anyone venturing out on this pool, however, better know how to use a boat or canoe. The currents are powerful and this pool is twice the size of a football field.

Other popular pools are the Little Eddy and Steep Bank Pool, and the former is a very dangerous place to put a canoe or boat, the only feasible way to fish it. Immediately below the Little Eddy lies a ferocious set of rapids.

These three pools are easy to find, and the two eddies are marked with signs and campsites. The Steepbank lies just below the Big Eddy. A powerline comes close to the river, so it's all open instead of woods. This pool is easy to see.

The Steepbank Pool has a characteristic so common on this river. Patches of slick water float on the surface with the current, and small, merry, undulating waves surround these flat spots. My favorite technique is to drop a dry fly onto these floating slicks and have it drift drag free as far as possible. If I can get a 20-foot float, I'm happy. To me, that's one of the keys to success on this river.

When you wade into the Steepbank Pool on the south side of the river, the most popular side because it's close to the highway, salmon lie along a drop-off 10 or 15 feet from the shoreline, depending on water level. This makes the pool easy to wade and fish.

The north shore of this pool, however, is so typical of the river. You step off the bank into waist-deep water and a powerful current. The bottom often has basketball-sized and bigger rocks, so wading is seldom easy. You can feel the current tearing at your legs, footing, even soul. If any river could sweep you away—body and mind—this is the one. Felt-soled waders, cleats, and a wading staff make sense on many pools.

Insect hatches are prolific. For dry flies, make sure to have a good selection of Elk Hair Caddises, Compara-duns, Henryville Specials, Flick March Browns, and a Hornberg-style fly tied with a yellow body, wood duck wings, and brown and grizzly hackles. This river has heavy hendrickson, sulfur dun, and blue-wing olive hatches. Fly choices should be between size 10 and 22.

One well-known hatch is a size 14 mottled brown caddis fly. To match this wonderful hatch, I've used the above Hornberg-style fly, a Flick March Brown (minus the tail and tied with downwings), or an Elk Hair Caddis with a tan body, cree palmering, and natural brown deer hair for a wing. My favorite of the three is the Elk Hair Caddis because of its durability and floating qualities.

Smelt imitations such as a Supervisor, Jerry's Smelt, Red Gray Ghost, or Nine-three also are important in sizes 2 through 6 on 8x-long-shank hooks. Smelts are a favorite food of landlocks, and typically, salmon are feeding on smelts early in the season.

Nymph fishing here often means matching the hatch, so sparkle caddis nymphs, stoneflies, Flick March Brown, Flick Hendrickson, Hare's Ear, and Zug Bug all have their place in sizes 10 through 18.

Another popular fly on this river is a wet fly series in varying colors. The body is fur dubbed, the hackle is semi-dry-fly style, and the wing is a breast feather from a duck, tied flat. A favorite pattern has a rust-brown body, dark ginger hackle, and a white-tipped, rust-colored breast feather from a mallard.

You can float parts of this river in a drift boat or canoe, but several portages for a canoe are a must. The rapids are impassable in anything short of a covered canoe with flotation bags and two expert paddlers. Most anglers drive their cars to pools and put the canoes in rather than running the river with its several portages.

Drift boats are uncommon in Maine so you don't see many of them. Some folks like that scarcity just fine. Some rivers, the Penobscot included, have sections that cannot be fished except with a drift boat. These sanctuaries offer salmon and trout a place to get away from anglers, and drift boats eliminate that safety zone.

Anglers take fish on this section from April 1 to September 30, even though snow covers the ground in early April. June and September generally are the best months.

A sporting camp and campsites exist on this stretch of river, but I never stay at them. It is a popular area for people taking rubber-rafting trips. They insist on partying the night away, and sleep is impossible under these circumstances. I prefer to stay in Millinocket, a 30- to 45-minute drive away. This town has several motels.

From April 1 to August 15, artificial lures only is the regulation, which does allow for spin fishing. You seldom see a spin fisherman on this river, however.

The daily limit is one salmon and the minimum length is 16 inches (general law requires a 14-inch minimum length for salmon on most Maine waters). The bag limit on brook trout falls under the general-law provisions and you can take 10 of them daily (nine if a salmon is in your bag limit). From August 16 to September 30 it's fly fishing only, and the daily limit is one trout or one salmon. In Maine, the daily limit and possession limit are the same. In other words, you can't take one salmon or 10 brookies a day, freeze them, and have more than the daily bag limit in your possession at any one time. Realize that all these laws are subject to change.

SEBOOMOOK LAKE TO CHESUNCOOK LAKE

This section of the West Branch stretches for approximately 24 miles, and much of it is flat, slow-moving water reminiscent of a bass stream—not a trout and salmon stream. A dam does control water levels, but it's such a long section that summer's glaring sun sends brook trout into spring holes and up feeder streams and brooks. It also forces adult salmon to head for the deep waters of lakes or springs or into the limited quick waters below Seboomook Dam.

When the spring run-off subsides in early June and the river flows at an optimal level for fishing until (hopefully) early July, salmon and trout angling can be good just below Seboomook Lake in a big pool and a series of runs and smaller pools for the first 500 yards below the dam. This is my favorite section of this 24-mile stretch. Another good spot is around the Rolls Dam approximately three miles downstream from Seboomook Dam.

Fish tend to be less selective here than in the Ripogenus stretch, so fly choice becomes less crucial. Folks who fish this section often like nymphs and Wooly Worms in yellow and green hues in sizes 8 through 12. Smelt imitations and Muddler Minnows, the standard pattern, and marabous are also good choices.

In September, cooler water temperatures and the spawning urge bring trout and salmon into the river. Salmon and trout run up from Chesuncook

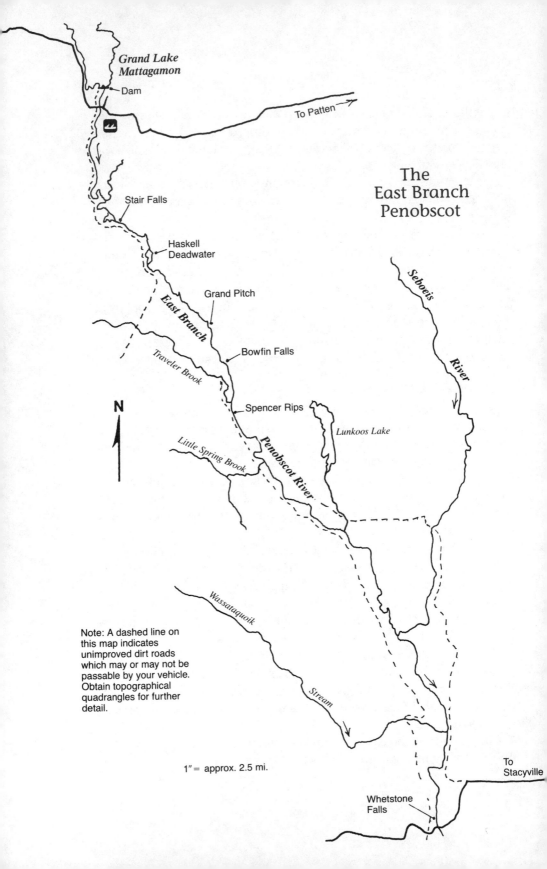

Grand Lake
Mattagamon

Dam

To Patten

The
East Branch
Penobscot

Stair Falls

Haskell
Deadwater

Grand Pitch

East Branch

Traveler Brook

Bowfin Falls

Seboeis

River

Spencer Rips

Lunkoos Lake

N

Little Spring Brook

Penobscot River

Wassataquoik

Note: A dashed line on
this map indicates
unimproved dirt roads
which may or may not be
passable by your vehicle.
Obtain topographical
quadrangles for further
detail.

Stream

1″ = approx. 2.5 mi.

To
Stacyville

Whetstone
Falls

and some may go all the way to the Seboomook Dam. Other fish may come from Lobster Lake up Lobster Stream to enter the West Branch.

Fish also drop out of Seboomook Lake over the dam or through a gate. No fishway exists, however, so it's a one-way street. No fish coming from Seboomook Lake can ever go back, and it's a shame the dam owner isn't forced by law to install a state-of-the-art fishway to remedy this unfortunate situation.

The runs and pools below Seboomook can produce top action in September, and so can the Rolls Dam downstream. Another favorite spot is the Fox Hole on the Chesuncook end of this stretch. The long deadwater sections also hold salmon and trout, but it can be a hit-or-miss affair.

Although this section lacks the fishing potential and beauty of the river below Ripogenus, fishing pressure is much lighter and forest campsites dot the river. Another plus is the float trip that begins at the Rolls Dam and ends anywhere you want to take out between there and Chesuncook. The water is flat and the only rapids are light.

Fishing from April 1 to August 15 is artificial lures only, and the daily bag limit on salmon is one fish. During this season the general-law bag limit prevails for brook trout, so anglers may keep 10 daily, nine if a salmon is in the bag limit. From August 16 to September 30 it's fly fishing only and the daily limit is one salmon or one trout.

EAST BRANCH—
GRAND LAKE MATTAGAMON TO SEBOEIS RIVER

Now we move from the West Branch of the Penobscot to the East Branch. The approximately 20 miles of river in this section flow through forests, part of it stunning white birch. Often, scenic mountains rise into view, including majestic Katahdin, the state's highest mountain at 5,267 feet. This area is Maine at its finest and the East Branch has landlocked salmon and a better opportunity for brook trout than the West Branch offers. In short, it's a grand place to visit.

The salmon run smaller than on the West Branch, and a one to two pounder is better than average. Brook trout get up to three and four pounds, and with rare exception, heavier. Brookies in the 12- to 15-inch range are somewhat common when water levels are right, and a string of them won't raise an eyebrow. On most of Maine's waters, a 15-incher is a trophy.

A dam on Grand Lake Mattagamon controls the water level, so fishermen are often dependent on the dam keeper, but generally, June and early July and again in September are optimal times to fish this lovely stretch. September sees spawning brookies and salmon, and the chance exists to hook into a real trophy, particularly a brook trout.

This water has heavy rapids, deep pools, and long deadwaters. It definitely is no place for a novice canoeist, and the only people attempting to run it should be experts with a daredevil nature. Fortunately, a road on the west shore parallels part of this section, and a trail covers the rest.

On the Grand Lake Mattagamon end, the road begins immediately west of the bridge and goes approximately 5 ⅔ miles downstream. The river is usually within a two to three minute walk of the road, and a top spot is the Haskell Deadwater right at the spot where the road veers away from the river. A trail (a four-wheel drive can go over parts of this in certain seasons) continues along the river here. Many lovely pools lie on this stretch, often at the head or foot of raging rapids. It's a calendar-photo river.

On the Seboeis River end, travel north on Route 11 from Medway (Exit 59 on Interstate 95) for approximately 20 miles and turn left at a 90 degree curve in the highway. It's the only major left. At a Y in this road, bear left and travel for one to two miles. Cross the river here and take a right onto the road paralleling the river. After approximately three miles, a bridge crosses Wassataquoik Stream. Continue for another three miles. The road is within a half-mile of the river. Sometimes it comes much closer, but it's never farther than a half-mile.

In recent years, the first few miles below Mattagamon have produced the best fishing, and fisheries biologists for the Maine Department of Inland Fisheries and Wildlife blame acid rain for the problems on the Seboeis end. The theory sounds plausible. Sharp mountainsides on the lower end create a much faster run-off of rain water, which in turn can create "acid pulses." On the upper end, this problem is much less acute. Heavy fishing pressure is also cited as a reason for the declining fishery. Probably, both factors contribute. Unfortunately, at the time of this writing, general fishing laws prevail on much of the East Branch, which in my view are much too liberal to provide a quality fishery under today's heavy fishing pressure.

Felt sole waders are a must and a wading staff is helpful. A fall above some of these heavy rapids would surely be fatal.

This river has excellent *Ephemerella* and *Stenonema* habitat, so bring along a good collection of Hendricksons, Red Quills, Blue-winged Olives, March Browns and Gray Foxes in sizes 10 through 18. Caddis hatches are also heavy so bring some caddis sparkle nymphs, Elk Hair Caddises, and Henryville Specials. Stonefly nymphs also work well here.

Smelt imitations, Muddlers in standard and marabous, and attractor patterns such as the Red and White, Mickey Finn and Wood Special have a place.

Campgrounds lie near Mattagamon Lake and campsites dot the river downstream.

From 150 feet below Mattagamon Dam to 2,000 feet down from the Route 159 bridge, it's artificial lures only. General law takes over from there down.

Anyone interested in fishing these waters should buy a copy of DeLorme's Maine Atlas and Gazetteer, DeLorme Mapping Company, P.O. Box 298, Freeport, ME 04032. This book of maps gives specific details of roads and trails in the area.

Because the West Branch sections are on paper company land, you must pay a small fee to travel and to camp on these roads.

Ken Allen is a full-time writer, registered Maine Master Guide, and editor for outdoor publications. In the past 17 years he has sold more than 1,000 articles to over 50 different magazines and newspapers, including *Fly Fishermen, Trout, Salt Water Sportsman, American Angler & Fly Tyer* and *Fly Rod & Reel.* He is also the author of several books, including *Cooking Wild* and *Guide to Upland Bird Hunting.*

Three

Maine Trilogy
by Al Raychard

The beautiful state of Maine is blessed with waters of every description, including some of the most significant trout and landlocked salmon rivers in America. But if you could choose just one good adjective to describe Maine's trout streams, it might be this one: short. There are a few exceptions of course (see Chapters One and Two). But often, Maine's premier trout and fly fishing streams are mere connecting links between two lakes or ponds. This does not diminish their appeal. It does, though, make discussing three of them in one chapter a feasible task.

Some offer consistent, predictable action throughout the season, while others reach a productive peak in late summer or fall as fish move out of the lakes to spawn. The rivers discussed in this chapter cover both categories. The Rapid River is one of Maine's most productive native brook trout and landlocked salmon flowages in terms of providing rather consistent action through the fishing season, while the Kennebago and Roach Rivers, although worth fishing whenever possible, have historically been "fall rivers," producing their best fish and most challenging opportunities in late summer and fall. Indeed, while each of these rivers can be considered short in miles, their aesthetics and quality angling are proof positive that length has little to do with providing an experience to be appreciated and long remembered.

RAPID RIVER
The Rapid River is located in Oxford County in Maine's western moun-

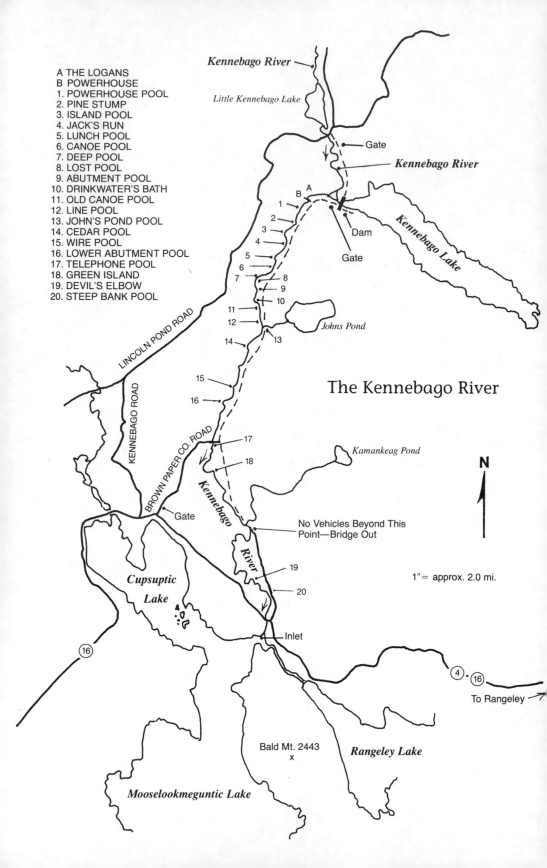

A THE LOGANS
B POWERHOUSE
1. POWERHOUSE POOL
2. PINE STUMP
3. ISLAND POOL
4. JACK'S RUN
5. LUNCH POOL
6. CANOE POOL
7. DEEP POOL
8. LOST POOL
9. ABUTMENT POOL
10. DRINKWATER'S BATH
11. OLD CANOE POOL
12. LINE POOL
13. JOHN'S POND POOL
14. CEDAR POOL
15. WIRE POOL
16. LOWER ABUTMENT POOL
17. TELEPHONE POOL
18. GREEN ISLAND
19. DEVIL'S ELBOW
20. STEEP BANK POOL

Kennebago River

Little Kennebago Lake

Gate

Kennebago River

Kennebago Lake

Dam

Gate

Johns Pond

The Kennebago River

LINCOLN POND ROAD

KENNEBAGO ROAD

BROWN PAPER CO. ROAD

Kamankeag Pond

N

1″ = approx. 2.0 mi.

Gate

Kennebago River

No Vehicles Beyond This
Point—Bridge Out

19

20

Cupsuptic Lake

Inlet

(16)

(4) (16)

To Rangeley

Bald Mt. 2443
x

Rangeley Lake

Mooselookmeguntic Lake

tains, about 25 miles southwest of Rangeley, and is just one of the legendary waters which helped to put this charming region on the map in the late 19th century. On the lower western shore of Lower Richardson Lake, one of several in the so-called "Rangeley chain," Middle Dam stands as a reminder of the great log driving days. Below that ancient barrier, now used to control water flow for generating power on the Androscoggin River system, the Rapid River begins its short but glorious journey.

No river in Maine is better named. From where it begins at Middle Dam to where it ceases to exist at Umbagog Lake on the Maine-New Hampshire border, the Rapid River travels just 4.5 miles, and drops 180 feet in that short distance for an average of 40 feet per mile. From start to finish, except for Pond-In-The-River where the current takes a hiatus, the Rapid is a continuous collection of rapids, riffles and runs separated by deep, dark mysterious pools, all holding native brook trout and landlocked salmon known to reach weights into the three and four pound class. The average fish is smaller, measured in inches rather than pounds. But the possibility of taking big fish along with the Rapid's swift current and consistent action, make it one of the most challenging and popular fishing retreats in western Maine.

Despite its relatively short length, the Rapid River offers no less than a dozen well known "pools" and fishing areas. All are reached by foot via the old "carry road" which pretty much parallels the river along much of its length from Middle Dam to Umbagog Lake. Some of the pools are marked with signs while others are not, but each is easy to find. The majority are fishable with chest waders or from rocks and boulders along the shoreline. The most heavily fished pools are those lying upstream of Pond-In-The-River, and include Dam Pool immediately below Middle Dam, Harbec Pool just downstream and Horsechop and Chub Pools just above the pond. The riffles above and just below the old barrier downstream of the pond known as "Lower Dam" are equally challenging and productive and offer more extensive wading opportunities. The area is perhaps a 45-minute hike from Middle Dam.

The Rapid is known for its season-long consistency. It continues to produce action on both brook trout and landlocked salmon in July and August (try nymphs and small wet flies) when other Maine rivers are typically slow. Due to its descent and the fact that water is released through Middle Dam right throughout the summer (to maintain a minimum flow as required by state law), the Rapid does not suffer from low or warm water conditions like some other Maine rivers. Until the middle or later parts of May, depending upon spring conditions, the river is high with run-off but can produce some big fish on traditional streamer and bucktail designs attached to a full-sinking or sink-tip line and short leaders in the three to four-pound test class.

Keep in mind that the river is full of smelt during the early spring so imitations such as the Grey Ghost, Black Ghost (either marabou or traditional design), Black Marabou, Yellow Marabou, Supervisor, Ballou Special and other classic designs work well. Sizes 4 to 10 are recommended, the larger ones doing best from late April through late May. The smaller offerings work better as water levels start to recede.

June and July are traditionally the peak fishing months on the Rapid River. During this time, starting about Memorial Day, try wet flies such as the Coachman, Hare's Ear, Leadwing Coachman, Picket Pin and Professor in sizes 6, 8, 10 and 12. Also try nymphal patterns such as the March Brown, Hendrickson, the Otter Nymph, Zug Bug, Tellico, Atherton Dark and other mayfly and caddis patterns in sizes 12 thru 16. These should produce fish whenever surface action is down.

Lower dam and Lower Dam Pool on the Rapid River.

The Rapid does, however, experience some wonderful and rather prolific insect hatches straight through the spring, summer and early fall. In fact, some of the best action in June and July will be found on the surface during a hatch which generally starts in the early afternoon hours or early evening. Sporadic hatches may occur at any time, and often do, offering a brief opportunity to work the surface during the morning hours.

As for dry offerings, many of the conventional and traditional designs used in the northeast work well. Rapid River landlocks and brook trout are not overly selective, but the fly fisherman must recognize where they are holding and be capable of getting the fly to them in proper fashion. Dry flies to try include the Adams, Grasshopper, Humpy, Mosquito, Hendrickson, March Brown, Light and Dark Cahill, Royal Wulff, Quill Gordon. Grey Fox, Henryville Special, Hairwing Caddis, Woodchuck Caddis and blue-wing olive. Flies as big as 10 to as little as 16 might be called for so bring a selection of dries in various sizes.

In August, surface action is pretty much limited to late afternoon, with hatches much more sporadic and sparse. Nymphs and wet flies perform well at this time, as they do in September. So do attractor type streamers, such as the Mickey Finn and Red and White. Typically, the action is slower during the last weeks of the season, but some of the biggest fish are caught at this time as the larger trout and salmon move into the river from Pond-In-The-River and Umbagog lake, in anticipation of the spawning season.

The Rapid River is restricted to fly fishing only along its entire length for the whole fishing season, which extends from April 1 through September 30. No catch-and-release regulations are in force on the river, although fishermen do return the majority of fish to the water. It is hoped that anyone visiting the Rapid River follows suit. Be sure to check the current fishing regulations for specific bag limits if fish are to be retained.

Compared to Maine's other top trout and salmon rivers, the Rapid receives less pressure largely due to its location and inconvenient accessibility. There is, however, a respectable contingent of dedicated Rapid River fly fishermen who fish it each season, and that number seems to be increasing. They accept, even appreciate the fact that the river is accessible only by boat from South Arm on the extreme south end of Lower Richardson Lake, for they know it is the lack of vehicular access which makes and has kept the Rapid River unique.

For those willing to make the effort of crossing the lake, a campground complete with general store, showers and boat ramp is located at South Arm, reached by paved road from Andover. On the river side, Lakewood Lodge offers clean cabins and meals in the traditional Rangeley fashion within short walking distance of the upper river. Arrangements can be made for the lodge to pick you up by boat for the journey "across lake," or you can take your own boat; launch at the state ramp just past the campground on the east side of the lake. Once you're at the lodge, they will arrange to bring you to the lower pools in case you don't care to make the trek by foot. Advance reservations are recommended for the lodge, particularly during the peak fishing weeks in June, July and early September.

KENNEBAGO RIVER

Few other rivers in the famous Rangeley region of western Maine, or in all of Maine for that matter, receive as much attention from fly fishermen during the fall as the Kennebago. Few are better known. Offering a variety of water characteristics, ranging from rapids and riffles to long stretches of smooth flowing current and deep, secretive pools (the vast majority of which can be easily waded) the Kennebago, bordered by black spruce and fir, is one of the most aesthetically pleasing rivers in the state. At certain times, it is also one of the most productive in terms of quality fly fishing for native brook trout and landlocked salmon.

In the traditional sense, the Kennebago River is considered a "fall run" salmon river, offering its best fly fishing for landlocked salmon in late summer and fall as the fish move into the river from Cupsuptic and Mooselookmegun-tic Lakes. The Kennebago is the most important spawning tributary for these lakes, with that section downstream of Kennebago Falls dam contributing upwards of 12,000 salmon and more than 4,000 native brook trout to the fishery annually.

The Kennebago River is located in Franklin County in Maine's scenic western mountain country. It originates from a series of small ponds in Seven Ponds Township on the Quebec, Canada border. Flowing in a southerly direction, the Kennebago travels a total of 22 miles before dumping into Cupsuptic Lake just below Route 16 west of the Town of Rangeley. Although much of the river is accessible by vehicle or foot and restricted to fly fishing only throughout the fishing season, the 12-mile stretch from Kennebago Falls Dam to Cupsuptic Lake is the most popular and heavily fished.

Accessibility to a large number of pools in this section is by foot only. There is an old railroad bed, now a gravel road paralleling the Kennebago's east shore, that provides some access. It starts just before the Route 16 bridge over the river and travels north to the Brown Paper Company Road leading to Big Kennebago Lake, but it is blocked to vehicular access a short distance past Steep Bank Pool. Limited parking is available at this point, and it is an easy walk along the road to upstream pools, all of which are open to the public.

Unmarked but obvious trails lead to the various pools which are just a short trek off the road.

In all, approximately twenty well known pools are available on the Kennebago River downstream of Kennebago Falls Dam, the vast majority upstream of Steep Bank Pool and requiring a lengthy hike to reach. The easiest pools to reach are downstream of where the Brown Paper Company Road crosses the river, about three miles above Steep Bank Pool, and include Telephone Pool, Green Island, Devil's Elbow and, of course, Steep Bank Pool, perhaps the most famous and popular pool on the entire river.

Trout will be found along the river's entire length, but the best fishing is upstream of Big Kennebago Lake. This section of river is accessible to the public by vehicle via the Kennebago and Lincoln Pond Roads, both dirt but well maintained, which leave Route 16 west of the Brown Paper Company Road. The river is quite small in this area, freestone in nature and best fished in June, early July and again in September when water conditions are most favorable.

Brook trout are also found downstream of Kennebago Falls Dam all the way to Cupsuptic Lake. In fact, some of the biggest trout produced each season are taken in this lower stretch. Again, the best trout fishing occurs in mid and late spring to early summer with the average brookie running 10 to 11 inches. During this period, brook trout make up 72 percent of the Kennebago's rod and reel catch. There is also some good fishing in the fall for larger trout as they move upstream from the lakes with the salmon. Trophy squaretails in the one to four-pound class are possible.

In September, however, fishing for landlocked salmon takes over as the fish leave the downstream lake system and move upstream. Salmon contribute upwards of 60 percent of the total sporting catch in September, and average 16 to 18 inches. Landlocks in the two, three and four-pound class are not uncommon, and even larger fish are possible. It is the possibility of taking such big salmon (some up to six and seven pounds), along with the beauty of the Kennebago in September, which makes this one of the most popular angling destinations in Maine.

The key to successfully fishing the Kennebago is being there at the right time. Technically there are two runs of salmon which migrate into the river each year, both of which are considered spawning runs even though spawning doesn't occur until October and November. The early run commences in June and reaches Kennebago Falls Dam by early July. It may be large or small in terms of number of fish, depending upon water conditions. The larger and more popular "late" or "fall run" begins in late August or early September, depending upon water conditions. Heavy rains in late August can bring the fish up early, while a dry fall can delay the run into mid or late September. Under normal conditions, the peak of the fall run occurs between September 10 and 20, although good fishing can be found before and after this time.

During the spring, the Kennebago is usually high and cold with run-off water, and salmon and trout will be feeding heavily on smelt and other baitfish. At this time streamers and bucktails often produce the best results. Try patterns such as the Grey Ghost, Light Edson Tiger, Black Ghost, Blue Smelt and other imitator designs in sizes 4 through 8. In the fall, salmon will continue to nail these patterns along with the Mickey Finn, Red and White,

Supervisor, Tri-Color and other bright designs in sizes 10, 8, 6 and perhaps 4, depending on water conditions. Various nymphs and wet flies in sizes 10 down to 14, sometimes 16, work well too.

It should be noted that fly selection in the fall is less important than at other times of the season on the Kennebago, since migrating salmon are not overly interested in feeding. What counts here most is knowing where fish are apt to be holding, approaching the area with extreme caution, and consistently making delicate and precise casts to fish that can be downright spooky. This is the real challenge of fishing the Kennebago during the fall. Failure to move a fish or find action is a strong possibility in this game, but when success comes it means you did everything right and the taste of that success is all the sweeter!

Reaching the Kennebago River is quite easy from points south. Route 4 travels to the Rangeley Lakes from Exit 12 on the Maine Turnpike at Auburn, and connects with Route 16 a few miles west of Rangeley Village near Oquossoc. From that point finding the river is simple.

Lodging facilities in the form of motels, cabins and rustic lodges will be found throughout the Rangeley area. Campgrounds are available on Route 16 a few miles west of the river. Specific information may be obtained by contacting the Rangeley Lakes Region Chamber of Commerce, Box 317, Rangeley, Maine 04970. A fly and tackle shop will be found in Rangeley Village. It's on the edge of town on the right hand side of Route 4 traveling west towards the river. This is a good source for up-to-the-minute river information and conditions.

ROACH RIVER

Of the tributaries flowing into Moosehead Lake, the Roach River is the most important in terms of providing spawning and nursery areas for the lake's landlocked salmon and native brook trout. Among fly fishermen, it is also the best known, as it offers some of the finest moving water opportunities in that vast region encompassing Maine's largest lake.

The Roach is born in a series of remote, wilderness ponds and lakes in Piscataquis County in north-central Maine. Flowing generally west, it is impounded as First Roach Pond, formed by a dam at the hamlet of Kokadjo, then runs freely again to Spencer Bay, in the northeast corner of Moosehead Lake. It is the 6.3-mile stretch downstream of First Roach Pond which is of primary interest to fly fishermen.

So much so, in fact, that the State of Maine in 1990 purchased what is now a 1,000-foot-wide public corridor along the entire length of the Roach River from First Roach Pond downstream to Moosehead Lake. The river will forever remain in its present state for future generations to enjoy. Also included in the purchase are several rights-of-way over private land. These allow fishermen to reach some of the more remote stretches with relative ease.

To call the Roach River an important landlocked salmon and brook trout flowage would be an understatement. Studies have shown that the river contributes about half the native salmon found in Moosehead Lake. The trout production is significant as well. As for the river itself, while there are good angling opportunities available right through the fishing season, the Roach is primarily known for its mature salmon and trout which ascend from Moosehead in the fall. Landlocks measured in pounds rather than inches are not uncommon, and trophies of four and five pounds do mix in. Some large brook trout are also taken. A few are in the one to three-pound class, although the average is 10 to 13 inches or slightly smaller.

There are actually two prime times to fish the Roach River. Both salmon and brook trout move into it from May to early June in pursuit of spawning smelt. There is good fishing with smelt-imitating streamers and bucktails at this time. Fair action continues into early summer on resident fish with conventional and locally popular dry flies, wet flies and nymphs. Those mentioned earlier in this chapter can all be productive at times.

Traditionally, once the spring run is over water temperatures will have warmed and the Roach will have reached normal, or below normal levels (often the case through July and August). Now, the river has little to offer except in some of the deeper pools close to the lake—and even this it is a hit or miss proposition with action slow at best and with early morning and later afternoon and evening the best times.

That period between late August and late September is the best time for big fish and consistent action. Salmon can start their upstream migration by the third week in August given proper water levels and temperatures, and a few fish are generally taken at this time. But the fishing generally improves from this point, and reaches a peak in the second or third week of September. By then, fall rains working alone or in concert with water releases from the dam at First Roach Pond, have increased water flow, and seasonal changes have cooled water temperatures so as to bring the fall run to a crescendo.

Fishermen can expect nearly every pool along the Roach River to be holding salmon and brook trout by September 10 or 15, drawn upstream by the flush of water, cooling temperatures and growing urgency to reach spawning grounds. Fish will continue to move in, with the action remaining good until

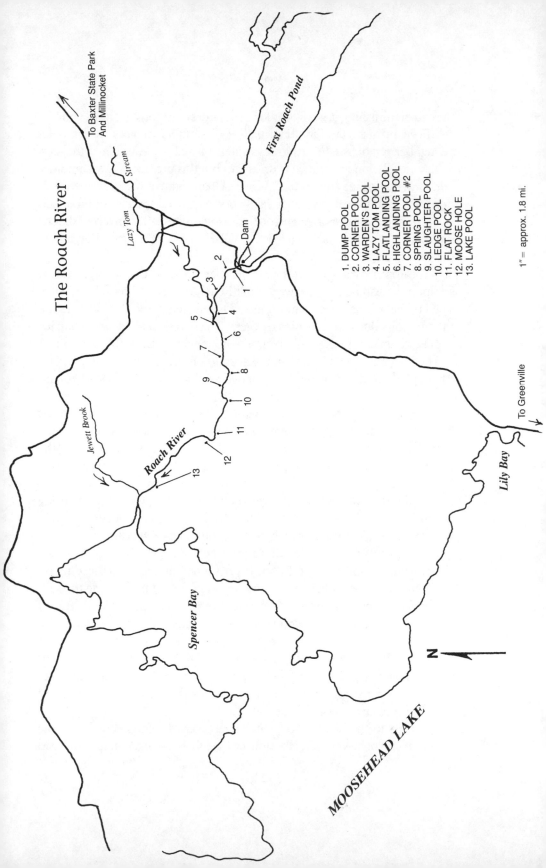

The Roach River

To Baxter State Park
And Millinocket

Lazy Tom Stream

First Roach Pond

Dam

Jewett Brook

Roach River

1. DUMP POOL
2. CORNER POOL
3. WARDEN'S POOL
4. LAZY TOM POOL
5. FLATLANDING POOL
6. HIGHLANDING POOL
7. CORNER POOL #2
8. SPRING POOL
9. SLAUGHTER POOL
10. LEDGE POOL
11. FLAT ROCK
12. MOOSE HOLE
13. LAKE POOL

1" = approx. 1.8 mi.

To Greenville

Lily Bay

Spencer Bay

N

MOOSEHEAD LAKE

the end of the fishing season, or as long as water conditions remain favorable.

Keep in mind that an abnormally dry summer or fall can delay the September run of fish. In such cases, water is usually released from the dam at First Roach Pond to bring fish upstream but this provides only temporary relief and may or may not induce the run. Chances are it will draw some fish upstream, but the action will not be as good as it would be if a period of rain and cool days and nights in August or early September changed river conditions naturally. Nor will the action persist; it will drop off dramatically the minute the dam shuts down.

The Roach River is relatively short but there are more than a dozen known and popular fishing areas between First Roach Pond and Moosehead Lake. The first half-dozen areas start off immediately below the dam and are the most popular due to relatively easy access. The pools stretch downstream for about one mile to where Lazy Tom Stream enters on the right, and can be reached via a dirt road (rough in the spring) on the north side of the river. Although the Roach is not overly big or deep in this section, chest waders with felt soles will make fishing easier.

From Lazy Tom Stream downstream to the lake, access to the river takes some time and hiking. Directions on how to reach these sections can be obtained from the general store on the right immediately after crossing the bridge over the river, or at the sporting camps on the left. Essentially, access is via a series of dirt roads and trails that cross Lazy Tom Stream north of the dam leading to Jewett Brook. These lower pools are worth getting into during the spring and fall, but be prepared for a trek through the northern Maine wilderness over sometimes rough, washed-out roads and difficult-to-follow trails. Allow plenty of time for your return before dark.

During the spring when Roach River salmon and trout are feeding on smelt, and in the fall when an increase in water flow is influencing the run, streamers and bucktails produce excellent results. The patterns mentioned earlier in this chapter are all good choices. Nymphs and wet flies such as the Black Nymph, Otter Nymph, Hare's Ear, Olive Heron, Leadwing Coachman and Picket Pin are good producers as well. The fly shop in Greenville, about twenty miles to the south, and the general store on the north side of the river can make other suggestions. Each carries a good selection of popular and productive offerings.

Getting to the Roach River is relatively easy. From Greenville on the southern end of Moosehead Lake follow the Lily Bay-Baxter State Park Road on the east side of the lake north to Kokadjo where the road crosses right over the river. The road is paved the entire distance. The only lodging within twenty miles is Kokadjo Sporting Camps, within view of the river (advance reservations recommended in September). Lodging is also available in Greenville, with camping available at Lily Bay State Park several miles south.

Al Raychard is a well-known outdoor writer residing in Saco, Maine. He has authored five regional books on fly fishing, including *Fly Fishing In Maine* and *Fly Fishing the Salt*. His articles have appeared in *Fly Fisherman, Rod & Reel, FlyFisher, Flyfishing* and other national and international magazines as far away as England and Japan. Raychard is also a contributing editor for *Canadian Sportfishing Magazine* and *The Atlantic Salmon Journal*.

Four

The Androscoggin
by Gene Parker

When the publisher of this book called and asked for a chapter about fishing on the Androscoggin River the reply was a delighted affirmative. Only thirty miles of the river is fishable (so I thought) and that thirty miles has been my favorite mecca for forty years. This was going to be a labor of love.

That bubble burst when word arrived that the river all the way through New Hampshire and Maine has been cleaned up and stocked with trout. The task of research and writing suddenly covered another 158 miles of unknown territory (20 in N.H. and 138 in Maine).

That Maine has good trout fishing on the "Andy" after over a hundred years of almost no fishing at all is big news indeed. It means that you have about five years of great fishing before it is rediscovered by the rest of the fishermen. Maine wardens told me they see almost no anglers on the river, even on the parts most heavily stocked.

Right now it is great for the catch-and-release devotees. This is not because of any law. It is due to dioxin contaminating the water. Maine authorities warn that it is unsafe to eat more than one Androscoggin fish per month. Hopefully, in time, the dioxin threat will lessen or even be eliminated. That will encourage local anglers (most of whom want fish to eat, not release) to try the river. With that increasing pressure the abundance of big fish may wane. However, if the state of Maine can effectively set aside some catch-and-release segments there should be enough trout to continue to attract sport fishermen.

Since there has been no point in residents fishing a heretofore rolling sewer there are almost no paths leading to the water, or well-trodden trails along the banks. It is almost like fishing a remote Alaskan river. Launching sites are almost non-existent.

Now is the prime time to enjoy some of the best fishing in New England. Try the Androscoggin not only in northern New Hampshire, but from Gorham N.H. through Maine. Really good looking trout water diminishes downstream of Livermore Falls although trout are stocked in the few fast water stretches almost all the way to the sea.

The Androscoggin River rises in New Hampshire about thirty miles south of the Canadian border at the junction of the outlets of the Magalloway River and Lake Umbagog. For almost two hundred years it has been part of the waterway carrying logs from the Rangely region downriver through sluices to mills along the river or to the sea for export.

The Andy flows south parallel to the eastern border of New Hampshire. At Gorham it swings east into Maine and meanders across the state to the ocean. In both states the river alternates between long vistas of smooth, slow-moving water, faster ripply stretches, rock dotted rapids, and white water hazardous or impossible to fish. In some sections ponds are formed where any of the twenty two dams slow it's 1,245 foot descent to salt water.

Hundreds of boom log cribs stand in midstream, forlorn sentinels now providing havens for fish. These rock-filled, log- and iron-pinned log cabin-like structures shelter some big trout. Many of the tributary stream mouths are also lies for trout and salmon which seek out prey fish there.

UMBAGOG TO ERROL DAM

We launch the boat at the public launch site on Route 16 two miles upstream of Errol Dam. The 6 h.p. outboard pushes our fourteen footer at a dignified pace against the smoother current. The alder lined Andy is fifty to a hundred feet wide. We pass openings to hundreds of acres of marsh. Three miles upstream we arrive at the confluence of the Magalloway River and the panorama of Lake Umbagog. Two bald eagles stretch their wings on a ten foot wide nest atop a large pine.

Turning off the motor, we drift with the current, fishing as we go. Occasionally we anchor to cast to rises. Here, alder lined wetlands preclude fishing from shore.

The best fishing is in spring and autumn. Trolling for landlocked salmon

Indian Pool, looking north to Errol Dam. White water is just below this.

and trout begins after ice-out in April and gets good in May. By mid-July the trout and salmon are in the cold depths of Umbagog. Weeds in the backwaters hide pickerel during the summer months. Bait anglers fish from piers just above the dam.

Lake Umbagog is partially in Maine. Check the current N.H. boundary water regulations for seasons, size limits, and catch limits, which apply all the way downstream to Errol Dam. Trout fishing ends with the salmon season on the last day of September above the dam. (Below the dam the last day for trout ends October 15. Salmon ends statewide September 30.)

ERROL DAM TO BRAGG'S BAY

Here it is fly fishing only. There is a two fish limit, and each must be 12 inches long or longer. A 150-foot-wide channel of very fast water rushes out of the dam's hydroelectric plant outlet before spreading out into Indian Pool some 800 feet downstream.

Salmon and trout lie under the outlet's foaming torrent safe from anglers' frustrated casts. At dusk I have watched five pound landlocked salmon roll in the current as they headed for the pool to feed on bait fish.

Rainbow trout splash in the swift water of the channel. Two mid-channel rock shoals at the entrance to the pool attract trout leaping for insects. Most trout are caught from the shores on both sides of the channel. It is possible to drive within a hundred yards of the east side of the channel's upper end via a dirt road that leads north off Route 26 some 300 yards east of the bridge.

On the west side of the pool, adjacent to Route 16, are located two next-to-your-car canoe launch sites. One is near the hydro outflow and the other is at the lower end of the pool, perilously close to the suction of the beginning of white water. Here is where white water kayakers begin their mile long bronco ride down to Bragg's Bay. Fly fishermen in waders brace their feet against the current to cast out to the lip of splashy water.

Each year on or about the twentieth of June the river becomes alive with fishermen. It is the annual alder fly hatch time. The fish go crazy and so do the anglers. It is possible to hook a trout on almost every cast.

Brown trout lie in the calm water of Indian Pool, brookies in the eddies among the rocks, and the rainbows cavort in the swift races.

The white water mile down to Bragg's Bay is difficult to fish because of trees shouldering up to the river's edge.

BRAGG'S BAY TO SEVEN ISLANDS

Beginning at Bragg's Bay, worm, bait, lure, and fly are legal all along the Androscoggin. Check F&G laws in case of changes.

At Bragg's Bay the current widens and slows as it spreads out over the predominately shallow gravel and sand bottom. A half-acre sized twelve foot deep hole is located midstream about sixty feet downriver from the tail of white water. The bottom contours shift from year to year.

A well worn path leads to the pool from Route 26 next to the bridge. It is a 200 yard carry to launch a canoe. That bridge is the only public vehicle crossing on the Androscoggin anywhere north of Milan.

Worm, bait, spin, and fly fishermen cast from shore or wade out on the sand bars at Bragg's Bay. A few good-sized trout are beached but most are of moderate size. Along the lower east side of the bay a backcurrent curls along a trench close to the alders. Bigger fish frequent this shaded bank, which can be reached only by canoe or boat. Caution: Much of the Androscoggin does not lend itself to float tubes, tiny rafts, or tricky canoes. If you get caught in the current of the many rapids you could be in sudden trouble.

At the lower end of Bragg's Bay the current splits around a large island and slows as it rejoins below the island. The easterly channel periodically offers good rainbow fishing for float fishermen. It's for expert canoeists only.

As the bottom shelves downward to an average depth of six feet below the island, fishing slows down with the current.

On nearby Route 16 South a sign announces the beginning of 13 mile woods. The road generally parallels the river. Watch out for moose on the road.

The river is wide and deep for the next 2½ miles. Big browns are caught on float trips mostly along the east bank.

Four miles below Errol the river bends sharply to the west at the Mollidgewock campgrounds directly opposite Mollidgewock Brook which enters from the eastern banking. The current quickens and becomes a series of rapids for the next 3½ miles to Seven Islands. This is one of my favorite stretches of river. Guides launch Mackenzie River boats above the tent grounds and drift past Seven Islands to take out opposite Bog Brook mentioned later.

It can be a wild ride in a canoe. It is best to use a canoe made of ABS material. Unlike aluminum or some plastics ABS will slide off rocks like soap. You can kick the dents out later. You must be an expert to handle a canoe in these treacherous waters. Always wear a flotation vest.

Immediately above Seven Islands (ten miles downriver from Errol but less by road) is a steel and concrete bridge. The gate on the bridge is normally locked to vehicles but not to pedestrians. This is the only access to the east shore between Errol and Milan. One of the idiosyncrasies of the upper Andy is that the east shore is heavily wooded and is difficult or impossible to fish from shore. That is why drift fishing the east bank is more successful.

Felt or abrasive soled waders are the rule on the slippery pebbles and rocks. There are shallow runs where you can wade almost to mid-stream to cast to deep channels. Wading anglers catch some good trout in and below each rapids. Worm fishermen recline in chairs at roadside pools.

SEVEN ISLANDS TO WHEELER BAY

Below Seven Islands, smooth water extends for the next three miles to Bog Brook outlet. There is a good sand launch/take out site on the highway side of the river. The opening into Bog Brook provides decent fishing. Below the brook the current picks up momentum. It runs briskly for a mile until it enters Five Acre Bay, where small dry flies can be used without drowning them so easily.

The next three miles is all part of Pontook Reservoir. Some trout are caught in the submerged original river channel. Mainly, you will hook pickerel and fallfish (a "chub" that can weigh three pounds and grow to two feet long).

One of the best and most accessible rapids below Pontook Dam was ruined when a hydroelectric channel bypass, over a mile long, was built. The original channel has water in it only during periods of high water.

At the bottom of this ruined stretch is Wheeler Bay into which the hydro facility discharges its water.

WHEELER BAY TO THE TWELFTH ST. BRIDGE

This is the only N.H. portion of the Andy where you can legally fish for browns twenty four hours a day. At dusk the big browns move out of their hidey holes to cruise the shallows for minnows and other large mouthfuls such as frogs or wayward mice. See chapter end for a "how to catch 'em" secret.

During the daylight hours fish the downstream side of the many boom log cribs on this portion of the river. Some very nice trout are caught using cut bait in the early spring. Both sides of the river have access points.

TWELFTH ST. BRIDGE TO THE MAINE BORDER

The Twelfth St. Bridge in Berlin divides countryside to the north from city to the south. It is below this area that fishermen are cautioned not to eat more than one fish per month due to chemical contaminants in the river.

Although trout are present in the river in Berlin it is hardly likely that readers are going to travel any distance to come fish here in the railroad lined backyards of houses, businesses, and factories. Certainly, few would come to cast a line next to the huge paper mill that sprawls in its miasma of chemical odor in Berlin.Let's move downstream three miles to get out of Berlin's city clutter. We now see a mixture of backyards and trees by the river.

At Cascade in Gorham a two mile length of rapids offers a promise of trout. Another half mile and we come to the dam above the railroad bridge. This dam deflects much of the river down a channel to a hydroelectric installation. The current quickens in small rapids opposite the outlet of Moose River. Access to the river has become easier. The water slows as we approach another dam above Peabody River. Below the junction of Route 16 South and Route 2 East, Route 2 parallels the river several hundred feet away on its south side. Access would mean a steep downhill scramble from Route 2, crossing a railroad track, and a hike through dense brush. Better to drive three miles east on Route 2 (you are now in Shelbourne N.H.), turn left at North Rd. and cross the bridge adjacent to a hydro dam. About two hundred yards beyond the dam is Hogan Rd., a dirt road that closely follows the river upstream back to the dam above Peabody River. The N.H. F&G department stocked the Peabody River with rainbows and browns which swam downstream and populated the Andy. Both sides of the river are forested, providing a background of wilderness as though you were miles from houses.

The upper two miles is mostly rapids. There are several passable launch openings beginning one mile down from the dam. Two miles farther east is a pond formed by the hydro plant. From dam to dam is good fishing.

Below the hydro dam you will catch trout which were released in Maine, which is five miles to the east. The river alternates between rapids, smooth fast water, and slower pools. There are several islands that divide the flow.

Two and a half miles east on North Rd. from the hydro dam look for a 4WD "road" that descends through the woods, zigs left at a clearing and zags right into more woods to a slide-down-the-bank canoe launch. There is a take-out at the bridge almost a mile downstream.

Since the area has been fishable only recently, there are no other established accesses, nor are there any bankside trails.

MAINE ANDROSCOGGIN

It seems strange to go to Maine and see a river with good trout fishing but with nobody angling for fish. I never saw one fisherman during the week spent looking for paths leading from road to river. A few farm tractor trails through corn fields led me to brush that had to be pushed aside to find the Androscoggin. Bridges affording access are miles apart.

Don't let this discourage you from fishing. It should encourage you. It means that you are one of the few to know about a hidden bonanza. Go for it!

I saw a rainbow at a stream mouth that would go six pounds. You can bet that I am going back, fishing rod in hand.

N.H. BORDER TO RUMFORD

North Road is sometimes near and sometimes as much as a half mile away from the river as you travel east toward Bethel. Route 2 does the same on the south side of the river. At Gilead, three miles from N.H., there is a bridge and canoe launch. It is hill country ravined by rivers and brooks. Rocky cliffs lining sweeping turns in the Andy are a photographer's paradise. Seven water miles downstream is West Bethel with a canoe launch on the south shore where there used to be a bridge across the river. On the north shore opposite and a half mile upstream is a canoe launch of sorts.

At Bethel the river swings north to Newry. There is a canoe launch at a picnic area on Route 2 in North Bethel. A mile downstream the Sunday River enters the Andy. The Bear River enters another three miles downstream. Because the Sunday and the Bear were never polluted, both have always been heavily fished. Another fishing hangout is at the confluence with the Ellis River at Rumford Point. The river has now become wider and slower.

Route 2 continues to follow the river on the north side to Rumford. Rumford Falls drops eighty feet. Even before the white man's coming this was as far as Atlantic salmon ever came. They did, however, spawn in the Swift River at Rumford, and in rivers and streams below Rumford.

From the N.H. line to Rumford the river has been stocked with rainbows and brookies. Trout also descend from tributaries as they grow larger.

There is a boat launch ramp off Route 2 above Joe's Pond Brook one and three quarter miles above the big dam at Rumford. There is a lesser dam one-fourth mile below the big one.

RUMFORD TO AUBURN/LEWISTON

Rapids alternate with slower water from Rumford to the West Peru/Dixfield bridge. Route 2 borders the northeast side and Route 108 the southwest side of the river. After passing a mile of rapids below Dixfield, Route 2 turns away from the river. Instead, go straight ahead on Dixfield Rd. to follow the river for eight miles to Canton Point. Long stretches of poison ivy discourage walking to or alongside the river. In time, as fishermen rediscover the Andy, entry trails should appear.

The river veers northerly at the Route 140 bridge at Gilbertville a mile south of Canton Point where we leave the Dixfield Rd. The water slows to meet a dam five miles down the road. I am told that there are trout aplenty. There are two places where the road is at waterside where a canoe launch is possible.

Below another dam at Jay, where there is a large paper mill, white water rushes for a hundred yards before smoothing for a three mile calm extending to a dam at Livermore Falls. Within a mile another dam is followed by eight miles of slow water. We begin to see more posted signs. As the river squeezes under a bridge at the junction of Routes 219 and 108 a couple of hundred yards of rapids break the monotony of smooth flowing river.

Seven miles below the bridge we come to a long span of bridge on Center Bridge Road in Turner. The river has become a long narrow lake. At a beautiful picnic ground on the west shore the state of Maine has installed a wide, ridged, concrete boat ramp. There is plenty of parking space. There is concern that hot weather here warms the water to deplete oxygen to lower than what trout need. Smallmouth bass and pickerel fishing is good in this "lake" which extends to Gulf Island Dam eight miles below the Turner ramp.

LEWISTON/AUBURN TO THE SEA

We skip over the seven miles of river that runs between Lewiston and Auburn and go to the Route 495 (Maine Turnpike) bridge. The twelve mile length of river down to the dam at Lisbon Falls has been stocked with rainbows and browns. The upper end of this reach is alternately rapids and pools. The lower end is slow water. There is a drag-the-boat-to-the-water launch on Cedar Pond Rd. opposite Lisbon Falls.

At Worumbo, a now defunct large mill in Lisbon Falls, there is a fish lift at the dam. This is one of three lifts now operating to bring Atlantic salmon up the river. Four miles downriver, at Pejepscot dam, and five miles further, at Topsham dam, are two more fish elevators. Over a hundred salmon passed Topsham in 1990. These were from stock that had been liberated from other rivers along the coast.

HABITAT, FLIES, BAITS, LURES, AND TECHNIQUES

The Androscoggin River abounds with a wide variety of trout food including prey fish, small swimming creatures, larval insects, hatching insects, and terrestrials. Bottom cover is widespread so that it harbors enough aquatic life to sustain a large sport fish population.

The following tips apply to both the N.H. and Maine Androscoggin.

Worms are still the number one method of trout fishing. My only objection to this method is that, in the part of the river that contains dioxin, a gullet or gill hooked fish that is released will die. If you aren't going to eat it, why kill it? Better to use single-hook lures or flies so that the lip-hooked fish can be released to be caught again, and again. That is sporting. Having said this, let's return to reality.

In the spring cut bait catches a lot of big trout when the water is too cold for fish to move about much.

Spinning lures should be bright and shiny for dark water and dark days, and dull for bright days. The Mepps spinners, the Phoebe gold, small Mooselook Wobblers and Sutton spoons, Panther Martins, and yes, some of the Mr. Twister type wiggly swimmers are effective. Small to tiny minnow-like lures do well. Heavily weighted streamers fished on ultra-light spinning tackle can be deadly.

Popular fly fishing streamers are: Grey Ghost, Supervisor, and Nine Three in the spring for salmon on the upper Andy; Black Ghost, Black Nosed Dace, Light Edson Tiger, Maynard's Marvel for rainbows and browns; and Little Brook Trout, Warden's Worry, and Mickey Finn for all. In autumn the Red and White Deceiver tantalizes brookies. Try sizes 6 to 10.

For mid to bottom depths use what I call semi-streamers (because they are tied on a streamer hook). These are the Muddler Minnows, Zonkers, Crystal Wooly Buggers, Dark Wool-Head Sculpin, dark leeches, and the leech-like "fuzzy wuzzies" (tied with marabou). Suggested are sizes 6 to 10.

Wet flies to try include: Hornberg, Hare's Ear, Blue Dun, Sulphur Dun, Yellow Dun, Black Gnat, and Brown Hackle. Some, like the Hornberg, Brown Caddis, and the Brown Owl can be fished dry or wet.

Dry flies on the rambunctious parts of the Andy should be big and buoyant. Even if you know how to mend the floating line a small dry can easily be dragged underwater.

Western type flies tied extra bushy are buoyant. Use a good floatant cream or spray. At dawn or dusk break the rules. Go huge. Size 4 or 2 is not too big. You can even use them during the day in turbulent water.

Dry flies include: Elk Hair Caddis, Humpy, Trude, Goddard's Caddis, Wulffs, Sofa Pillow, and the large Royal Coachman. Go a size or two larger in the faster water. Use the Alder Fly in late June, terrestrials such as ants, caterpillars, and beetles in summer, and the grasshopper fly in later summer to fall.

Nymphs: Dark Stone Fly, Pheasant Tail, Hellgramite, Green Caddis Larva, Zug Bug, Feather Duster, Dragon Fly, Crane Fly Larva, and LaFontaine Sparkle Pupa.

O.K., here is the promised secret for catching big browns at night. Use an 8 weight rod with #8 floating line. Cut the leader down to four feet long tapering to a 10 lb. test tippet. Tie on a bass-sized deer hair mouse, a huge salmon dry fly, or a bass bug that doesn't chug or pop. Cast a short line because you can't see what you are doing at night. No lights. Even a cigarette lighter may spook the fish because they will be in very shallow water. Slap the fly on the surface to attract the attention of a five (or more) pound brown. Retrieve fast to make a wake. Cast towards shallow shores or brook outfalls where the browns look for baitfish, frogs, or swimming rodents. Cast and cast and cast. Eventually a big brown will smash that fly with a splash and swirl that will make you think you have foul-hooked a beaver.

This technique works on big browns anywhere it is legal to fish after dark.

Gene Parker lives in the North Country near the upper Androscoggin, and is a registered New Hampshire fishing guide. He has written magazine articles on scuba diving, fishing and hunting, and books on diving and fishing. Being an artist, he frequently illustrates his own work. Gene is North Country editor for *New England Out of Doors,* and is a member of both the Outdoor Writers Association of America and the New England OWA.

Five

The Saco
by Stewart Bristol

The Saco is one of the largest, most diverse, and most scenic rivers in the Northeast. Cold mountain springs and snow melt from New Hampshire's Presidential Range feed this 125-mile-long-river, which is home for brook trout, brown trout, rainbow trout, and landlocked salmon, as well as trophy largemouth and smallmouth bass. In the lowland sections of the Saco, migrating Atlantic salmon ascend in increasing numbers, and the river's estuary is well known for its annual runs of striped bass, mackerel and bluefish. You may recognize the Saco estuary as one of the favorite fishing spots for President George Bush, whose summer home is a few miles south in Kennebunkport, Maine.

The Saco's mileage is split almost evenly between southwestern Maine and the foothills of the White Mountains of New Hampshire. The river's basin consists of 1,697 square miles, offers an impressive drop in elevation of 1,515 feet, and encompasses more than 1,000 miles of tributary streams.

The river begins at tiny Saco Lake, a small pond just north of Crawford Notch, New Hampshire. As it leaves the lake, it begins to tumble through steep granite ledges where brookies and rainbows can be found in good numbers. Due to the rapid drop and the bottom scouring effect that tumbling boulders have on the river, most fish in this section of the Saco are stocked by the New Hampshire Fish & Game Department and rarely grow larger than a pound.

Just north of Bartlett, off Route 302, Dry River, Sawyer River, Stony Brook and Albany Brook (each only several feet wide, with a gravel bottom) feed into the Saco, giving fishermen ample opportunity to explore small trout waters.

The section between Bartlett and Conway is heavily travelled by tourists, but fishermen seldom hit the stream anywhere other than at roadside. Access to the river and tributaries is easy, most of the time alongside Routes 302 and 16 but, paradoxically, fishing pressure is always light. Many highway department pull-offs are located within sight of this section of the river. Because of the heavy tourist traffic, campgrounds and motels are in abundance along both routes.

The Ellis River, Wildcat Brook and the East Branch can be reached alongside Route 16 just north of the junction of Routes 16 and 302. These tributaries are similar in character and small, usually stocked brookies and rainbow trout are what you'll mainly find. In these smaller tributaries, there is a native population of rainbows, and some holdovers in the larger pools will exceed two pounds. But native brook trout are the dominant fish species and while they average only about seven inches here, squaretails exceeding two pounds will occasionally be yielded by the larger pools.

Just north of Conway, the Swift River empties into the Saco. It is the mountain stream all fishermen picture in their minds when dreaming of the northeast. Its spectacular mountain scenery, and fast-moving cascades of cold, clear water make this a joyous stream to fish.

Nearly two dozen small tributaries pour into the 23-mile length of the Swift, each a haven for native brook trout in the five- to nine-inch range with larger pools holding an occasional 12-incher. Of particular interest to fishermen is Sabbathday Brook, at Passaconaway along Route 112, known for its deep, although narrow pools and unmatched scenic splendor.

Almost the entire main stem of the Swift follows Route 112, better known as the Kangamangus Highway, where fishermen find exceptionally easy access. Here, again, most take advantage only of the roadside pools, leaving the river away from the highway pull-offs to the more serious fishermen who are willing to walk a bit. The deeper pools of the Swift, bordered by heavy boulders and fed by cold spring water off New Hampshire's Presidential mountain range, have been known to yield large brook trout in the two and three pound class.

Throughout the headwaters of the Saco, the hendricksons appear quite late, sometimes not until mid-May. Until they emerge, a Muddler Minnow, especially one tied with elk hair has been an early producer. As the water warms, the hendricksons give way to stoneflies and March browns. Late

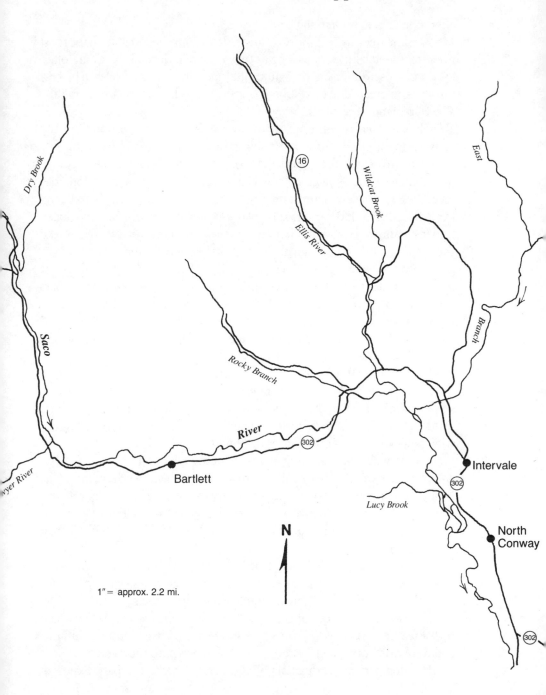

The Upper Saco River

Dry Brook

16

Wildcat Brook

Ellis River

East

Branch

Saco

Rocky Branch

River

302

Intervale

302

Bartlett

wyer River

Lucy Brook

North
Conway

N

1" = approx. 2.2 mi.

302

afternoon fishing is often the best.

The first week in June the huge green drakes appear and remain the most important food source for as long as they continue to hatch. They are often joined or closely followed by light cahills and blue-winged olives. The best numbers of green drakes will be encountered in late afternoon, along the slower-moving large pools.

The water temperatures stay in the mid-50's to lower 60's throughout the summer months, and trout in the six- to nine-inch range are plentiful.

Of the river's total drop in elevation of 1,515 feet, 1,100 of that occurs in the 40-mile stretch situated in New Hampshire. Only two major tributaries enter the Saco in New Hampshire: the Ellis and the Swift Rivers, both falling from the 2,000-6,000 foot elevation of the White Mountains. Nearly a dozen feeder streams and larger brooks flow into these tributaries or directly into the Saco, offering uncrowded small stream fishing opportunities.

Once the water reaches the Maine-New Hampshire border, the river slows and widens, but still travels through granite ledges and over gravel bars and eventually through southern Maine forests and farmland. Except for the topsoil and clay composition of stream banks and stream bottom in lowland sections near where the Saco empties into the Atlantic Ocean, shorelines are of a rocky and sandy composition.

Springtime fishing in the New Hampshire section of the Saco is seldom productive until late May or early June, due to the heavy run-off from melting snow off the White Mountains. As the water temperature climbs into the high 50's and low 60's, the brook trout and rainbows become active, pursuing the wide range of insects common to the region.

Think small when selecting nymph patterns. Size 10-16 is preferred, but an occasional size 8 may be called for in some of the larger holding pools. Nymphs are preferred over streamers or dry flies most of the year and have proven to be more productive. For those who spin fish, small casting spoons (1/16 oz.), garden worms, grubs and hellgramites work well when fished without weight.

Hip boots will suffice in any of the feeder streams or the main stem of the Saco between Conway and Fryeburg. However, cold water temperatures make the use of waders highly desirable a big part of the season.

Access is no problem along the entire length of the Saco, as it follows main highway routes. Both New Hampshire and Maine highways feature pull-offs and rest areas from which fishermen can gain access to the river.

Development and industrial pollution have somehow bypassed most of the Saco River. Individual housing is scattered along its length, but in some stretches the river is protected by "greenbelt" and floodplain zoning which prohibits development within 200 feet of the river's edge.

Industrial pollution has only become a problem in downstream communities, near where the river empties into the Atlantic Ocean. Until recently, water quality in the Saco at Biddeford has been below standards. After the closing of a tannery and a textile plant and the installation of a water treatment plant at the site of a major arms manufacturer in southern Maine, the water quality has improved dramatically.

Community sewage discharge problems have been nearly eliminated by modern treatment facilities and strict septic discharge prohibitions have been enforced all along the river in recent years. Watchdog environmental groups such as Trout Unlimited, The Saco River Salmon Club and the Maine People's Alliance carefully monitor the river for abuses.

As the Saco nears the Maine border, the river slows and becomes wider, making navigation by canoe and small cartopper boats possible. In recent years, the increase in popularity of canoeing and the magnetic natural beauty of the Saco have combined to create a bottleneck of river traffic. On a busy weekend, beginning at the New Hampshire border and for 40 miles downstream, dozens of canoeists can be found using the river, usually to the consternation of fishermen.

Fryeburg, Maine, has become the headquarters for canoe rentals and access to this section of the river; it has half a dozen major rental companies. Even with the large number of canoes on this section of the river, fishermen can still find room to cast for brown trout, some of which will tip the scale past the six pound mark.

The majority of canoeists are out for a leisurely paddle down this scenic river. The many sandy bars and peninsulas which jut out into the main current are the usual stopping points, and each is a picnicker's delight. Few canoeists stop to cast for trout, and the early morning fisherman can have the river to himself during the prime fishing hours, until mid-morning and then again near dusk.

There has been a great deal of publicity concerning the hordes of canoeists in the section of the Saco River between Conway, New Hampshire and Hiram, Maine. Until measures were taken to control canoeists, gangs of party-seekers crowded this section of the river. Beer, liquor and drugs were common, and many boaters would raft their canoes together in a kind of intoxicated embrace. The noise and sometimes obscenities cast from these parties have given the Saco River a bad name. In 1988, the Maine Department of Inland Fisheries and Wildlife set up riverblocks in the area, aimed at stopping the rowdy actions and uncontrolled drinking.

Although the riverblocks were later ruled unconstitutional, the actions taken by the Maine game wardens and sheriffs caught the media's attention and the rowdiness was brought to an end. Today, during a summer weekend, the river is still somewhat crowded along this section, but the crowds have become quieter and fishermen can cast with less interference and distraction.

A recent development along this section of river is the landowner's co-operation with canoeists and fishermen. Some residents encourage camping and picnicking provided the users clean up after themselves and are watchful of the fragile environment. In Fryeburg, a courtesy patrol known as the "River Runners" operate in well-marked canoes, directing canoeists to picnic and camping areas.

Open fires are not permitted on the Maine side of the Saco River without written permission of the nearest Fire Warden. It is suggested that you bring a cold lunch or a portable gas grill rather than use an open fire.

Trophy brown trout are taken along this section, as are landlocked salmon and a few large brook trout. Much of the river is wide (200 yards) but still has a sandy or gravel bottom with very little silt.

Brown trout are most often taken during cloudy or rainy days or at night. During periods of heavy rainfall, when the river is high, is one of the premier times to fish for large brown trout. Large wet flies, copper colored spoons or lures and live bait top the list for Saco River browns. River bends and large, slow eddies are common places to find the larger browns while the younger fish hang out in the rapids in typical holding runs alongside large boulders and downstream from fallen logs and along undercut banks.

Commonly used fly patterns include the Hornberg, Humpy, Hairwing Caddis, Henryville Special and both the Light and Dark Cahill. Spinfishermen will do well with hardware in the small sizes, for example 1/16 ounce. Super Duper, Mooselook Wobbler, Thomas, or Al's goldfish are all popular here. Bait fishermen should look to garden worms, large nightcrawlers (fished with a willowleaf or Colorado Spinner), golden shiners or, if you can find them by turning over rocks, hellgramites.

Farther east, or downstream, you will encounter a limited number of landlocked salmon. These fish will be found primarily in that section of the Saco between Hiram and Limington. This 15-mile stretch of the Saco holds the finest fast-water fishing on the river, with whitewater rips that can be waded or fished from shore. Felt soles and a wading staff are recommended due to the algae over the gravel bottom and the fast moving water.

Inexperienced canoeists should plan their options before heading into this section of the river. The white water just south of East Baldwin, at Steep Falls, must be portaged on the left shore about 100 yards above the bridge and farther downstream the Limington Rip should be canoed by only those with experience. Many of the smaller brown trout taken in this section are of stocked origin, but fishermen take larger holdovers and some natives up to six pounds.

Again, access is easily gained and this 15-mile stretch makes an excellent weekend experience. Be sure to obtain landowner permission for overnight camping. Local country stores and town offices will assist you in finding camping sites. It is important to stress your interest as a fisherman concerned with preserving the environment when asking for permission to camp. Smalltown communities in Maine can sometimes be a bit unfriendly to non-resident requests.

Downstream from Limington, the Saco flows through flat farmland and the river grows ever wider. The bottom retains some silt at this point although it remains sandy rather than muddy. Occasional sandbars make great lunch stops and the rocky shorelines offer good habitat for large brown trout. Water is shared downstream from here by brook trout, landlocked salmon (in the tributaries) and warmwater species including trophy sized smallmouth bass. Larger boats can be used in this stretch of river although access is by 4-wheel drive for anything larger than a cartopper. River depths average 6-10 feet with occasional deep holes to 40 feet.

The flow below any of the 10 dams which obstruct the Saco River is an excellent place to find any of the fish species. Caution should be exercised in these areas due to the unpredictable rise and fall of the river from water releases at each dam. Water flow is computer controlled and no warning horn is sounded before discharge. Do not wade the river immediately below any of the dams.

The final section of fresh water, from below the Skelton Dam in Dayton to Biddeford, is wide and slow-moving with an occasional rip. Brown trout are common along the rocky shorelines and downstream of large mid-stream boulders. The water is seldom deeper than 15 feet, though an occasional pool will bottom out at 20 feet.

With only one other dam (located in Biddeford) between Dayton and the Atlantic Ocean, Atlantic salmon return each spring and have become more popular than brown trout in this portion of the river. Ongoing negotiations with Central Maine Power Company, the Maine Department of Inland Fisheries and Wildlife and Federal wildlife agencies promise to improve the Atlantic salmon fishery in the Saco.

Although fish passage around all 10 dams on the Saco seems a distant goal, construction of improved fish passages at Biddeford has begun. While more than 300 Atlantic salmon are estimated to return to the lower Saco each year, 1989 and 1990 rod and reel catches have been in the mid twenties, with a 1986 high rod & reel catch of 85 fish.

Fishing for Atlantic salmon in the Saco is attempted by very few fishermen due to the small return of fish. The area most often targetted is just below Skelton Dam in Dayton, but the entrance to feeder brooks along the river will also hold Atlantics during the warm months when river water can reach as high as 80 degrees.

Small boat and canoe access is available at Skelton Dam both above and below the dam (limited parking) and larger boat access in Biddeford at Rotary Park (no fees required). Power boaters should note that Maine law prohibits boats from being operated at more than headway speed within 200 feet of any shoreline, including islands, anywhere in the state. Much of the Saco River is less than 400 feet wide.

Below Biddeford, the Saco River becomes affected by the tides. Small returns of coho salmon occur in September with two noted runs of Atlantic salmon in May and August. Saltwater species such as striped bass, mackerel and bluefish comprise the bulk of sportfishing in the lower Saco River and Saco Bay.

Access to this section of the Saco is gained at the Department of Conservation facility at Marblehead, just off Route 9 south of Biddeford. A $257,000 renovation was completed on the facility in 1990. There are no fees to launch and parking is available for up to 75 trailered vehicles.

Large brown trout, an occasional trophy brook trout, Atlantic salmon and the illusion of being in the wilderness while civilization is just a few hundred yards away: All this makes the Saco River an unusual resource, worthy of exploration.

Stu Bristol is a free-lance writer currently living in southern Maine. He has written about hunting and fishing since 1968, and has had articles published in *Sports Afield, Outdoor Life, New England Game & Fish* and other magazines. He has also written two books on turkey hunting, the most recent being *Hunting Wild Turkeys in New England*. A member of the Outdoor Writers Association of America and New England OWA, he is also a newspaper columnist and lecturer.

Six

The Connecticut
by Robert Panuska

There is a place below Stewartstown, New Hampshire, where the Upper Connecticut River shows itself like no other. It has just boiled over a small dam at West Stewartstown and its character is about to change from a wilderness freestone stream to a pastoral, meandering river. You can pull your car off the road on the long grade that terminates at the Coos County old folks home and take a good look at a loop of river that will tell you a lot about what to expect on the Connecticut.

The first thing you notice is that it's no small river. The long riffle facing you as you look towards Canaan, Vermont, is over 200 feet across. There is usually enough water covering the whole riffle to make wading a careful, thoughtful proposition, though during medium to low water conditions this is a great wading stretch. Swinging a small streamer will usually produce a good number of rainbows in the nine to twelve inch range. The water is always cool here. Nine miles above this point Murphy dam at Lake Francis releases from sixty feet below the lake's surface. This cold water races though a heavily forested valley in pretty short order and it arrives in Stewartstown pure, cold, and full of trout.

The long riffle foams and bubbles towards you and drops off at your feet into what must have been the greatest salmon holding pool on the upper river when bright fish ran as far as Bellows Falls. The pool is deep and sheltered so the surface is only disturbed by coiling current tongues and tiny whirlpools and rising fish. There are almost always rising fish—big fish. The river pushes its way around the pool and meets a huge rock that sticks out like a big toe at the base of the County Home. The seam where the resulting eddy meets the main current is always dimpled with rises.

This pool is tough to work, though you can approach it from the Vermont side below the riffle and wade out a few feet on a soft sand ledge that drops very quickly into deep water. Big maples and birches crowd you from behind; you soon discover how far you can shoot from a short cast. The dimples in the eddy beckon. The fish are eating emerging caddis pupae and they'll take an olive number 12 imitation or an olive and partridge soft hackle served up with a Liesenring lift. The trick is serving it up. When you do everything right you have big fish hitting aggressively on a tight line. These trout will pop 4x tippet like thread unless you cushion the strike with a gentle fingertip on the line and a few inches of slack behind.

It's deceptive to call the Upper Connecticut one of the East's greatest trout rivers and leave it at that. It's really a system, a collection of waters. It begins at Third Connecticut Lake on the New Hampshire-Quebec border and flows through and connects three more large lakes before finally emerging to form the border between New Hampshire and Vermont. The system supports a diverse cold water fish population: brook, brown, and rainbow trout, land-locked salmon, smelt, and lake trout. The end of the Upper Connecticut trout water is arbitrarily marked at the bottom of the three mile no-kill section at North Stratford, though good fishing continues for miles downstream. Warm water species—smallmouth and largemouth bass, perch, and pickerel—become more abundant below North Stratford. The nearly fifty miles of water between Quebec and North Stratford offer some of the best trout fishing in the east.

To begin to get a handle on the fishery it helps to break the Upper Connecticut into upper and lower stretches. The river above Stewartstown is a north country wilderness fishery. Not that you leave civilization; there is an abundance of comfortable lodges and beautiful campgrounds along Route 3, but civilization is only a crust here. There are loons and ducks and a lot of beavers. Rolling green hills of mixed conifer and deciduous forest bracket the river with nary a farm in sight. You will seldom be able to drive from Third Lake to Second Lake without seeing a moose, especially early or late in the day.

The Connecticut is smaller here, more a big stream than a river. Its ultimate source is actually Fourth Lake, a boggy little pond a stone's throw from the Quebec border. A tiny, brush covered outlet brook, the infant river empties quickly and without fanfare into Third Lake…cold, clear, deep, and

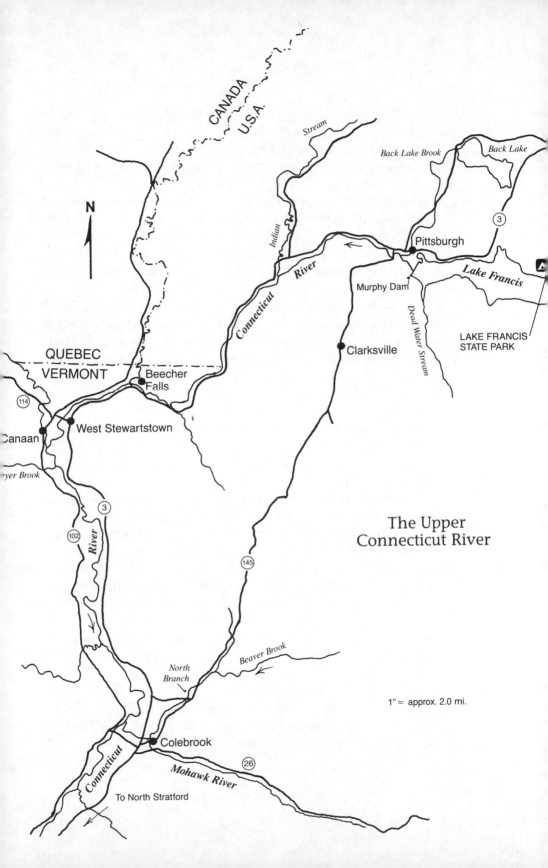

The Upper
Connecticut River

1″ = approx. 2.0 mi.

covering a little under three hundred acres. Third Lake is home to good populations of rainbow and lake trout.

Of interest to the stillwater fly fisherman, Third Lake gets the *Hexagenia* hatch, plus other smaller mayflies and numerous caddis emergences. During warm, still evenings at the end of June or the first part of July, big yellow mayflies pop out of their shucks and cover the surface of shallow mud bottomed coves like regattas of tiny sailboats. While their wings are drying the duns are helpless, and the rainbows know it. The biggest fish in the lake begin feeding with deliberate, slurping rises. It doesn't happen every night, and it's dark so soon, but the hex hatch has a magic that never fails to accelerate the pulse.

The river drops from Third Lake to Second Lake as a wilderness brook trout stream. The banks are often boggy and bordered with crowded clumps of alder and willow. Thick stands of black spruce are common. This area gets very little fishing pressure except where the stream actually borders the road. It's a tough place for a fly rod, but an ultralight spinning rod and a cup of worms can produce a breakfast of brilliant small brookies that never saw a hatchery.

At Second Lake the Connecticut system begins to show some muscle. This is a big lake, four times the size of Third. It's blessed with good populations of brook trout, landlocks, and lake trout. Second Lake is an impoundment with the tailwater released from forty feet below the lake's surface. Below the dam there is a short fly-fishing-only stretch followed by closed water reserved for salmon spawning; no fishing at any time. Another small piece of river at the inlet to First Lake is open to fishing. This spot can be very hot for salmon at ice-out in the spring, a fact that is not a secret to local fishermen.

First Lake is the biggest of the Connecticut lakes, nearly three thousand acres. It holds lake trout and salmon and is formed by a dam that releases from forty feet below its surface. The tailwater between First Lake and Lake Francis is posted fly fishing only, with a limit of two brook trout bigger than twelve inches and two salmon bigger than fifteen inches. In this stretch the Connecticut begins to develop as a river. It is swollen and enriched by its first major tributary, Perry Stream.

The preponderance of conifer forest and boggy conditions in the surrounding flats seems to indicate poor, high acid soil conditions. The water here is a light tea color from tannin stain, but the soil is limy and buffers the naturally acidic tannin runoff with enough alkalinity left to neutralize the effects of acid rain. The pH in this stretch is just a hair above seven, just about right for intense stream insect life. Clinger mayflies, caddis, and stoneflies abound in the cold, slightly alkaline water.

Early spring is best for landlocks. They follow the smelt spawning run at ice-out, and for two weeks the salmon fishing can be very good. All summer long, especially during periods of high water, some landlocks wander up this stretch, but the salmon fishing is most dependable in late April or early May. The brook trout fishing is good from January 1 through October 15, however, if you don't mind chipping ice from your guides for the first few months. Some large brookies continually trade between this stretch and Lake Francis. This water is heavily stocked and it is accessible from two roads, so it gets more pressure than most of the river.

A word about water temperature: the water in the tailwater wilderness area of the river is always cold. Not just cool, cold. In this stretch of the river look for water in the low to mid forties. On the warmest days of the summer you might see it at sixty, but don't count on it. Insulated waders can be a real asset, hypothermia a real possibility.

I fished this stretch years ago in a pair of sweat pants covered by thin, stocking foot waders. After about a half-hour I noticed I was beginning to shiver from time to time, but the June sun was warm and the March browns were just starting in the big bouldered run I was fishing, so I didn't pay much attention. After a few more minutes and a pair of decent fish that fell to a drifted nymph, I noticed a good fish taking emergers just out of comfortable casting range.

I started to move and my legs felt like lead. They had lost nearly all feeling and I had real trouble controlling them. I felt a twinge of panic and decided to lurch for shore. On the way my knee bumped a boulder and the waders split like a ripe melon. The feeling returned immediately to that leg; it felt like someone had fanned it with a blowtorch before it went numb again. A vision of remaining there forever, a frozen warning to other careless anglers, flashed through my mind. This scared me enough so that I floundered the last ten feet to the bank and dragged myself out of the water. It took an hour of sun and a full Thermos of hot coffee to stop the shakes. When I could hold something without dropping it I fished the stream thermometer from my vest and found the water temperature was forty two degrees.

Lake Francis is the last Connecticut Lake, and it is plugged by Murphy

Dam, which releases water sixty feet below the lake's surface. On warm mornings and evenings a blanket of fog often covers the river below the dam. The tailwater of Murphy is another good place for insulated waders. It is also a good place for big fish. The trip through the dam stuns and disorients the smelt and sculpins lucky enough (or unlucky enough) to make it. Just below Murphy the first deep holding water is in the little town of Pittsburg, and here the groggy baitfish meet an awesome reception committee. Here Ken Reed caught the New Hampshire record brown trout, sixteen pounds six ounces, on the fourth of July in 1975. The fish ate a black-backed gold Rapala in the long pool with the big rock, right in the center of downtown Pittsburg. Another brown of nearly thirteen pounds was caught by the same plug and the same man during the same week of fishing. If you're curious what a sixteen pound brown looks like, as I was, you can see it hanging on the wall of the main lobby of The Glen, a charming lodge and rustic cabin complex on the shore of First Connecticut.

Below Murphy the river seems to be trying to make up its mind. Most of the water between Pittsburg and West Stewartstown is fast riffles and short, quick pools like the river between the lakes. The water is cold and the banks are heavily timbered, but now and then the leaves and needles are broken by the picturesque expanse of a dairy farm, complete with black and white cows. Long pools near the confluence of Indian Creek and at Beecher Falls hold enough silt on their bottoms to have good populations of burrowing mayflies, supplementing the predominant clingers of the upper water.

The river is bigger here, and though accessible, it doesn't seem to get the heavy pressure of the stretch between First Lake and Lake Francis. Perhaps the bigger water is intimidating to the casual wader, but this stretch is great wading water for advanced fishermen with proper equipment. Chest waders, felt soles (best with aluminum cleats), and a wading staff are needed. With care the river can be crossed often. The water is big and I'm sure the average fish is bigger here than in the headwater stretches. The water is slightly more alkaline and the biomass is thriving and diverse. More minnows and sculpins live here and trout put on meat quicker. Runs of clean spawning gravel make the river a better nursery and native fish outnumber the stockers.

Below West Stewartstown the river makes up its mind. After it rolls its bulk into the big rock at the base of the County Home, the flood plain broadens. The Connecticut is now a major river meandering its way majestically through the verdant patchwork fields of some of the east's most beautiful and fertile farming country. There still are rapids and riffles and deep pulsing runs.

Uplifted rock and humps of glacial gravel dramatically hinder the river's flow in many places, but the Connecticut flows deep and wide and mysterious for long stretches.

Wading must be done selectively now, as the flow can seldom be crossed. You must plan how you are going to work the water, but the planning is worth it. There are very big fish in this part of the river. Men who have spent years of days fishing here talk of fish sighted and hooked that would shatter Ken Reed's record. Monty Montplaisir tells of a tarpon fishing fanatic from Florida who fished with a heavy ten weight salmon rod and saltwater multiplier reel

loaded with 150 yards of twenty pound backing. He used only big streamers, 1/0 and 2/0 sculpin patterns, and fished a lot in the late afternoon. He wasn't interested in a lot of action, only big fish.

He fished every day for almost a week without a strike. Cast and strip, cast and strip, the same routine all day long for nearly five days. Late one afternoon they were finishing their day in the next big pool below the County Home. This pool is another slow curve of quiet, very deep water that whispers incessantly, "big fish." Monty was standing on the high undercut bank of the west side of the pool. The sun, about to slip behind the Vermont mountains, was directly behind him, probing the depths. At the head of the pool his client was wrapping it up for the day. Just a few more swings of the big fly and it was back to Colebrook for a beer and a thick steak.

The sculpin imitation thudded against the bank at Monty's feet and plopped into the black, shadowed water. Monty's eye casually followed its swing through the shadow to the sun line. When the fly broke into the light he noticed a huge dark shape coasting behind it and in a heartbeat the fish rolled up and took the fly. When his client raised his rod he hooked the fish and rolled it slightly, and Monty had a good look at a brown that he estimated at between twenty and twenty five pounds.

Monty saw the fish hang in the water and shake his head a few times, not realizing he was connected to something. Then he darted for the depths, boiling the surface with a sweep of his broad tail. For a few minutes the fish charged around his home pool, the activity alternating between short, powerful runs and frantic reeling when the fish ran towards the head of the pool. Then the fish slowed and sulked in the deepest part. The Floridian, no stranger to fighting big fish, tried to pressure the giant brown into movement, but the huge trout wasn't buying. The combination of bulk plus deep, fast water allowed him to stay just where he was. Monty says it was as if the fish stopped to rest and think the situation through.

After two minutes of stalemate the brown turned and very deliberately, without panic, headed for the tail of the pool. The Floridian followed, exerting as much pressure as he dared. Monty was the last person to see the fish. He glimpsed a broad spotted flank as the brown rolled in the riffle at the end of the tail of the pool. It was as if the fish was waving good-bye. The west bank of the run below the riffle was studded with blowdowns and other debris piled and scrambled by winter ice. The huge fish deliberately swam into the jumble of limbs and tree trunks. When he succeeded in wrapping the leader a simple lunge popped the tippet. Monty is a quiet, conservative New Englander, but he never fails to get excited when he tells this story.

This is my favorite stretch of river, the twenty six miles of meandering, deep water from West Stewartstown downstream to past Colebrook, the largest town on the upper river. A very civilized little town, Colebrook is the commercial center of the area and offers about anything the visitor might need, including accommodations, restaurants, fly shops, and sporting goods stores. This piece of water ends at the no-kill section in North Stratford. It is big and deep and often mysterious. Even though it can be fished by every lawful method from worms to flies, it gets very little pressure. It is bordered, but not closely, by major roads on both sides, but there is no true public access. Landowners will usually allow you to cross to its banks, but you must ask permission.

You can't see much of the river from the road; you'll need a canoe or drift boat to explore its potential. Refer to the detailed maps from *The New Hampshire Atlas,* available in Colebrook, and use two cars. Plan the distance you think you can cover in the time you have, then cut that distance in half. Good fishing is everywhere on the river and you need time to savor and discover it. Secure launching and take-out permission from the appropriate landowners. Beach your boat and wade the most tantalizing riffles and runs. Fish from your boat in the deep sections.

You'll discover one of the east's finest trout fisheries. From the bank the water appears deceptively slow and looks like it would be warm, but once you launch you'll realize it is big water moving swiftly through a smooth channel. It is continuously cooled by underwater springs, and your stream thermometer will barely touch sixty degrees in mid-summer at the no-kill section at North Stratford, thirty five miles from Murphy Dam.

The fertility and fish holding capability of this stretch is exceptional. The pH averages a perfect 7.2 and the fertility of the agricultural flood plain produces an incredible abundance of life. *Hexagenia limbata,* March browns, *Potamanthus,* hendricksons, green drakes, *Isonychias,* blue-winged olives, tricos, and pale evening duns: these are some of the mayflies represented. At least four species of stoneflies, a plethora of caddis from 12's to 20's, uncounted chironomids, and a continual sprinkling of terrestrials from the lush meadows and hardwood forests that border the water make fly selection the observational challenge that defines superb fishing.

Numerous stretches of clean gravel provide good spawning opportunities for both browns and rainbows. The brookies prefer to spawn in the numerous cold feeder streams and tend to hold near their mouths. Icy springs in the bed of the river hold good brookies; these are usually invisible, so brookie action comes and goes as you move downriver. Some rainbows are stocked on this stretch, but not many, as stocking is simply not necessary. The healthy juvenile populations of all three trout species attest to the natural fertility of the river and the lack of fishing pressure.

Even on long summer weekends canoeing purists outnumber fishermen on the river. This is one of the few places in the Northeast where you can fish productive trout water on Fourth of July weekend in solitude. Forked sticks near accessible areas indicate some bait fishing pressure, but I have seldom seen one filled with a rod.

The float itself is a rare and special experience. You slip silently along, surprising a watering herd of Holsteins at one turn and a family of dabbling black ducks at the next. The mood of the river and the fishing challenge constantly change. I always float with two rods rigged: one a delicate four or five weight with a floating weight forward line, the other an eight or nine weight with a big Zonker or Matuka knotted to a 3x tippet and a fast-sinking-tip line. When nothing is showing I chuck the streamer into the bank or near other obvious good lies. I use the delicate smaller rig for rising fish. Both rigs will often see action in a short stretch.

The barely perceptible edge currents of the smooth sections must be carefully observed. Tiny *Baetis*, or blue winged olives, hatch in vast numbers near the banks and the duns quickly disperse into the bordering vegetation. Big browns and rainbows take up feeding stations and suck down stillborn duns and helpless emergers. The rises are tiny little dimples like chubs taking midges and the fish are very selective. Tiny soft hackles, #20 or 22, dead drifted in the surface film, take these fish with surprising ease. At least, fool them with surprising ease. Landing a two or three pound fish on a 6x tippet and a #22 fly in a current is a pretty dicey proposition. A strike indicator at your tippet knot saves a lot of frustration, for it is impossible to see your fly.

The same kind of fishing—big fish on little flies—continues through the late summer into the fall with the late morning spinner fall of tricos in most of the slower, mud bottomed runs and pools. In mid-morning the tiny spinners flutter down like crystal flakes and big fish move to the surface to tip and sip the trapped bounty. These fish are right under the surface mirror and can't see very far. Work on one close fish at a time and concentrate on putting your fly right on his nose in synchronization with his feeding rhythm. Patient accuracy catches fish.

The no-kill section, three miles of river above North Stratford, is faster and more riffled. It gets more pressure, but it holds plenty of fish. The rules are artificials with a single hook only, so spinning gear with the right lure is OK. This is good stonefly and caddis water, but heavy populations of clinger and swimming nymph mayflies, like March browns, *Isonychias*, and *Potomanthus* are also represented. This water can be waded with care and there is a lot of river to wade. A serious angler could spend a week on the no-kill section alone and not totally cover it.

The Upper Connecticut lingers in the mind of any fisherman lucky enough to have sampled it. There are few rivers in the east that match it for fertility and variety of angling experience. It drifts into your thoughts when you least expect it, beckoning with its promise of big clean water and wild fish, of green mountains and crisp pink sunsets, of feeding moose and herds of black and white cows against bright green grass. It whispers of the good things of our earth.

Robert Panuska was born and raised in the midwest, attended school in the east and far west and spent 20 years as an advertising photographer in Miami. Though an avid salt water fly fisherman, he is addicted to cold water and rising trout, and the Connecticut has been his favorite eastern stream for more than 10 years. His writings have appeared in *Fly Fisherman* and *Trout*.

Seven

The White
by Mark Scott

Vermont evokes images of rolling hills, covered bridges, and pristine water so clean you can count the pebbles. If that's what you want when you fish trout in the Green Mountains, then by all means your first stop should be the scenic White River.

Beginning in the high peaks of central Vermont, the White drains a watershed of 710 square miles and offers nearly 100 miles of challenging fishing for three species of trout. Along its course, the river ranges from small pools and riffles to long shade-lined pools, heavy rips, and pools that drop 20 feet or more. The White River is, in effect, many rivers in one.

The White has a reputation for trophy trout, but like any river it does not give them up with any regularity. I fish it frequently, catching wild brook trout and rainbows in the 10- to 13- inch class along with an occasional 18- to 20-inch brown trout. But I've yet to land one of those really big trout this river produces every year.

Fishing guide Paul Albertazzi of Stockbridge knows about the big trout that lie in the White and has seen many of them firsthand. But it's more than just the trophy fish that attracts Albertazzi to the White. "Diversity in the watershed is what I like about the White," Albertazzi admits. "This river offers fast water, slow glides, undercut banks and deep pools, all within easy access of a road."

The lower stretches of the White consistently produce big rainbows and browns every summer, while the middle reaches are a fly fisherman's paradise and the headwaters hold wild brook trout. The insect hatches are decent, though sporadic. In some stretches, brook, rainbow and brown trout are all present. All in all, the White River offers some of the best trout fishing opportunities in New England.

In fact, the White River is receiving considerable attention in the Northeast because it's Vermont's best chance for return of the Atlantic salmon. Back in the late 1700's, twenty-pound salmon spawned in the White in large numbers. They disappeared at the end of the eighteenth century when a dam was constructed on the Connecticut River below Miller Falls, effectively preventing them from ascending the White.

Since 1971 the U.S. Fish and Wildlife Service and the Vermont Fish and Wildlife Department have stocked over a million young salmon in this watershed in an attempt to establish a wild run of salmon from the ocean. To date, salmon returns have been dismal, although biologists continue their efforts. Strong encouragement came when the first salmon returning to Vermont waters, in modern times, was spotted in the White on July 17, 1986. It was seen from the Route 107 bridge in Stockbridge and was estimated to be 22 inches long. If you catch a small salmon, return it carefully to the water. A young salmon is characterized by seven to 12 vertical dark bars or "parr marks" on its sides with several small red dots between the stripes. Young salmon can be confused with a small brown trout, but the salmon will lack any red coloration on the adipose fin or halos around their spots. They are strictly protected under Vermont's endangered species law.

The White's selection as a salmon restoration site underscores its water quality. Its upper reaches have five branches of clear, cold water. Although the best trout fishing is found in the main stem, each contributory branch is unique and offers its own set of angling opportunities and challenges.

Given the White's length, you could fish for days and catch nothing. Some sections are definitely worth trying, and others quite simply aren't. Here's how I see the fishing opportunities.

WEST BRANCH

The water of the West Branch is well oxygenated, as it rushes down from mountain peaks that tower to 3,000 feet. The brook flows about seven miles through a heavily forested valley along a winding dirt road called the Bingo Valley Road to Route 73, where it enters the main stem in Rochester. Brook trout claim the upper reaches, and rainbows take over where the stream reaches Route 73. You'll find brown trout near Rochester.

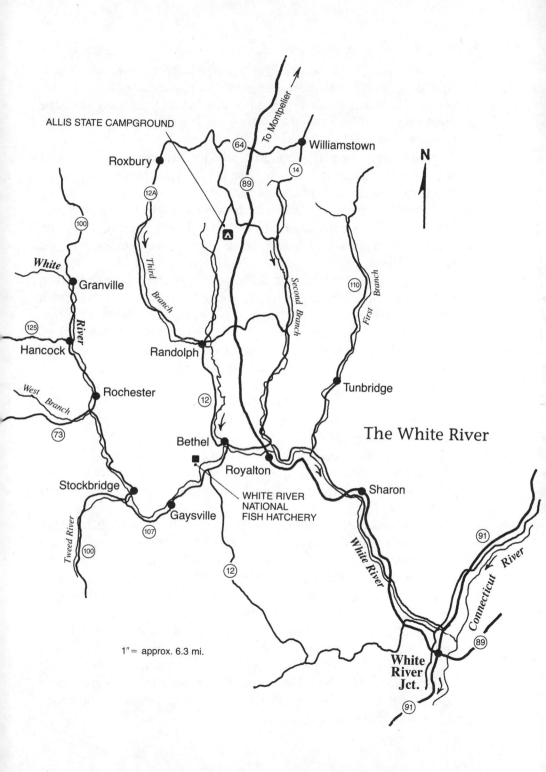

ALLIS STATE CAMPGROUND

Roxbury

12A

To Montpelier

64

89

14

Williamstown

100

White

Granville

Third Branch

Second Branch

110

First Branch

125

Hancock

River

Randolph

Tunbridge

West Branch

Rochester

12

The White River

73

Bethel

Royalton

WHITE RIVER
NATIONAL
FISH HATCHERY

Sharon

Stockbridge

107

Gaysville

Tweed River

100

12

White River

Connecticut River

91

89

White
River
Jct.

91

1″ = approx. 6.3 mi.

N

Bingo Valley is in the heart of the Green Mountain National Forest Service's land. While here, you get the true sense of wilderness country. Wildlife such as bear, fisher, and grouse live in this valley. Primitive camping along the brook is permitted. For more information, contact the Green Mountain National Forest Service, Box 519, Rutland, Vt. 05701.

The clear water and five-foot-deep pools formed from the rapid drop of water over the mountain boulders make this stream appear like top-notch brook trout water but it just doesn't pan out.

John Claussen, regional district fisheries biologist with the state agrees. "The waters of the upper reaches of the West Branch just aren't very productive. The water is so clean that it lacks nutrients. A seven-inch brookie is a good one here," he observes.

The lower reach of the West Branch offers better rainbow and brown trout fishing. Big fish from lower reaches of the White move into this stretch during summer, as water from Brandon Brook helps cool the temperatures. It's easy to reach this stretch as it meanders within eyesight of Route 73. In fact, there's a public fishing access site on Route 73, well-marked and with ample parking, about two miles from the center of Rochester.

UPPER MAIN STEM

The upper main stem of the White trickles down from the spine of some of Vermont's tallest peaks, tumbling through the town of Granville. This section typifies what most anglers look for in a wild trout stream. The brook flows clean and clear through a tangle of dense hardwoods and alders. Tree blowdowns and streamside brush render the upper stretches fishable for only the most agile.

Wild brook trout are the primary inhabitants. The fish don't get large, but come summer they do get very hungry. The best way to fish this section is to walk down the middle of the stream with a number eight hook baited with a small worm. A secret approach to the hidden pockets of water beneath boulders, fallen logs, and undercut banks is the key to catching them. You fish here more to catch dinner than anything else.

A little farther downstream, between Hancock and Rochester, all three trout species are found. Brown trout become more common, and some of the best fly fishing on the White occurs near Rochester. The river is easily accessed from Route 100. A good place to park is next to the river along Route 100 just north of where it meets Route 73. Most people fish this stretch by wading upstream.

THIRD BRANCH

The Third Branch starts above Roxbury with the convergence of several small mountain brooks. It joins the main stem of the White in Bethel. This branch covers more than 20 miles of good looking trout water along Route 12, although only the upper reaches near Roxbury are worth fishing. Here, small brook trout with an occasional brown or rainbow, predominate. The lower part winds through a series of farms that send forth a lot of silt, killing aquatic insects. A flood in 1984 widened the White in many places, including this branch, resulting in warmer water and loss of cover for trout. The other stretch worth trying, especially for big browns in the spring, is between Randolph and Bethel.

"Most of the browns are taken in the bigger pools early in the season just after spring runoff," comments state game warden Doug Lawrence, who has patrolled the entire White for the past eight years. "I know a lot of people come

to the White to fly fish, but the big browns are taken on either garden worms or nightcrawlers fished on the bottom early in the year. Later on they catch some on small gold and black or silver and black Rapalas at twilight," he adds.

SECOND BRANCH

The Second Branch flows from Williamstown Gulf almost 20 miles south to Royalton where it enters the main stem of the White. For the fisherman, this is probably the least desirable branch of the White. Like most headwater streams in Vermont, the upper section of the Second Branch holds some wild brook trout, but serious erosion from agriculture along this branch has severely damaged the trout population. In fact, the U.S. Fish and Wildlife Service has reported this section as having zero potential for salmonid reproduction. Outside of where Route 14 crosses the Second Branch several times, access is difficult because of pastures.

One favorite fishing spot on the lower reach of the Second Branch is the natural waterfalls at Spaulding's Farm, located off Route 14, just north of where it meets Route 107 in South Royalton. These falls act as a natural barrier and hold big rainbows in spring and big browns in fall. These fish are spawning, of course, and since they're migrants from the main stem they are unaffected by the relative infertility of the Second Branch.

FIRST BRANCH

Outside of the main stem, the First Branch used to offer the best trout fishing on the White. Today, fishing on the first branch is fair at best. From Chelsea downstream to Tunbridge there is good fly fishing for rainbows. This stream parallels Route 110 and it offers a good combination of fast riffles and deep pools. Below Tunbridge, a few big browns are taken every spring. Most of the upper reaches of this branch are posted.

MAIN STEM

The main stem of the White, from Rochester to its junction with the Connecticut River in Hartford, is what makes this river one of the finest in the Northeast. You will find about 45 miles of fishable river uninterrupted by dams. Rainbows are the principal fish with some large browns in the bigger pools. The lower 13 or so miles of the White also offer some good fishing for smallmouth bass. Like most big streams, certain stretches of the White produce better than others.

From Gaysville upstream to Hancock is a popular fly fishing stretch.

What makes this section choice, beyond its nice blend of riffles, pools and some slow-moving runs, is its relative seclusion. Routes 100 and 107 bring you near the river; however, you should expect to walk a half mile or so to get to the hidden runs. Easiest access can be obtained by stopping and asking a farmer for permission to park in his yard and fish his "back forty." Most times he'll tell you about an exceptional area worth trying because he usually doesn't have time to fish it himself. Either way, he'll probably appreciate your taking a few minutes to ask.

The stretch of the main stem near Gaysville is very popular, at least partially because it is easily accessed from Route 100. Even from the highway you can glimpse the nice combination of runs and pools that characterizes this stretch.

The White forms an exceptionally large pool just upstream of Gaysville, under the bridge on the road from Route 107 to the center of Stockbridge. Summer depths in this pool average from 12 to 15 feet. I was fishing here one early summer morning and had an experience I'll never forget. I was drifting a nightcrawler through the tail of the pool when a huge trout hit so hard that instinctively I yanked hard. It took only a second for the entire experience to begin—and end. The six-pound test monofilament line broke instantly, and I watched the large trout dart downstream. I've heard similar stories from others about this same pool. My guess is that this fish was a large rainbow, since downstream from Gaysville to Bethel there's a good mix of moderately flowing riffles and deep pools. It is usually this stretch that each spring gives up some of the bigger rainbows.

The rainbows spawn in the spring, and you can find them where small tributaries enter. Nightcrawlers are one very productive bait. Some of the more popular gathering spots early in the season are the big pools just below the White River Fish Hatchery in Bethel on Route 107.

Below Bethel, the river becomes big water with deep aqua-hued pools. It is this section that is prized by Vermonters who fish the river regularly. "I love this section," says guide Albertazzi. "There's just so many places to fish. There's pools 25 feet deep, one after another, all the way to the Connecticut River. The trout run bigger here and there's plenty of easy access from Route 14, which parallels the river downstream. My favorite section is in Sharon, just off exit 2 from I-89. It's a peaceful and beautiful stretch to fish, plus there's plenty of hard-fighting rainbows here."

The current slows in the lower sections, making the waters more suited for big brown trout. This beat also receives a heavy stocking of rainbow trout, which tend to stay in the swifter runs. You'll have better luck fishing for rainbows in the faster waters at the heads of the pools. The faster the water you can find, the better your luck because this is where the rainbows concentrate when they feed.

July and August fishing really drops off on the main stem. During hot weather, some fish migrate upstream to above Gaysville; some will congregate where the water is cooler near the confluences of the smaller tributaries like Locust Creek between Gaysville and Bethel, Broad Brook in Sharon, or Mill Brook in West Hartford; and still others become inactive and wait until dark to feed.

WHEN TO FISH

Vermont's trout season traditionally opens the second Saturday of April and continues until the last Sunday of October. Spring in Vermont means melting snow and high, roily water. It's a tough time for stream fishermen. You have to be a little bit daring to wade much in April, when the water temperature hovers around 40°F.

Early season fishing on the White is about as predictable as the weather in the Green Mountains. The amount of snow melt plays a big role in determining water flow. Invariably, the upper branches of the White are unfishable until mid-May because of heavy runoff. The main stem offers the best fishing for trophy trout early in the season. A key to catching fish early is to fish deep along the bottom. As I mentioned earlier, spawning rainbows can be found near the entrances of some of the smaller streams on opening day.

According to surveys conducted by the Fish and Wildlife Department, about 70 percent of the anglers use bait to catch fish on the White. In spring, it's often the most productive way to fish. Nightcrawlers or small golden shiners weighted with a few split shot on six-pound test monofilament line seems to be the standard set-up. A local tactic bait fishermen use for the rainbows is to break a nightcrawler in two, using just half. This is one of my best tactics, but I take it one step further and use only the lower half of the nightcrawler, hooking it once at the break. During high water, place the bait in back eddies or behind boulders because trout cannot stay in the fast current long.

Lures and spinners work well in the deeper pools. In the spring, it's a good idea to retrieve lures slowly and weight your line with a couple of splitshot like you would bait so it drags across the bottom. That technique worked for Rick McGarry several years ago when he took the state's annual record rainbow, a nine pounder on a Colorado Spinner. Rapalas, Panther Martins, Sidewinders, Al's Goldfishes and Phoebes are all favorite lures for the White.

Most people planning a trip to the White pick the first or second week of June. By then spring runoff has waned and warming water temperatures mean mayfly and caddis hatches for the trout and a special time for the dry fly fisherman. For the most part, the White is not a fertile river. As with most relatively infertile rivers in Vermont, insect hatches tend to be irregular, small and localized. There will be some mayfly activities. March brown nymphs are good to try all through June because they emerge sporadically all day long.

Fly fishers who look to cast to rising trout pay an attentive eye to caddis hatches. Like caddis everywhere, you won't find common names for the ones that hatch on the White River. As with most other Vermont rivers, olive-brown caddis adults in sizes 12 to 14 are the most prolific. For that reason, the Elk Hair Caddis with gray caribou wings and olive body is a very popular fly.

On the White, the Vermont Hare's Ear Caddis, designed by Farrow Allen, often makes a superior general adult caddis imitation. The dark olive Henryville Special, while an effective fly on more turbulent runs, offers a bushy profile on the water. On the transparent White, such an effect often sends fish darting to the bottom. The Vermont Hare's Ear Caddis floats in the film. It is a simple fly to tie, as there are no wings. Just wind one grizzly and one brown hackle over a body that has been dubbed with hare's ear fur (with the guard hairs). Natural gray brown is good but died colors can be used to create more accurate imitations. A short tail of mixed brown and grizzly hackle fibers is optional, but is added by some tiers.

For bigger trout, streamers may be best. For that reason, the slow clear water of the White demands precision for the streamer angler as well as the nymph or dry fly angler. The Thunder Creek Series tied with maribou rather than bucktail offers a pattern which replicates closely the natural bait fish in the White and at the same time permits fly fishers to "work" in the stretch waters of the White.

Slaymaker's series of little brown, brook and rainbow trout streamers offers a good imitation of the trout and salmon fry food throughout the White. Close attention to detail with these streamers might pay off with a trophy trout. The White River is noted for big browns, but you won't catch many on size 20 dry flies.

From about mid-June on, fly fishermen have the White pretty much to themselves as the bait fishing activity peaks in May and comes to a halt in summer. Most non-residents visit the White to fly fish the clean, clear waters. For early season fly fishing, weighted stonefly nymphs often bring results. Tie and fish them as big as #4 4x long. Fish can be caught early in the season by casting these large nymphs upstream in the slow water of the larger pools. You should also be prepared for a sudden hatch of hendricksons in April or the first two weeks in May. The activity may be brief, but the trout will ignore everything else except some close imitation of *E. subvaria.*

My friend, Marcel Rocheleau, relayed this incident to me about fishing the White one evening near Bethel.

"I had an experience on the White a few years ago that fly fishermen dream of. It was in early June just before dark and this particular hatch (the hendrickson) occurred. The water boiled with voracious trout. Casting after the first 15 minutes was strictly by sound, but I managed to catch and release several trout, including some over 15 inches." His story reminds me of my first experience on the White.

It was about 20 years ago and I was fishing with worms, the only way I knew how then, on the main stem in Bethel. The river was quiet until the sun began to set. Large mayflies began hatching, and trout were splashing in every

riffle and pool. My evening was topped when a brown trout of at least six pounds came almost full body out of the water after an insect. But experiences such as these remain exceptions.

Newcomers fly fishing the White can experience a lot of frustration. In fact, Guide Albertazzi attributes the difficulty beginners have on the White to their inability to read the water. Without consistent and predictable insect hatches, you must look to the fast water at the heads of the glides and pools to find the feeding rainbows.

White River trout become wary in summer, and the clear waters allow them to scrutinize every offering. By mid-summer, flies grow increasingly small, with the exception of the *Potamanthus,* that large cream mayfly. Slate-gray tricos work best early in the morning during the hot dog-days of August. Now, fishing the faster waters with lighter leaders, can be a good approach. Anglers should be prepared to encounter caddis hatches in June and July in sizes 12 through 16 and shades of buff, light green and brown.

For every trout in the White River that rises to an adult caddis, five will take a caddis pupa. Like caddis pupae on most other trout rivers, those in the White have bodies that range in color from light green to olive. One of the most effective materials for these pupa bodies is Antron, used in patterns that approximate those in LaFontaine's master work on caddis flies. Antron traps air bubbles to imitate the caddis shooting up to the surface just before or while it is shucking its pupal case.

Fishing slacks off on the White from mid-July through early September because of the lower stream flows and warmer temperatures. You can catch fish then, but success might well be limited to early morning or the last 45 minutes of daylight. On the other hand, fall fishing is fantastic on the White, barring heavy rains. Water temperatures will drop to the high 50's in October, and at this time the rainbows go on a feeding spree before winter.

Regardless of the month, runoff from five mountain basins can change the White quickly. Adaptability, then, is one of the keys to success here. For example, your plans may call for fishing the main stem near Gaysville. Yet if you find high water, you might be better off to venture up north to fish smaller water or fish the big pools below Bethel.

In spring, high runoff attracts a lot of recreational canoeists to the White. Few people fish the White from a canoe, probably because you can get to just about all parts of the river from shore. If you wish to fish one of the better sections of the White from a canoe, Warden Lawrence recommends this five hour float: put in at the Foxstand Bridge in Royalton (jct. of Route

14 and Route 107) and float downstream to the Sharon Village bridge (jct. of Route 14 and 132). For canoeing, one helpful publication is the *A.M.C. River Guide, New Hampshire/Vermont,* available from the Appalachian Mountain Club, 5 Joy St., Boston, MA 02108.

FINDING LODGING AND SERVICES

Many facilities, ranging from private campgrounds to motels, cater to anglers along the White River. For information on these contact the Vermont State Chamber of Commerce, Box 57, Montpelier, Vt. 05602 and ask for the telephone number of the Chamber of Commerce nearest to where you wish to stay and fish.

A number of fishing guides specialize in trips to the White River. You can obtain a list of these, as well as a *Vermont Guide to Fishing* and license and season information, by contacting the Vermont Fish and Wildlife Department, 103 South Main St., Waterbury, Vt. 05676.

A valuable aid to visitors of the Green Mountain State is an official Vermont highway map, available free by writing the Agency of Development and Community Affairs, Vermont Travel Division, 134 State St., Montpelier, Vt. 05602.

Mark Scott has been fishing Vermont's waters for almost 30 years. He is a freelance outdoor writer with work appearing regularly in *Outdoor Life, Northeast Woods and Waters* and *The Vermont Sportsman.* He also works full time as Education Coordinator for the Vermont Fish and Wildlife Department. Mark holds a B.S. in Wildlife Management from the Univ. of Maine and an M.S. in Wildlife Biology from the Univ. of Vermont.

Eight

The Battenkill
by Bob Zajac

The charming Battenkill is a river richly steeped in the history and tradition of fly fishing. It begins gently as a soft southerly trickle in the Otter Creek-Emerald Lake area, deep in the Taconic Mountains in southern Vermont. Its flow gradually increases, nurtured by numerous small icy springs that well up within the shadows of mountains that rise more than 3,000 feet above sea level. The Battenkill sneaks through East Dorset and then meanders somewhat surreptitiously through Manchester. Here, its currents are mostly hidden by the growing expanse of factory outlets and tourist boutiques that have recently taken root in this bustling resort town. Its escape from the tourist center is hastened when the West Branch joins the river and the ever-widening headwaters next follow a placid, winding trail through valley meadows until they meet the Roaring Branch just upstream from Arlington. Shortly, the river turns east to leave Norman Rockwell country. In the angular valley downstream, it gathers momentum as it runs rather swiftly past white clapboard houses where pot-bellied stoves glow cherry red on long, cold winter nights. After twenty-four miles, the river enters New York but not before adding its presence to complete such bucolic scenes as found at Benedict's Crossing. It was here that the great painter, Odgen Pleissner, was inspired to create still another exquisite watercolor depicting a special moment in an angler's life.

In New York, the river widens quickly yet gracefully as it passes Lee Wulff's former home. Several miles later and still averaging less than seventy feet in width, it coils through Eagleville where it is graced by a remarkably well-groomed, covered wooden bridge of Civil War vintage. The river then rolls north past Shushan, home of Lew Oatman, the creator of numerous innovative fly patterns tied specifically for the Battenkill. His Shushan Postmaster and Battenkill Minnow streamers are still effective patterns here today and on many other trout streams as well. The river continues over the next three or four miles as if seeking a direct route to Rexleigh where it bends to the west toward Greenwich and then loops south to Middle Falls. In Schuylerville, where England's General John Burgoyne surrendered his five thousand soldiers to an emerging American nation in 1777, the Battenkill, some forty-nine miles from its source, quietly surrenders to the Hudson.

Along most of its length, the 'Kill is bordered by alders and willows that shield the cool, well-oxygenated water from the heat of the sun. It's this canopy factor that also contributes to the river's exceptionally low temperatures when compared to many other trout streams. The Battenkill rarely exceeds seventy degrees, except during drought conditions, and though higher water temperatures may postpone hatches, the fish remain in relative comfort. The riverbed itself is often a mosaic of limestone and marble gravel that can sometimes stare back at you through the gin-clear water. Timeless wooden covered bridges span its width at several locations, each marking a pool born of the bridge's construction. Their aging, graying shells elicit lengthy gazes from those who view their historic designs.

The seasons on the Battenkill are visual studies of panoramas: the harsh stillness of winter as a chiaroscuro of lead-colored water and white snow; the bright spring as its sun bounces light from a dazzling surface of countless diamonds; and the comforting summer as it brings a delicious verdant warmth in its prelude to the explosive autumn tapestry of crimson and gold. It is truly a beautiful river.

The Battenkill is an American treasure, a pristine, rural waterway, where brook and brown trout thrive and reproduce naturally in a delicate ecosystem carved in a magnificent setting. The river is an integral part of a sportsman's paradise where deer, turkey and ruffed grouse thrive in a mixed terrain of farmland, mountains and vast tracts of deep woods. For more than two centuries the river has captured the spirit of artists, writers, naturalists and fly fishermen. Guests of the river are attracted by the magical vistas, the endangered bald eagle or the rare Hooker's orchid. Anglers come to be taunted and teased by the rising native trout that are crisply marked, living palettes of color as beautiful as trout anywhere.

In Vermont, some of the upper river can only be accessed by crossing

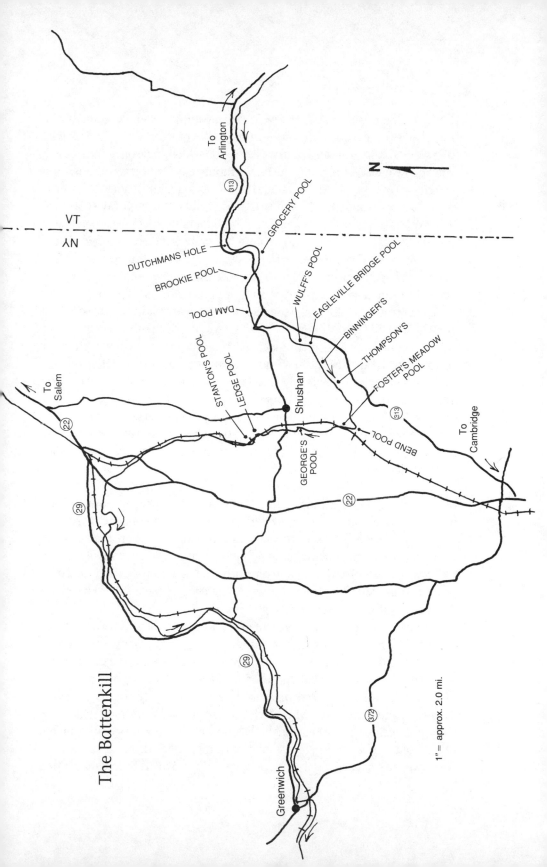

The Battenkill

VT
NY

To Arlington

GROCERY POOL

DUTCHMANS HOLE

BROOKIE POOL

DAM POOL

WULFF'S POOL

EAGLEVILLE BRIDGE POOL

BINNINGER'S

THOMPSON'S

FOSTER'S MEADOW POOL

STANTON'S POOL

LEDGE POOL

Shushan

GEORGE'S POOL

BEND POOL

To Salem

To Cambridge

Greenwich

1" = approx. 2.0 mi.

private property along Route 71, but permission is generally granted to a polite and sincere request. You could also reach a quiet section of the river by following the railroad tracks north of Arlington which angle off to the east just south of the little 7A bridge. There's a Vermont State Department of Fish and Wildlife access area in Arlington and below this quaint hamlet the river is rarely far from Route 313, a well maintained ribbon of highway shared by New York and Vermont. A five minute hike is about the longest you'll take to pools in this section, but heavy fishing pressure is the obvious negative to such easy access. One progressive landowner has even instituted a "slot limit" along his property in an attempt to upgrade the quality of fishing. Conceptually, slot limits serve to remove a higher number of smaller fish and an occasional trophy while leaving significant numbers of mature fish to continue growing, thereby giving the river the chance to produce more fish of greater size. Hopefully, if successful, this idea will be replicated elsewhere as the river is heavily fished and the vast majority of trout taken are in the eight to eleven inch range. Some local bait fishermen have been accused of a rather liberal interpretation of the daily creel limit which the State of Vermont has presently set at twelve fish or five pounds per day. Many years of this somewhat cavalier attitude toward conservation may have had its effect on the river, but any new regulations promulgated by either state seem to invoke controversy. Vermont stopped stocking the Battenkill in 1975.

Big fish continue to become more scarce each season but the flats below Manchester in Vermont and the deep holes around Shushan in New York are the preferred holding areas for the very small proportion of fish that survive long enough to reach the sixteen inch mark. Nonetheless, there remain some dream fish to be encountered and their existence is verified annually. There are always stories of a twenty-inch plus brown that somebody "wormed out" of one of numerous deep holes during the high waters of early April when the smell of wood smoke was lingering in the air.

In New York, there are approximately fifteen miles of widely varied trout water stretching as far downstream as the Rexleigh area. Below this section, the river loses its intimacy as it widens, deepens and warms to the point where it becomes marginal trout habitat. The Empire State's DEC has designated the first 4.4 miles of the river from the State Line to the covered bridge at Eagleville a Special Regulations Area where live bait of any kind is prohibited and the daily limit of three fish over ten inches is imposed. There is no stocking in this section of the river and here, in spite of numerous environmental threats, there exists a substantial population of naturally spawned brook and brown trout. Log cribbings in this section reflect the efforts of Trout Unlimited's stream improvement projects. An hour from Albany, New York, the Battenkill is the lovely adopted daughter of the Clearwater Chapter.

Streamside chatter echoes theories that the size limits serve only to cull out the larger fish, leaving a smaller sized population to breed a genetically inferior trout. Further, the theories go, due to the absence of these larger carnivorous trout, undesirable coarse fish populations increase.

In the Special Regulation Area, the river is never very far from Route 313. A short, brisk hike from the road, from the 313 bridge, or from the DEC parking area a few miles downstream of the Eagleville bridge at the end of the Special Regs Area will put you on good water rather quickly. On the north side of the river, Hickory Hill Road provides immediate access; other roads worth exploring include Camden Valley Road, Robinson Road and the Eagleville Road. The Special Regs Area is open all year long and it's not unusual to see some fevered soul plying his craft on a cold but bright and sunny February afternoon. No wonder: there can be risers seen even during this harsh and most difficult month. The tell-tale rings of feeding fish mark the demise of Diptera, stoneflies, tiny blue-winged olive mayflies (generally referred to as TBO's) and other minutiae amidst seemingly glacial environs.

Below the Special Regs Area the stream receives modest numbers of hatchery fish whose colors and spirit pale significantly when compared to the native residents. From the Eagleville bridge downstream to Shushan, the river gradually widens and slows as it passes through several miles of fertile farmland in its flight from the area of heaviest angling pressure. Access below Eagleville becomes as good an excuse as any for a healthy stroll.

Downstream from Shushan, the 'Kill winds through still another pretty valley and weaves itself through a D&H Railroad crossing which provides access to this more remote section of the river. For the adventuresome, solitude, hatches and rising trout can be found there, away from the crowds. This same area can also be entered from farther downstream by following the railroad tracks near the Rexleigh Bridge parking area on Rexleigh Road off Route 22.

The major hatches on the Battenkill are fairly dependable and their timing is generally about a week to ten days after the Catskills and a few days to a week or so before the Adirondacks. The 'Kill's insect populations have been assiduously researched by pioneering angling entomologists such as Preston Jennings, Ernest Schwiebert, Ed Koch and countless others of lesser reputation.

The anxious early season fisherman will find trout sipping size 18-20 blue-winged olives *(Baetis vagans)* and size 16-18 blue quills *(Paraleptophlebia adoptiva)*. These hatches begin as early as midday and can continue through the afternoon in spite of the moody, if not blustery, mid to late April weather. Light hatches of quill gordons *(Epeorus pluralis)* in size 14 follow as the temperatures warm, but the hendrickson *(Ephemerella subvaria)* is generally acknowledged as the true guarantor of excellent spring fishing. The hatch usually starts between two and three in the afternoon and allows the angler to arrive at a gentlemanly hour. The consistent strength of this hatch coupled with the size of the insect will usually bring on a heavy rise. Knowledgeable fly fishermen are aware that the nymph of this species becomes very active a few hours before the surface activity begins. A size 12 or 14 Hendrickson or Gold Ribbed Hare's Ear nymph fished below the surface can be deadly just prior to the hatch. These patterns and caddis emergers in sizes 12-18 are productive throughout the year.

Depending on the water level and temperature, the hendrickson duns generally start appearing during the last days of April with the hatch usually peaking in early May. Spinner activity will often bring the fish back up in the early evening after the hatch has been on strong for several days. Although most of the river's bed slopes gently, aggressive waders should be alert as the substantial spring runoff from the mountains will fill the river from bank to bank. Caution is advised as the flow is deceptively strong due to its sheer volume. Heavy rain, lusted for during mid-summer droughts, is the nemesis of the early season. A wading angler distracted by rising fish won't realize the true strength of the current until he's thigh deep and sometimes that can be too late for a graceful, dry exit.

After the hendricksons have waned, various caddis hatches intensify and help carry the action through May. They emerge in a variety of sizes and colors but the most prevalent species at this time seems to be an olive-bodied, brown-winged size 18. An Elk Hair Caddis or Henryville Special in the appropriate size and color combination are excellent choices for selective fish.

The warmth of late spring generates size 16 sulphurs (*Ephemerella dorothea*), size 10 March browns (*Stenonema vicarium*) and size 14 gray foxes (*Stenonema fuscum*) and by early June, although there is some afternoon activity, the fly fisherman's priority becomes the evening hatch. Between six p.m. and dark, the river will produce a variety of insects including cahills (various *Stenonema* species) in sizes 10-16, and huge green drakes in size 8, 4x-long (*Ephemera guttulata*). Although they do occur elsewhere on the river, the green drake hatch seems to be strongest just below Eagleville. Here, the silt beds formed by run-off from the adjacent cornfields provide optimal habitat for these burrowing nymphs of the *Ephemeridae* family. The strikingly handsome, size 10 cream variant (*Potamanthus distinctus*) begins to show in late June with peak activity in July, but unfortunately the best hatches occur right at dark presenting still another challenge to middle-aged eyes. In addition, the evening hatch will include a diversity of caddis activity as well as mayfly spinner falls that will cause the angler to search his fly boxes for the correct imitations. Observation is critical at this time as success will be the product of not only noting which insect is being taken but pinpointing in what life stage as well. When in doubt, do not hesitate to fish a spinner imitation!

In the heat of summer afternoons and low water conditions, the persistent angler will find himself in midstream, where possible, casting terrestrials to risers holding close to the alders on either bank. This is difficult fishing as one-rise-wonders abound and any fish taken is well earned. Stealthy wading, long leaders, fine tippets, flawless casting and precise imitations are mandatory. Other than very early morning, the best fishing at this time is the evening hatch which has now been sadly reduced to the last half hour or so of light.

From July on, the Battenkill becomes home to that peculiar and esoteric

A beautiful Battenkill brown fooled by a #24 trico imitation.

group of fly fishermen known as "7x Freaks." They are drawn to the river in pursuit of their quarry which will now be feeding on size 24 tricos (*Tricorythodes stygiatus*) followed shortly thereafter by tiny blue-winged olives (*Baetis, Cloeons, Pseudocloeons,* etc.) in sizes 18-24…and smaller! The tricos usually start in July, often as early as five a.m., and are usually followed by the TBO's. By the first week of September, though, these hatches have progressed to the point that the trico spinners are now hitting the water at about 9 a.m. and can mercifully be fished after a good night's sleep. A solid trico hatch on the 'Kill can sometimes last two hours or more and the TBO's all afternoon, which, when conditions are right, can make a wonderful day, especially during the peak of the spectacular change of foliage. These hatches continue well into autumn and anglers should take advantage of New York's Special Regulations Area which knows no closed season. Regulations in both states are subject to change so be sure to consult the appropriate syllabus before fishing.

Because much of the river's character is accented by long, swift, smooth-surfaced runs, first time visitors may not be aware of the rather unique situation that occurs on the surface. To be consistently successful fishing dry flies here, you must first consider each rising fish to be holding beneath a particular area of the surface that is dramatically affected by an extremely complex weave of braided currents. This point cannot be emphasized enough. Although the surface may appear only slightly riffled or almost as smooth as glass, there is often more going on than meets the eye. These currents, because of their intricate nature, have a penchant for inducing what has often been referred to as "invisible drag." Make no mistake about it, the fish can discriminate a dragging fly from their vantage point far better than we can from ours. If your best efforts prove fishless, you can turn the odds in your favor by lengthening your tippet by 50% or so and while you're at it, go one x finer to accommodate the fact that these trout are fished over and often very skittish, not to mention picky. For the sake of example, if you're fishing a size 16 dry fly on a 12 foot leader with a 5x tippet 24 inches long and are reasonably certain that you've matched the hatch and still have not had a take, definitely move to 36 inches of 6x. Also, concentrate on presenting that fly with a reach or curve cast to ensure a drag-free float. Such a change in tactics can often be the difference between the neurotic frenzy of failure and the soothing satisfaction of success.

For the intrepid anglers of the night-fishing persuasion, the Battenkill lends itself quite nicely to the task. Most of the water on both sides of the state line flows over a moderately gentle gradient with long riffle sections of consistent current and sufficient depth for hunting big fish in the dark. As with any river, one should not attempt limited vision wading on the 'Kill without first arming one's self with a thorough knowledge of the terrain in daylight. Scouting trips can pay huge dividends by offering opportunities to make mental notes of where you think the big fish will be feeding. Huge browns seem to show a marked tendency to gravitate to the heads and tails of pools under the cover of darkness. Daytime expeditions will also serve to enlighten you as to the locations of deep holes, fallen trees and other hazardous obstructions that could diminish the pleasure of your night's fishing.

Standard night fishing techniques will work well on the Battenkill. Fishing a series of two or three wet flies across and down through pre-selected areas should bring action in the dark of night. Another excellent method is to fish a large Muddler or similar type fly across and down so it drags across the surface at a steady pace creating a wake. The idea is to make the fly move water. This variation on Atlantic salmon fishing's Portland or Riffled Hitch technique can result in violent, jarring takes, the kind that make wonderful memories to recall in that last moment before deep sleep. Although certainly not for everyone, night fishing offers definite advantages for those among us who are more than just slightly maso: the big fish are surely feeding, the competition from other anglers is eliminated, there are no canoes to contend with and you definitely won't get a sunburn.

The politics of conservation on the Battenkill are far more complex than the hatches. The fragile ecosystem of the river has been increasingly threatened by forces that range from waste disposal and second home construction to recreational overuse and industrial abuse. Here in the '90's, we should be thankful for the efforts of such organizations as the grass roots Friends of the Battenkill as well as the Battenkill Conservancy, the Vermont Natural Resources Council, the Nature Conservancy, Vermonters Organized for Clean Up, Trout Unlimited and the Orvis Company for their efforts in preserving the river thus far. Their strength and determination helped stop a proposed toxic waste dump which was to be located in tiny Sunderland, Vermont, a double haul cast away from the river. Federal and state testing found the metals in the ash to be extremely toxic to aquatic life at concentrations of less than one part per million. Even a minor leaching accident involving such volatile chemicals could have resulted in unquantifiable disaster.

The state of Vermont is currently under considerable pressure by these groups to declare the Battenkill an Outstanding Resource Water which would place conservation oriented restrictions on any further development. The river is also being studied on the Federal level under the Wild, Scenic and Recreational River Systems Act. A "wild and scenic" designation would heighten the scrutiny on any proposed construction or land use on or near the banks of the river.

Until recently, the aluminum hatch was simply regarded as somewhat of a minor nuisance on the Battenkill. In the past decade or so it has come to be viewed with increasing consternation by fishermen. Because there are no dams along the river's trout water and because the river is easily paddled, the number of canoeists seems to be expanding at a geometric rate. Anglers must occasionally bite their tongues as fleets of canoes compete for the finite amount of river that the relatively small Battenkill affords. During the heat of the summer, the canoeists are accompanied by tubers and rafters whose presence makes things even tougher for the fisherman. Whether there can be any resolution to this remains to be seen, but it is a factor to be considered if you're heading there to fish.

If you go, you'll find no shortage of accommodations in the Manchester-Arlington area. Lodging is readily available to suit a variety of needs and budgets. Campsites, inns, bed and breakfasts, motels and posh hotels are located throughout the region. Food offerings range from fast-food chains to true gourmet restaurants. There is a nationally known fly shop in Manchester and a smaller one on Route 313 in New York a few miles west of the state line. Confirmed addicts of the sport, however, should definitely include Manchester's fly fishing museum on their itineraries. After all, in order to plan for the future, we must first look to the past.

Bob Zajac is an active outdoorsman who focuses his attention on fly fishing and big game hunting. In the spring, he can be found harassing trout on the Battenkill and many other New York streams. June through August are reserved for Atlantic salmon while in autumn he is out pursuing Adirondack whitetails. He has contributed to several other books and has had articles published in the *Atlantic Salmon Journal*.

Nine

The Housatonic
by Denis Rice

The Housatonic River flows from north to south through the entire state of Connecticut. From its source in the foothills of the Berkshire Mountains in southwestern Massachusetts to its drainage into Long Island Sound near Milford, Connecticut, the Housatonic, or Housey, stretches for over 120 miles.

Along its flow, the Housatonic takes on a variety of characteristics. In some areas it may be deep and slow, while in others it may be a series of rapids, riffles and runs. It is punctuated by numerous dams, waterfalls and gorges, which ultimately slow the river and transform some sections into lake-like stretches.

The section of the Housey which is of primary interest to the trout fisherman is a six and a half mile beat of water located in the northwestern area of Connecticut. From approximately one and a half miles north of the covered bridge in West Cornwall (an area referred to as Push 'em Up Pool), downstream to the bridge at Routes 4 & 7 in Cornwall Bridge, lies the Housatonic Trout Management Area (TMA).

Within the confines of this area all trout must be released. Approximately half of the management area is designated as "fly fishing only." The fly fishing area begins a mile or so south of the covered bridge and extends to the end of the TMA.

Outside of the fly fishing only section, but within the TMA, any type of lure or bait may be used. For a catch-and-release trout fishing area this may appear unusual; nevertheless, such is the case.

The Trout Management Area is truly beautiful. Within its breadth are tree-lined banks, long pools and oxygen rich rapids. The trout angler can travel along the Housey and literally find every type of fishing condition which may fit his or her fancy.

Having a width of up to one hundred yards or more, dotted with large boulders and fast runs, the Housatonic resembles some of the legendary trout rivers in the western United States.

Its natural beauty aside, the Housatonic is not without its problems, both past and present. Considering all of the factors which may affect any trout stream, it would probably be safe to say that there are few today which are problem free. The Housey, however, has endured several rather unusual situations.

In 1975, an experiment by a prominent scientist led the United States Environmental Protection Agency (EPA) to conclude that polychlorinated biphenyls (PCB's) were life threatening carcinogens. A year after this study, PCB's were detected in the Housatonic River. In 1977, a ban on the keeping of trout caught in the Housatonic was put into effect. Stocking programs were reduced and, finally, came to a complete halt in 1980.

A suit was instituted by the Housatonic Fly Fisherman's Association (HFFA) against the State of Connecticut in 1980, protesting the cessation of trout stocking in the Housatonic River. The HFFA won the suit. The Housey would be stocked again in accordance with a catch-and-release policy and, at long last, the Trout Management Area would be established.

Word travels fast when problems like this occur. Anyone who fished the Housey shortly after the 1977 ban on fish consumption will tell you of the ghost town feeling of the river. The meat fishermen were definitely going elsewhere, and many of the devoted recreational anglers abandoned their home river. Those of us who stayed on were privy to some fine trout fishing.

In spite of intensive research on PCB's and their toxicity, controversy still reigns regarding what constitutes a safe maximum level in fish tissue. As in many other northeast waters where PCB's occur, "advisories" are more common than outright bans on the taking of fish. Within the Housey's TMA, rainbow and brown trout remain a catch-and-release species. However, six black bass may legally be taken.

Another man-made problem on this beautiful river is its water level. The Falls River Power Plant, owned and operated by Northeast Utilities,

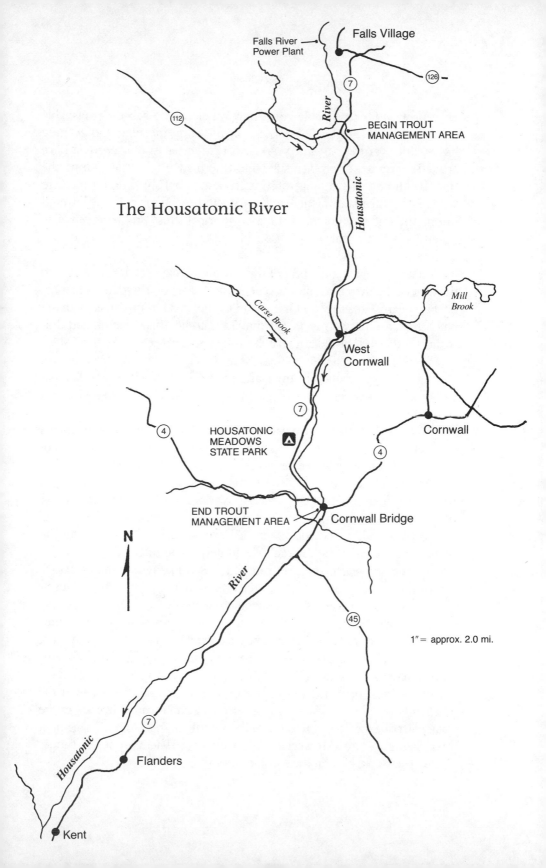

Falls River
Power Plant

Falls Village

126

7

River

BEGIN TROUT
MANAGEMENT AREA

Housatonic

112

The Housatonic River

Carse Brook

Mill Brook

West
Cornwall

7

4

HOUSATONIC
MEADOWS
STATE PARK

Cornwall

4

END TROUT
MANAGEMENT AREA

Cornwall Bridge

N

River

45

1″ = approx. 2.0 mi.

Housatonic

Flanders

Kent

once provided a reasonably consistent water release schedule. Fishable conditions could generally be found in the early morning and evening hours. But over the past few years, inconsistencies in the schedule have created a number of problems for the fisherman. High water during the "fishable" hours creates dangerous wading and poor fishing since trout here tend to go off-feed during high water. When the water is radically lowered during the mid-day hours, in summer, thermal stress problems can arise upsetting both the balance of insect life on the river and in extreme conditions, the life of the fish.

Low water during the heat of the day allows exposed rocks to absorb the heat of the merciless sun. Insect eggs and cases on these rocks literally bake to death. This situation has created problems for a number of insect hatches on a variety of rivers. On the Housatonic, this situation had dramatically affected the alder fly hatch in the southern section of the TMA.

Worse, when water covers these heated rocks, water temperatures rise. During the summer months there are times when the Housey walks that very fine line between water temperatures at which fish can survive and those at which they die.

To the trout fisherman, a water release program which would show a preference and advantage for the total ecosystem of the Housatonic is of much more importance than any concern for recreational activities.

As alluded to previously, the Housatonic River can be as difficult a river to wade as any in the Northeast. Wading can be tricky even under optimal conditions, and downright treacherous when the water is high. Slippery rocks, large boulders, and deep runs are found throughout the management area. A wading staff is definitely recommended.

During low water, the river can be crossed in any number of places, but care should be taken as the water level may rise at any time. Signs at streamside state this, and should be taken seriously.

From late morning through the afternoon, canoe traffic is quite common. Some of these canoeists are knowledgeable and courteous, but there are a few who are inexperienced and in some cases, quite ignorant. Be alert, as you may find a canoe trying to share a space with your waders. Canoe activity is most prevalent from late morning to mid-afternoon, with the weekends being the busiest time. There are several canoe liveries in the area, with one located on Route 7 in the middle of the Trout Management Area. Being able to fish weekdays is a blessing. There are fewer canoes during the week, even in the summer months.

One of the things I really enjoy about certain sections of the Housatonic is that "getting away from it all" feeling. Yes, Route 7 does run along much of the river, but there are plenty of places to find peace and quiet with beautiful surroundings. The fact that you can have all of this and yet be within a reasonable drive of the urban world is noteworthy. A variety of motels and bed and breakfasts are located in the immediate area within fifteen minutes of the TMA. Beyond lie the larger towns of Canaan, Kent, Sharon and Torrington (respectively to the north, south, east and west), all of which offer a wider range of services.

A greater abundance of bed and breakfasts, motels and eating establishments are located in these areas, only a fifteen to thirty minute drive from the river. If you should find yourself with a hook in your ear, or if any other calamity should occur, Sharon Hospital is about twenty minutes away.

The general store in Cornwall Bridge offers a deli-counter and a variety of other food and drink items. West Cornwall also has a general store for sandwiches and other snacks to stay the hungry piscator. A restaurant and a pub are also located in West Cornwall, to take the sting out of an afternoon with too many canoes or too few flies.

The Housatonic Meadows State Park is a 451 acre park which braces about a mile and a half of river within the Trout Management Area from Cornwall Bridge north to the end of the fly fishing only section. Park property extends to both sides of the river in the course of this mile and a half stretch, but does not in any way alter the fishing regulations or access to the river. The Housatonic Meadows Campground is located along the western shore of the river. This is a 94-site campground with a dumping station, flush toilets, and showers. Pets are not allowed. A number of campsites are located within casting distance of the river. Across the street from this is a well-stocked fly shop where one can obtain the latest hatch information.

The just named amenities and facilities play a role in drawing recreationists from all around the tri-state region: New York, Connecticut and Massachusetts. Thus while the trout mileage of the Housey is not exactly close to a major population center, the river gets considerable recreational pressure. You can find a quiet beat of water for yourself at times, but deep solitude is not the attraction here.

To assist in handling the pressure, the state trout stocking program (influenced by local sportsman's groups) has continued to increase the number of fish per year put into the TMA. The stocking of approximately nine thousand brown trout per year continued through much of the 1980's. Then, Bitteroot Trout, a strain of wild brown trout from Montana's Bitteroot River, were also introduced. These trout proved to be very hardy and showed remarkable growth. The German brown trout introduced here appear to grow a little slower, but overall, yield larger adults. In recent years, both browns and rainbows have been stocked. The number now approaches fifteen thousand fish annually.

In 1985 the Rainbow Club, based in South Kent, began adding rainbows to the Housatonic. Several large fish (3-5 pounds) were added to various pools throughout the TMA, adding a special bonus for those who were fortunate enough to hook one of these leapers.

Accessibility to the various fishing spots in the management area is relatively easy compared to many other trout rivers. Route 7 parallels the western side of the Housey throughout the five mile stretch of water between Cornwall Bridge and West Cornwall. To gain easier access to the mile and a half section of the TMA north of West Cornwall, you simply have to cross the rustic covered bridge and take the second left, which is River Road. This becomes a narrow dirt road after you are on it for a short distance. Push 'em Up Pool, which is the northernmost pool in the TMA, is about 1½ miles north on this road. The section of river beyond this is generally deep and slow flowing, and eventually leads to the dam at Falls Village.

One can also fish the eastern side of the river by taking the first right over the covered bridge in West Cornwall. This road takes you through property owned by the Trinity Parish Church Camp; it can legally be closed to any traffic, but seldom is. Drive slowly and be aware of pedestrians who may be participating in various camp functions. Traveling down this road seven-tenths of a mile, you will come to a parking area and a trail which will take you along the eastern side of the river.

At the southern end of the management area, you can fish the eastern bank by crossing the cement bridge on Route 7 and turning left past the National Iron Bank. If you follow this road down to the river and park near Furnace Brook, you will reach Church Pool, the home of large, finicky browns.

If you have been a fly fisherman for any length of time, you will know the frustration of traveling to an area with the hope of hitting a particular hatch only to find that (a) it has not started yet, (b) it came and went, (c) it should be happening, but the water is too high or low or hot or cold, or (d) "you should have been here last week." Considering all of these factors, the discussion of hatches on any stretch of water can be a tricky business.

Hatches on the TMA section of the Housatonic are very similar to those found on other trout streams in the Northeast. Varieties of mayflies, caddis of about size 12 and stoneflies are all present within the Housey's ecosystem. Ask any regular on the Housatonic and you will undoubtedly be told that one should never go forth without having caddis pupae or adult caddis imitations in one of your fly boxes. The Housatonic is a river which is extremely rich in caddis hatches. Nearly three quarters of the caddis families known to science hatch at some time or other during the spring and summer months.

The most popular of these hatches would be the alder fly, a huge caddis which makes its appearance in mid-May and continues through the month of June. The trout are practically feeding on shore when this hatch is on.

Tan, brown, and green bodied adult caddis imitations in sizes 14 and

The Housatonic looking up toward the famous covered bridge in West Cornwall. Much of the best fishing on the Housey is from this bridge down to the large cement bridge at Cornwall.

16 are effective throughout the season; a black caddis comes off from mid to late June, and you should have an imitator for this hatch, too.

Mayflies begin to make their appearance starting in late April with the hendricksons. To many anglers, this hatch represents the unofficial opening of the Housatonic fishing season. This hatch generally lasts through early May.

During the middle of May, March browns and grey foxes show up. Blue-winged olives *(Baetis)* and brown drakes come off during the latter part of May and continue into early June. Green drakes also begin hatching in early June, followed by light cahills and cream variants. The cahills and variants overlap into early July.

July and August can be tough months anywhere, depending upon just how hot and dry the summer is. These months can be particularly difficult on the Housatonic.

One of the other regulations within the Trout Management Area deals with fishing those pools which are fed by brooks or springs. These areas are posted, stating that fishing within one hundred feet of such places (read the signs for specifics) is prohibited. Such a regulation is excellent for the fish population, but can create tough fishing for the summertime angler. Nevertheless, early morning and late afternoon fishing can be productive outside of these off-limits areas during July and August.

Tricos in sizes 24 and 26, ants and various attractor patterns along with such flies as The Usual can be very effective in July, along with cream variants (10-14), blue-winged olives (sizes 16-20) and of course caddis (black, tan, and green bodied).

In the middle of August, the ever popular Housatonic quill enters the scene. This is also known as the white fly hatch. This is an evening hatch, with some of the best action occurring at dark with a tremendous spinner fall mixing in with the newly hatched duns. Tricos and ants continue to be good bets in August. A blue-winged olive *(Pseudocloeon)* makes its appearance in late August and remains a good hatch throughout the fall.

In September, along with the *Pseudocloeons,* certain *Stenonema* and *Diptera* provide the angler with some interesting fishing.

October still sees surface activity in the form of lingering *Pseudocloeons.* However, in mid to late fall, weighted nymphs and streamers may be the best bet depending somewhat on weather and water conditions.

Practically every pool or run in the management area has a name associated with it. The Housatonic Fly Fisherman's Association has published a map that names nearly every possible pool, run, hole, and flat within the management area. Their address is given a little farther on.

You should know that during high water conditions, very few of these areas are fishable. The Sand Hole (located south of Turnip Island), Church Pool and the Corner Hole may be your best spots during high water. If you arrive at the Housatonic and the water is high but dropping down (remember that water levels are controlled by a dam), head towards the Push 'em Up Pool area. Since the dam is located north of the TMA, when the flow of water from the dam decreases the more northerly pools of the management area will become fishable an hour or more sooner than the pools in the southern section. The reverse is true if the water is low and begins to rise due to the opening of the dam.

Every angler has his or her favorite fishing hole. My largest brown trout (20½ inches) was hooked and released at Split Rock, while my friend Peter Phelps released one over twenty two inches near Rainbow Run. Church Pool also has some dandies in it, as does the Corner Hole. As a matter of fact, I saw a beauty released at Push 'em Up and another +20 incher at the Carse Pool. Needless to say, there are some big fish in the Trout Management Area. A good stocking program, catch-and-release restrictions, and anglers who know how to release a fish properly all assist in keeping a trout river alive and well with quality fish.

The water level of the Trout Management Area of the Housatonic River is controlled by a hydro station which is located in Falls Village, Connecticut. This hydro station has a twenty-four hour phone service recording which gives a daily report of the water release schedule. The number is (203) 824-7861. The information given includes the date, number of units which are being run, time each unit will be run during that particular period, water temperature, and a statement that water levels may change without warning due to weather conditions or load demand. Water release is stated in terms of units: three, two, one or "shutdown." One unit, or a shutdown, means that the water level is down; this is the water level that's prime for fishing. With two units running, the water level is up, but many sections of the Trout Management Area are fishable. In particular, the stretch of water from Church Pool north to Turnip Island can be particularly productive when the water release is two units.

Three units means high water, and in most sections of the Trout Management Area, this results in extremely difficult wading conditions. Fishing near the shoreline with weighted nymphs and additional split shot will probably be your best bet when three units are running. Personally, I would only fish under these conditions if I knew that the water release would be decreased well before I planned to quit fishing.

Again, I must stress that these water release schedules are not etched in stone. Changes can and do occur. On several occasions I have driven the forty-five minute trip from my home to the Housey with the expectations of finding prime fishing conditions (in accordance with the recording) only to find that the water level had been raised. Such an experience is more the exception than the rule, but it can happen and does.

As we already discussed, the Housatonic is not without its problems. Fortunately, there are two organizations who are concerned about this blue ribbon River. They are The Rainbow Club, P.O. Box 11, South Kent, CT 06785; and, the Housatonic Fly Fisherman's Association, P.O. Box 5092, Hamden, CT 06518.

If you are interested in doing any further research on the Housatonic River, there are two sources which you may find to be of particular interest. First, a good article by Dale Spartas ("The Housey") appeared in *Fly Fisherman* magazine, July 1985 Volume 16, Number 5. It's worth looking up. And second, a booklet published by the Housatonic Fly Fisherman's Association provides an in-depth study of the various pools located on the river.

Some things to remember: watch your footing and wear felt sole waders, be aware of rising water and canoes, stay out of the restricted pools in July and August, release each trout with tender loving care, and enjoy the Housey as often as you can.

Denis Rice has been a dedicated fly fisherman for the past twenty years, and has been fishing the Housey even longer than that. A full-time physical education instructor (plus football and wrestling coach), Denis makes time each year for both trout and Atlantic salmon, and summer is apt to find him on the great *salar* rivers of eastern Canada. He has also fished in such far-flung places as Alaska, the Keys and Montana.

Ten

The Ausable
by Francis Betters

A book on great trout rivers of the Northeast must include a chapter on the fabled West Branch of The Ausable River, which emanates from the highest peaks in the Adirondacks and, after joining the river's other main branch, flows eventually into Lake Champlain. The 30-mile-long West Branch is considered by many top outdoor writers and a multitude of fishermen who have visited it to be one of the best trout streams in the East. Man in all his wisdom and expertise on trout could not have drawn a better blueprint for the perfect trout stream than Mother Nature has provided in the West Branch of the Ausable.

The Ausable River consists of two main branches, but it is the West Branch that has received the most attention and rightfully so. It is this river to which thousands of fly and spin fishermen from all over the United States and many foreign countries come, to try their luck at hooking one of the lunker brown trout that inhabit the many deep pools found here.

To understand why the West Branch is so good, it is important to know what ingredients go into producing a premier trout stream. This in turn necessitates knowing what the trout's requirements are...what it takes to ensure an abundant and healthy population of fish. To sum these requirements up briefly: 1) clean, unpolluted water; 2) a proper temperature range and a good supply of oxygen; 3) a plentiful food supply; and 4) cover.

How does the West Branch stack up in each of these four categories?

The water is still very clean in spite of increasing development in the area, and there are no great pollution problems menacing the river. The rich mineral water from the mountain feeder streams and the rich soil that is found along parts of the West Branch provide a good foundation for the food chains that eventually feed the trout. The river provides good nourishment for both of the major sources of food the trout feed on, namely insects and bait fish.

Traversing a very cold part of the Adirondacks, the West Branch usually runs in a very favorable temperature range for the trout. The shady conditions brought on by steep gorges and overhanging foliage help out in this regard so that even in summer the West Branch is often surprisingly chilly. As for the oxygen content, it is very good, thanks in part to the steep gradient. An abundant supply of oxygen is infused into the river as the water tumbles over the millions of rocks and boulders that make up the stream bottom in a large part of the West Branch.

The lower forms of life that the trout feed on are found in large numbers. The Ausable has an abundance of all three of the most important species of insects: mayflies, stoneflies and caddisflies. These insects are a good source of protein and their abundance promotes good trout growth.

Finally, in regard to requirement number four—cover—the West Branch is hard to beat. Not only are there many deep pools, but there are a multitude of hiding and holding spots created by rocks and boulders and, in places, undercut banks.

It might be added here that another virtue of the Ausable is its very remoteness. It is far from any of the major cities of the east, and this has so far prevented overuse. Also, it is one of the most heavily stocked rivers in New York State.

The West Branch begins its infancy stage in the mountains. The headwaters comprise several brooks which flow essentially north from the Mt. Marcy High Peaks area. As these tumbling mountain brooks converge, they gather strength and at the junction of Marcy Brook and South Meadow Brook the West Branch is officially born. This is at the western edge of the South Meadows area, and just south of the Village of Lake Placid. The West Branch then winds its way down past the Olympic ski jumps just outside Lake Placid, picking up Indian Pass Brook on the way.

For the next four or five miles the river is fairly calm as it makes its way through more meadowland, picking up a number of other small feeder streams. This is the part I refer to as the "Sweetwater" section of the Ausable. The river continues to grow, reaching the Rt. 86 bridge about three miles north of Lake Placid. After this crossing, the river really begins to gain character, passing

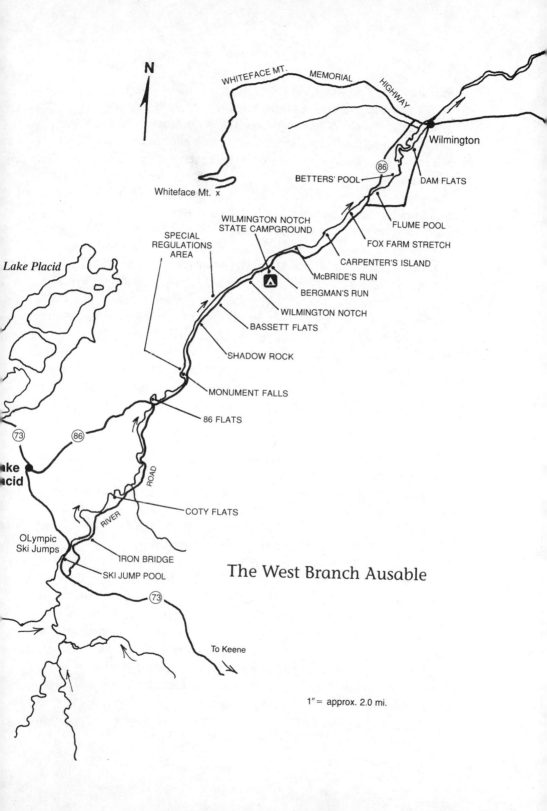

N

WHITEFACE MT.   MEMORIAL   HIGHWAY

Wilmington

Whiteface Mt. x

BETTERS' POOL   86   DAM FLATS

Lake Placid

FLUME POOL

FOX FARM STRETCH

SPECIAL
REGULATIONS
AREA

WILMINGTON NOTCH
STATE CAMPGROUND

CARPENTER'S ISLAND

McBRIDE'S RUN

BERGMAN'S RUN

WILMINGTON NOTCH

BASSETT FLATS

SHADOW ROCK

MONUMENT FALLS

86 FLATS

73   86

ROAD

COTY FLATS

ake
acid

RIVER

OLympic
Ski Jumps

IRON BRIDGE

SKI JUMP POOL

The West Branch Ausable

73

To Keene

1" = approx. 2.0 mi.

through its rebellious and energetic teenage stage, if you will. A few miles farther downstream, ancient glaciers have carved out a series of deep gorges in what is now called Wilmington Notch. As it tumbles through these gorges, the river takes on the personality by which it is chiefly known. The rocky West Branch is extremely scenic here, with one of the most dramatic spots being about a mile upstream of the Wilmington Notch State Campground. Here, the river roars over a falls that is more than 100 feet in height. Through the millennia, the countless billions of gallons of water churning over this great falls (called High Falls) have gouged out a deep pool within which large trout can hide amid the boulders and ledges. The trout here are comparatively safe from both anglers and from the large chunks of ice that come crashing down each spring when the ice breaks up from the slower sections of river upstream.

For the next two miles, the river sort of catches its breath as it forms numerous pools and pockets before taking another spectacular plunge over another series of falls known today as "The Flume." Beneath this falls, there is another large, deep pool that has become famous over the years and where big trout are taken each spring after ice-out. There is rarely a day during the open trout season when there aren't fishermen lining the ledges along both sides of this famous pool. Surprisingly, in spite of the pressure most of them catch some fish. Over the years, I have taken many good trout in the 15-20 inch range and can recall a half dozen or more lunkers that weighed from four to seven pounds. My largest was a 7 1/4 pound brown taken on a Hornberg streamer.

About a mile below the Flume Falls, the river seems to rest after its arduous journey and it flows now in a more peaceful fashion until it eventually meets the constraint of a dam located in the center of the Village of Wilmington. This dam forms what most of the old-time residents of the village refer to as Lake Everest, but it is merely a dammed up section of stream about two miles long, a hundred to four hundred feet wide and with depths to about twenty feet. This beat of the West Branch holds some lunker trout, and each spring one or two very large fish are bested by lucky anglers fishing the local beach. A few springs ago, for example, an 8½ pounder was taken by one of the local residents. This two mile section of slow water above the dam is an ideal spot for bait fishermen, but aside from the section between the bridge in town and the dam, and the small beach section, it must be fished from a canoe or small boat.

Beneath this dam at Wilmington, another large pool measuring some

400 feet across holds a great many trout, with some over three pounds. A fairly adept fly fisherman can wade out near the center of the stream below the pool and cast up towards the dam. It is an ideal place to fish large streamers and weighted nymphs. It's also a good spot to try big dry flies just before dark, and in the spring after ice-out it is one of the favorite pools of bait fishermen.

The section of stream from the Wilmington dam downstream about two miles is my favorite stretch for fly fishing. Here there are too-numerous-to-count pools and pockets formed by converging currents around boulders, and these create excellent fly fishing water. Access here is difficult, however.

After the river crosses beneath Lewis Bridge below Wilmington, it is posted for about one and a half miles. Fortunately, this is not one of the better parts of the West Branch. The river here is fairly wide and shallow for the most part, with only a few good holding pools. But from where Black Brook empties into the river at the lower end of the posted water, the river again has an increased number of pools and pockets, and these persist for the next six or seven miles. This beat of river from Black Brook to Ausable Forks is known as "The Bush Country." There are numerous old logging roads where one can reach the river, but for the most part it has to be gotten to by foot. New subdivisions and posting have made access here more and more difficult. As with the dammed-up section at Wilmington, the half-mile impounded part of the West Branch above the dam at Ausable Forks contains many trophy size fish.

For about a mile below this dam at Ausable Forks, the West Branch offers up some excellent pocket water for the fly fisherman. It is, however, one of the roughest sections of the river to wade. Its bottom is littered with segments of old bridges, broken boulders and pieces of cement blasted out when the old pulp mills were destroyed years ago.

Just downstream of the bridge in the center of Ausable Forks the West Branch converges with its sister stream, the East Branch, to form the main Ausable. Although the main branch contains some trout, it is not considered top quality trout water. The river is quite wide and shallow for the most part, and it contains a large number of chubs and shiners. There has also been a problem here with raw sewage flowing directly into the river from the Village of Ausable Forks, although a new treatment plant should end this problem soon. A few good pools can be found farther downstream, but as the river is quite shallow, it heats up during the hot summer months and doesn't produce well. Nonetheless, the Main Stem of the Ausable has its devotees and there are trout to be caught.

Let's now get a little bit more specific about a few of the better sections of the West Branch.

The stretch from the Olympic ski jump outside the Village of Lake Placid down to the Rt. 86 bridge is for the most part deep water with undercut banks, some faster currents, and a few pools. It may be that the largest trout in the stream are hiding beneath these undercut banks. The DEC once shocked one of the larger pools in this section and turned up three trout over six pounds apiece. (This same scenario also applies to the mile long section from the Rt. 86 bridge down to Monument Falls, where the trophy sections begins.) This section is best fished with nymphs, small streamers or large wet flies during the early season months. At this time, bait fishermen can excel on this part of the river. During the warmer summer months, small flies in sizes 18-22 work best. Terrestrials such as ants and grasshoppers are also a good choice during the summer period. There is

also an excellent trico hatch here in August and September.

From the beginning of the trophy section (discussed below) at Monument Falls all the way down to the Flume, the river is broken water with plenty of pockets and pools. Much of this is wadable fly fishing water, and it is very good. Another of my favorite stretches is the approximate one mile section below the Flume. Here, there are a number of islands below which large pools have been formed. These pools produce good-sized trout each spring and fall. This particular section is about two hundred feet off of Rt. 86, just north of the Flume bridge.

For the most part, the West Branch is governed by general statewide trout regulations, i.e. ten trout per day no size limit, with the season running from 4/1 to 9/30. However, there are two special regulations sections. The first is from the Rt. 86 bridge northeast of Lake Placid downstream to the Wilmington Dam. Here you can take ten trout nine inches or larger by any legal method, and the season is year-round. Section two lies within section one. This is the beat from Monument Falls downstream 2.2 miles, usually called the Trophy Section. Within this zone you may keep only three trout 12 inches or larger, and you may use artificial lures only. Again, the season is year-round.

Since the trophy section was initiated some dozen years ago, it has become a very popular part of the river. Although the size of the trout do not average much larger than those on the remainder of the stream, the DEC does stock this section from time to time with some of its large breeders. A couple of years ago, they put in about 800 large rainbows up to eight pounds. During the regular trout season, there is probably at least one large trout taken each week from the trophy section.

The East Branch of the Ausable has its origin in the Ausable Lakes area, southwest of the Village of Keene Valley. It flows northward along Rt. 9N past the villages of Keene, Jay and Upper Jay. It is a good trout stream by most standards but pales alongside the West Branch, in terms of both numbers and size of trout. The East Branch is relatively shallow, without much character, and during the hot months of July and August does not produce well. It is, however, a much tamer river than the West Branch and therefore much easier to wade. There are some good holding pools and the stream is a good choice for the less adventurous and less aggressive fisherman.

The deeper holding pools and runs are few and far between so you will have to explore a greater section of the stream to find them. One nice stretch is from Keene upstream to Hull's Falls. Unlike the West Branch, the East Branch has very few good feeder streams emptying into it. Styles Brook and

Clifford Brook are the only two tributaries big enough to contain fair populations of fish.

The West Branch, however, has some larger tributaries that offer excellent fishing. Black Brook, which empties into the river just below the Village of Wilmington, is large enough to fly fish and produces a good population of fish. I've taken trout up to four pounds from this brook. Other West Branch tributaries worth mentioning are Beaver Brook (excellent speckled trout fishing) Little Black Brook, Brown Brook and White Brook. All of these tributaries are a mile or less from the Village of Wilmington.

Many wonder what the best fishing periods are for the various types of fishing possible on the West Branch. In the spring from April first when the general season opens until about the middle of May is when bait fishermen often do best. The best natural baits are, of course, minnows and worms. In the faster sections of the West Branch, spinners are often the most effective spinning lures. Included here would be Panther Martins, Mepps, Roostertails, C.P. or Swiss Swings, etc. In the medium to slower sections, Phoebes and Rapalas are often deadly, but they do not operate as well as spinners in the white water. Fly fishermen during this same early period will do best using small streamers and nymphs fished deep, since the trout are not as active in the cold water and will be close to the bottom. Good early season patterns are the Grey Ghost, Muddler Minnow, Wooly Worm, and Hornberg.

The best fly fishing months for the dry fly fisherman are May, June, July and September into the middle of October. The first major hatch to emerge is the hendrickson, between the fifth and tenth of May. It is well to remember that the mayfly hatches on the Ausable come off about two weeks later than they do on Catskill streams because of the higher elevation and the colder water temperatures. There are heavy hatches of caddis during May and June and good hatches of stoneflies throughout the season. The longest hatch of the year is the *Isonchyia bicolor,* which comes off beginning around the middle of August and lasts well into October.

Since much of the river is comprised of fast water with many boulders and heavy currents, the most productive flies are usually the larger ones, sizes 10, 12, and 14; smaller flies are often the ticket in the slicks and the pools. The fly that seems to account for more fish than any other is my own Ausable Wulff in sizes 10 and 12. Some of the other especially productive patterns are the dark and light Haystacks, light and dark caddis, Light Cahill, Adams, March Brown and Hendrickson. The most productive nymph patterns are the black, brown and light stonefly nymphs, grey mayfly, all-purpose light, Light Cahill, Hendrickson and blue dun. During July and August, small midges and terrestrials are in order. A good imitation for the *Isonychia* dun is the Dark Haystack with a reddish-brown body.

Another aspect of fishing on the West Branch worth mentioning is the ratio of stocked fish to those spawned in the stream. In the center section of the stream between about Wilmington and the Olympic ski jumps, the trout

There are miles of quiet "sweet water" on the Ausable. But fast, rocky, slippery riffle and pocket water is how it is chiefly known.

are mostly stocked fish. A very high percentage of these fish are brown and rainbow trout. From the Olympic ski jump upstream there is a greater percentage of wild speckled trout (in smaller sizes). From the dam in Wilmington downstream you will also find a greater percentage of naturally spawned trout. The populations of fish here are mostly brown and rainbow but there is a fair number of speckled trout also. This six or seven mile section from the dam downstream is the most productive water on the river. Here is where you will find the best fly hatches from May through September.

A word of special advice is in order in regard to wading the West Branch of the Ausable. The river has one of the slipperiest bottoms I have ever encountered, thanks to the algae that covers the rocks in many areas of the stream. Combine this with the large and often jagged rocks and you can see why the West Branch is such a treacherous river to wade. It is wise to use both a wading staff and felt-soled waders, or felt soled wading shoes.

Those visiting this region for the first time will find several different types of accommodations. In Wilmington, there are a number of reasonably priced motels. The West Branch Fly Fishing Club has its own motel where fishermen can stay for a modest fee. It's located near the dam in town, right on the best fly fishing section. The lodge has its own lounge with color T.V. and a large kitchen where fishermen can cook their own meals. Although members get first priority on the rooms, other fishermen are given the same rates when rooms are available. For anyone wishing up-to-date stream conditions on the West Branch, there is a local hotline that you can call from April 1st until October 15th. That number is (518) 946-2605.

A more upscale and generally more costly village to stay in is Lake Placid. This scenic site of past Winter Olympiads is admittedly a little bit glitzy, but it does offer a wide range of accommodations and there are some very good restaurants. There is also good transportation (bus, etc.) in and out of Placid.

Many out-of-town anglers who come to fish the Ausable choose a campground as an economical way to spend a few nights. There are a number of choices. One is the Wilmington Notch State Campground, which is located right in the middle of the fishiest section of the river. Another is the Adirondack Loj which offers both indoor lodging and "primitive" outdoor camping. This is located just outside Lake Placid near the South Meadows area, and is administered by the Adirondack Mountain Club (ADK). Private campgrounds are also numerous in the Adirondacks, and can be found in the various campground directories or through chambers of commerce.

The West Branch of the Ausable is a river worth traveling to, and indeed, some anglers travel thousands of miles to fish its productive waters. It offers all types of fishing conditions for fishermen of all dispositions, from the timid to the most adventurous.

There is also the nostalgic presence of the many other well known anglers who have fished these same waters over the years. Bergman's Run, just upstream of the Flume Pool is named after Ray Bergman. Ray did much of his research for his book *Trout* here on the Ausable. He often fished this section of stream with my Dad and I learned much of my fly tying technique from this quiet and humble man. "Frustration Pool" located above the trophy section was named by another good friend and fellow angler, Jim Deren. Jim never missed fishing his favorite pool on his yearly pilgrimages to the Ausable. He fished this pool for the last time only a few months before he passed away.

The scenic beauty of its tumbling currents in the shadow of Whiteface Mountain, it's clean unpolluted waters and its abundance of trout make the West Branch of the Ausable a stream you will want to return to many times.

Fran Betters operates a large sporting goods business on the banks of the Ausable. He is a fly tyer of legend and has authored several now-famous patterns. He ties thousands of flies each year and conducts fly fishing seminars for beginners and experts alike. He has written five books on fishing and numerous magazine and newspaper articles. He is also president of the West Branch Fly Fishing Club. His latest book is *Fran Better's Fly Fishing, Fly Tying and Pattern Guide.*

Eleven

The Saranac
by John Spissinger

For anglers who relish variety in their quest for trout and salmon, relatively few northeastern rivers can match the bountiful opportunities found on northern New York's mighty Saranac River. Whether it's fishing for colorful native brook trout in a pastoral mountain stream, coaxing rainbows with dry flies in a boulder-strewn stretch of pocket water, or contending with the dazzling acrobatics of a fresh-run steelhead or landlocked salmon, the Saranac is bound to delight even the fussiest angler. On an extraordinarily good day, and with the right kind of luck, an angler could conceivably tangle with five different species of salmonids.

In terms of the variety it offers, the Saranac may be unique among Adirondack rivers. Not only does it hold an interesting blend of cold and warmwater gamefish, it also affords very different types of water that can be fished in different ways according to the individual preferences and skills of anglers. There is plenty of good water to suit the desires of spin, fly, and bait fishermen. Public access is excellent throughout the 65 mile stretch of river from Saranac Lake to Plattsburgh. Much of the river is navigable and can be fished from a canoe or small cartopper. Additionally, there is ample access for wading or bank fishing. Although there are a few seasonal hotspots where anglers tend to congregate, there's enough quality water spread throughout the river to ensure the peace and solitude that many anglers cherish. Combine these features and you have a river that has something to offer everyone.

Located in the northeastern sector of New York's Adirondack Mountains, the Saranac flows easterly through parts of Franklin, Essex, and Clinton counties. Less heralded than its neighbor, the Ausable, the geography of the Saranac has much in common with that great trout river. The headwaters of the Saranac and Ausable lie but a few miles apart in the High Peaks region of the Adirondack Park. The main stems of both rivers are formed by the confluence of their two branches: the East and West Branches of the Ausable, and the North and South Branches of the Saranac. With Lake Champlain as their eventual destination, the rivers traverse roughly parallel courses before entering the lake less than ten miles apart.

Unlike the Ausable, hydroelectric development has had a decisive impact on the Saranac's fishery. More than any other factor, the several hydroelectric impoundments along the Saranac account for the extensive variety, abundance, and local intermingling of cold, cool, and warmwater species of fish. Anglers and environmentalists throughout the country have been rightfully concerned about the detrimental effects of such projects. Frequently, habitat is severely altered or destroyed, and some species of fish are totally eradicated. Occasionally, though, hydro projects have actually had a positive impact upon fishery resources by creating or improving habitat. Arguably, the Saranac is one of the watersheds to have benefitted from its hydro impoundments. Presently there are nine hydro projects on the Saranac system, with the two largest being Franklin and Union Falls. Three smaller impoundments are sited on the main stem of the river just a few miles west of the City of Plattsburgh.

These projects are particularly significant from the standpoint of trout habitat. The high dissolved oxygen levels below the dams help offset summer water temperatures that would normally be marginal for trout. Thus, some very decent tailwater fishing for browns and rainbows exists below the Cadyville, Mill C, and Kent Falls dams. In the ponded waters above all the dams, smallmouth bass, northern and walleye pike, and various panfish are the predominant species. Each year, however, the impoundments surrender some very large browns that have taken up residence in the still waters.

The Saranac's reputation as a blue-ribbon trout river is borne out in the productive pools, riffles, and pocket water above and below the several impoundments. Trout fishing enthusiasts can easily explore and sample these stretches by taking a leisurely drive along Route 3, starting either in Plattsburgh or in Saranac Lake. About one-third of the South Branch, half of the North Branch, and virtually all of the main stem border this highway. There are many parking areas along the river which allow close-up inspections of

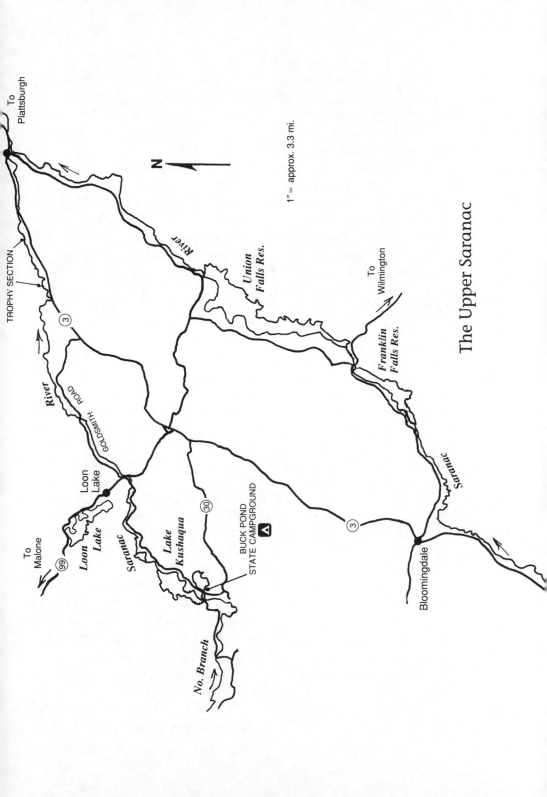

The Upper Saranac

1" = approx. 3.3 mi.

To Plattsburgh

To Malone

To Wilmington

TROPHY SECTION

River

GOLDSMITH ROAD

River

Union Falls Res.

Franklin Falls Res.

Saranac

Loon Lake

Loon Lake

Lake Kushaqua

BUCK POND STATE CAMPGROUND

No. Branch

Saranac

Bloomingdale

③

㉚

㊾

③

③

promising stretches of water. Moreover, additional information can be gleaned from local sources like the bait and tackle shops, small grocery stores, inns and campgrounds that are evident along Route 3. Assuming that you're embarking from Saranac Lake, the following paragraphs should give a picture of what to look for as you head downstream.

From the Lake Flower Dam to the hamlet of Bloomingdale, the South Branch wanders through meadow and swampland. Road access is relatively limited along this slow, deep run, and floating it by canoe is probably the best approach. Although a few trout are stocked in the Village of Saranac Lake on a put-and-take basis, smallmouth and northerns are more numerous. Just before Bloomingdale, the river veers away from Route 3 and quickens its tempo as it flows through pine and hardwood forests. Good access is found along the River Road in Bloomingdale which follows the river downstream to Franklin Falls Pond. Generally, the faster slicks and pocket water hold brown and rainbow trout while there's a mixed bag in the slower pools and runs. After passing through Franklin and Union Falls Ponds, the South Branch resumes its course and is largely inaccessible until it crosses the Silver Lake Road bridge. The river is heavily posted and patrolled on both sides of the bridge, but there are three public parking areas for fishermen just north of the bridge down to the junction with Route 3 in Clayburg. Anglers must descend steep banks to get to the river from these sites, but the excellent brown and rainbow fishing is worth the effort. This is a turbulent, boulder-strewn section with many deep pockets. Calmer waters are not to be found until the river merges with the North Branch in Clayburg.

For the beauty, solitude and enchantment that so many anglers feel to be the essence of trout fishing, few Adirondack rivers can match the charms of the Saranac's North Branch. It is a cold, quiet little river from the headwaters to its junction with the brawling South Branch in Clayburg. Dense overhanging alders and waist-deep oxbow bends and undercut banks provide ideal cover for the brook, brown and rainbow trout which thrive in its waters. The river is easy to get to from several well-maintained public parking areas on Route 3, from Clayburg five miles upstream to Alder Brook. During May and June this stretch sees some moderate to heavy angling pressure. However, few anglers bother to fish the headwaters of the North Branch, which can be reached via the Goldsmith Road which joins Route 3 a few miles west of Alder Brook. The river is much smaller here, in places no more than a few feet wide, and thickly forested. Native brookies are small but plentiful, and occasional wild browns are an added bonus. Although there are a number of private camps and posted property along the Goldsmith Road, the DEC has secured public fishing rights in various spots. The fish are highly selective on the North Branch and often you have to work hard to catch them. Still, there few places anywhere on the Saranac system that look as intriguing as the North Branch.

Reasonably good trout water continues on the main stem of the river from Clayburg to Saranac, six miles downstream. Because the river is so broad and shallow here, it doesn't appear to be a productive reach of water. However, the choppy riffles disguise deeper subsurface trenches and pockets. Trout hold in these protected areas and migrate to feed along the shallower edges. Although it takes practice to learn how to read this water, some surprisingly good fishing can be had. Several riverside parking areas are present along this stretch. Generally, the Hardscrabble Road bridge in Saranac marks the dividing line between cold and warmwater species. Shortly below the bridge the effects of the Cadyville dam are evident and smallmouth, northerns, walleye and panfish displace the trout.

The final stretch of trout water worth mentioning on the Saranac is the tailwater fishery created by the Kent Falls dam about two miles west of the Village of Morrisonville. Here the river is broad and fast-flowing, with many subsurface runs and pockets along with a few deep pools. Browns, both stocked and wild, are abundant in this section of river. In recent years the DEC has begun stocking landlocked salmon smolts in the Morrisonville area. While the smolts are aggressive and strong fighters when they reach the 10 to 12 inch range, their presence seems to have diminished the quality of the trout fishery. Because the smolts are remarkably similar in appearance to brown trout, anglers should heed the DEC signs along the river explaining how to distinguish between the two species. Different minimum size and possession limits apply to browns and landlocks.

Caution should be exercised when fishing this stretch because the water level fluctuates significantly during periods of power generation. Unsuspecting anglers can easily get stranded or swamped if they are not attentive to rising water. When fishing the Kent Falls-Morrisonville stretch, it is a good idea to pick out some indicator of the present water level, such as an exposed boulder or shoreline log, and to check it periodically while fishing to detect changes in flow. The swift currents and loose cobble bottom combine to make wading tricky under any circumstances. Access to this section is found along the Kent Falls Road which borders the river from Route 22B in the village of Morrisonville upstream to the Kent Falls dam. NYSEG maintains a fishermen's parking area below the powerhouse, and some roadside pulloffs give access farther downstream.

Because it is such a large and varied river, the best time of year to fish the Saranac pretty much depends on what you hope to catch and where you plan to go. May and September are probably the best months for coldwater species. Usually, the action is better on the lower sections of the main stem in early April and May, and then improves upstream as the waters warm. This is an especially provident feature for fly fishermen because it extends the duration of some of the river's major insect hatches. For example, with the right weather conditions the hendrickson emergence may begin in late April on the lower section of the main stem and continue through Memorial Day weekend in the cooler upper reaches of the North and South Branches.

During the hottest days of summer the North Branch, with its densely shaded waters and many spring seepages, is a good bet. Fall is probably the most enjoyable time of year to be on the Saranac. The radiant hues of autumnal foliage provide a pleasant atmosphere in which to fish, and nicely complement the river's browns and brookies that are now bedecked in colorful spawning attire. With cooler air and water temperatures, the trout are active and hungry again, and some late season hatches like the *Isonychia* provide nourishment for the fish and plenty of action for the angler. Best of all is the notable absence of the hordes of blackflies, mosquitos and no-see-ums that plague fishermen earlier in the season.

Generally, the flies, lures and baits that work well for trout on other northeastern rivers are also productive on the Saranac. Worms undoubtedly provide the most consistent action since there's not a fish of any species in the river that won't gobble one up from time to time. For best results with the Saranac's trout population, worm fishermen would be well-advised to vary their tactics and to use worms as a fly fisherman would use nymphs. Plunking heavily weighted nightwalkers into the Saranac's deeper pools will almost always yield a trout, and sometimes a nice one. But, over the course of the season it's better to explore the riffles and pocket water with smaller, very lightly weighted garden worms. A long supple spinning rod (a 9 foot or 10 foot noodle rod would be ideal), or a flyrod rigged for baitfishing, would be best for this type of worm fishing. The lighter the monofilament the better, with four-pound test being the preferred standard. Only minimal weight should be added, depending on the water conditions. Short, strategically placed casts should be aimed slightly above promising riffles and pockets. The idea behind this approach is to allow the river's currents to sink the worm naturally and to swirl and suck it beneath the rocks and depressions in the river's bottom. Strikes are frequently swift and decisive, and the angler has to have quick but controlled reflexes. This is a very demanding technique but for those who master it well the Saranac will give up some fine trout.

Plying worms in the Saranac has its drawbacks, mainly in that it entices strikes from fish other than trout. For this reason, live bait or salted minnows will greatly reduce the number of strikes by nuisance fish like river chubs and rock bass. Using live bait will also improve prospects for tangling with one of the Saranac's notoriously carnivorous trophy-sized browns. Spinners and spoons will occasionally produce the same results as baitfish, and they will usually take a larger number of pan-sized trout. Ultralight outfits are both sporting and fun in the upper Saranac, especially in the North Branch. However, on the main stem from Clayburg down to the mouth in Plattsburgh, sturdier outfits are in order. Besides larger trout and salmon, spoons and spinners are likely to draw the attention of smallmouth and northerns.

Fly fishermen have the chance to encounter all the major eastern mayfly hatches, starting with the hendrickson in early to mid-May. Some hatches are distributed throughout the entire river system, while others are more localized. Hendricksons, March browns and grey foxes, cahills, and blue-winged olives are emergences that occur up and down the river. Almost as widespread is the *Isonychia* hatch which begins in mid to late July; good populations are present in all sections of the Saranac that are characterized by pocket water or swift tumbling riffles. Examples of more localized emergences include the green drake hatch which tends to be concentrated in slower water above the hydro projects; the tiny *Tricorythodes* which is a very significant and prolific early morning hatch on the North Branch in late July and August; and the *Ephoron* or "white fly" hatch which is extremely prominent below the Kent Falls Dam in Morrisonville. The *Ephorons* are a late summer, late evening emergence.

In addition to the typical succession of eastern mayfly hatches, the Saranac also contains good populations of caddis which emerge regularly throughout the season. Even though the Saranac's green drake hatch (which begins in early June and progresses upstream in successive weeks) can be phenomenal, the trout often ignore these juicy morsels and instead feed heavily on the smaller caddis. By contrast, the river's smallmouths find the drakes irresistible and will smash them with a vengeance. Stoneflies are also quite abundant and large nymphal imitations are especially productive in the South Branch's heavy pocket water. During the summer, terrestrial insects like carpenter ants and various beetles, along with midges and Chironomid pupae, are important on the North Branch.

A good assortment of the standard mayfly patterns (including nymphs, wets and dries), supplemented by some Elk-Hair Caddis in various sizes and colors, will handle most situations on the Saranac. As searching patterns, the ubiquitous Adams, Hare's Ear Nymphs, Muddlers, and some Woolly Buggers are useful to have on hand. Not to be forgotten is the Ausable Wulff, a pattern that has proven itself as often on the Saranac as on its nearby river of origin, the Ausable. Sizes #12 and 14 are most popular, but it would not hurt to carry some #10s for night fishing or rough water, and some 16's and 18's for more selective trout in the quieter pools and runs.

Dry fly patterns for both the Saranac and the Ausable have historically emphasized the qualities of buoyancy and visibility in rough and tumbling

currents. In the past this has dictated more heavily hackled dressings of standard patterns than would ordinarily be needed on less turbulent waters like those found in the Catskills. The Compara-dun series, originated by Al Caucci and Bob Nastasi, has become very popular and effective on Adirondack rivers. This generic style of dressing embodies the virtues of floatability and visibility, and it accentuates realism in terms of wing silhouette. So, along with traditional hackled patterns, it would be a good idea to carry some of the hackleless Compara-dun ties on a trip to the Saranac.

Not all of the Saranac is characterized by rough water, and on its larger pools and flats, and in the meadow stretches of the North Branch, the fish are every bit as picky and demanding as those in the Beaver Kill and Battenkill. To successfully meet the challenges posed by these selective trout, more sparsely dressed and strictly imitative patterns are needed to carry the day. In these situations, too, the Compara-dun series has proven to be very adaptable and effective.

If there is one secret weapon to be stored away in the Saranac angler's arsenal, it is the use and value of smaller flies. Probably owing to its reputation as a western style river, fly fishermen here have tended to favor larger, bushier flies because they're easier to keep track of in swift currents. Consequently, anglers have overlooked or neglected the surprising productivity of micro-caddis larvae and pupae, midges and midge pupae, and especially Chironomid pupae. There are dense populations of these insects throughout the river, and while it is admittedly not easy to fish size 20 and smaller patterns in a river as large and as swift as the Saranac, the effort frequently brings handsome rewards. The trick is to be observant of rise forms, and to learn to detect "smutting-type" rises which indicate that the fish are feeding on small flies in or just beneath the surface film. Most experienced fishermen recognize these rises when they occur in flat water and in pools, but many are not good at seeing them in the faster slicks and pocket water. Keeping a watchful eye and summoning the courage to try a tiny fly on a fine tippet in an improbable stretch of white water can sometimes salvage an otherwise fruitless outing.

Although the City of Plattsburgh marks the end of the Saranac's journey toward Lake Champlain, it is also home base for the newest, and to many the most exciting dimension of the river's diverse fishery. In the 1960's, New York's DEC began experimental stockings of landlocked salmon in Lake Champlain's major tributaries. Historical records indicated that salmon were once native to the lake, but pollution, overharvesting and destruction of spawning habitat led to their demise by the mid 1850's. Results of the initial restorative stockings were encouraging as the salmon thrived on the abundant forage base in the lake and then returned to spawn in the lower reaches of the tributaries. The stockings continued throughout the 1970's and 1980's, and were augmented by the introduction of steelhead trout. Today, the Saranac supports modest runs of salmon and steelhead. Prospects for the future are even brighter as the DEC began an eight year sea lamprey control program in Lake Champlain in the fall of 1990. Reducing the fish mortalities exacted by the parasitic lampreys should significantly increase both the size and numbers of returning salmon and steelhead. Fish ladders planned at three hydro impoundments in and near the City of Plattsburgh will eventually provide access to nearly 14 miles of river. Salmon will once again be able to reach their historic spawning grounds in the Kent Falls-Morrisonville area, and the habitat there continues to be suitable for some natural reproduction to take place. If all goes well, Saranac anglers may one day have the pleasant opportunity to fish for wild, stream-bred (though lake raised) landlocks.

Salmon and steelhead fishing on the lower Saranac is very different from that found on Lake Ontario's tributaries. Lake Champlain's landlocks average about four pounds during the fall spawning run, with a few fish over ten pounds. Similarly, Lake Champlain's steelhead range from 16 to 20 inches, with some larger specimens over four pounds. Another key difference between Lake Ontario's and Lake Champlain's salmonids is that landlocked salmon do not die after spawning but return to the lake to feed, grow larger, and to spawn again. For this reason catching salmon by snagging or lifting is strictly prohibited on the Saranac. Although its fish will never match the size and number of Pacific salmon that ascend Lake Ontario's Salmon River each fall, the Saranac offers a qualitatively different angling experience more akin to traditional Atlantic salmon fishing. And the landlocks are no less spectacular fighters than their sea-going brothers.

The Saranac's spring salmon run usually begins in early April and continues through mid-May, depending on the water temperature and level. The run is triggered by the influx of the river's warmer waters and the salmon's pursuit of various baitfish, most notably the emerald shiner, which enter the lower reaches of the river to spawn in the spring. The best fishing occurs from the river's mouth to perhaps a half-mile upstream. Although not particularly large at this time of year, averaging between 18-20 inches, the salmon are voracious feeders and will hit worms, spoons, plugs, streamers, nymphs and even dry flies. More important than what to use is the task of getting your lure, bait or fly down near the bottom in the swift, heavy waters. Fly fishing anglers should come equipped with at least a seven weight line and rod system, and either a full sinking or fast-sink-tip line. Spin and bait anglers would do well to use a long sturdy rod and a reel with a dependable drag. Six to eight pound test line will normally handle the most challenging fish.

Early September marks the beginning of the fall spawning migration, with the peak coming by mid-October. The salmon ascend the river as far as the Imperial Mill dam three miles upstream. The fish are both larger and more temperamental than in the spring because they are not actively feeding. Patience, in the form of repetitive casts into likely pools and runs, is the only sure way to maximize chances for success. When the salmon are inclined to hit, they will strike almost anything. Worms and plugs continue to work, although fly fishing is perhaps more common in the fall. Some anglers have luck using traditional Atlantic salmon flies, with the Cosseboom and Rusty Rat being notable favorites. The majority of fly fishing enthusiasts use streamers and bucktails. Yellow maribou streamers, Grey Ghosts, and Muddlers, in sizes 2 through 8, are popular patterns. Again, though, the exact pattern seems less important than the mood of the fish at any given moment.

In spite of one's best laid plans, an angler should still never be too sure about what he'll catch when he visits this river. Steelhead, smallmouth, walleye, northerns, brown trout and even lakers swim in the same water as the migrant landlocks. And, they hit just often enough to remind everyone of the truth of the proposition that, when fishing the mighty Saranac, it's always best to "expect the unexpected."

John Spissinger lives in Peru, NY, a short distance from the mouths of both the Saranac and Ausable Rivers. A faculty member at SUNY Empire State College, John is also a Trout Unlimited activist, having been secretary and president of the Lake Champlain Chapter, and currently serving as the Region 5 Vice President for the NYS Council of TU. John has fished extensively in the Adirondacks and also teaches fly tying classes for TU members in the Plattsburgh area.

Twelve

West Canada Creek
by John Sweeney

West Canada Creek. It doesn't exactly roll off the tongue. It's not heatedly discussed at TU meetings from coast to coast. It's not to be seen in the paintings of Abbett or Pleissner, and no fly has been named after it.

And by the way, just where the hell is West Canada Creek?

It happens to be located in the southwestern Adirondacks, and it has the length, size, aesthetics and quality of fishing to make it one of the premier trout streams in the Northeast.

Starting in Hamilton County in the Adirondack Mountains of New York State, West Canada Creek begins where the outlets of West Lake, South Lake and Mud Lake join together. This is the beginning of the North Branch of the river. Some ten miles to the South, Twin Lakes Outlet marks the beginning of the South Branch. The South Branch of West Canada flows almost west while the North Branch flows southwest and the two join just above the hamlet of Nobleboro.

Fishing in the West Canada Lakes and The North and South Branches is primarily for the native brook trout with some stocking by the DEC along Haskell Road on the North Branch and Mountain Home Road on the South Branch. This is a legendary wilderness area where hiking and backpacking to camp and fish pristine waters is still the order of the day. In addition to the main branches there are many feeder streams which contain substantial numbers of brook trout and even a beaver dam where, at the right time, some large brook trout may be caught. The fishing here is like much of the brook trout fishing in the Adirondacks in that it tends to be erratic. It can be outstanding or discouraging.

Natives of the area have long recognized the quality of fishing here and local folklore highlights the exploits of one Louis Seymour, affectionately known as "Adirondack French Louie." French Louie was a guide, trapper, and fisherman who roamed the area from Nobleboro to the West Canada Lakes. He would take occasional time out for rest and rehabilitation at Speculator, N.Y., and sometimes walk the fifty or more miles to Utica. His diary of the 1880's indicates large catches of brook trout and even lake trout from West Lake. The lake trout were often ten to twenty pounds and brookies of two to three pounds were not uncommon. Parties measured their catches in total pounds rather than inches. To many, these were the "good old days."

At Nobleboro, West Canada Creek crosses state Route 8 and proceeds in a southeasterly direction toward Hinckley Reservoir. This stretch of some ten miles presents a variety of fishing opportunities. Brook, brown, and rainbow trout may be taken here. One may encounter both native and wild fish ranging in size from seven to sixteen inches. The area may be reached from N.Y. State Route 8 and other roads such as Jones Rd. and Harvey Bridge Rd. which cross the creek at various points. The nature of the stream is varied, ranging from fast water and large boulders in the area of the Wilmurt Gorge to some broad, slow sections along Route 8. The width varies from perhaps forty to two hundred feet in places.

Below Harvey Bridge, the creek empties into Hinckley Reservoir. The dam which created this impoundment was built in 1914, much to the chagrin of many naturalists since it virtually inundated a great natural attraction known as Trenton Falls. Hinckley Reservoir is about eight miles long and nearly three miles wide at it broadest point. The angling opportunities in the reservoir are substantial and large brown and rainbow trout are caught there each year.

In 1959 another dam was completed at the hamlet of Trenton which is about five and one half miles below the Hinckley Dam. Because of the very steep banks and rapidly rising water, the area between the two dams is very difficult to fish.

West Canada Creek flows below the hydropower dam at Trenton Falls for about twenty-five miles to its confluence with the Mohawk River at Herkimer, N.Y. This section of the stream presents the very best angling opportunities. It can be described as classic northeastern freestone water, and its size, length, and quality deserve careful examination.

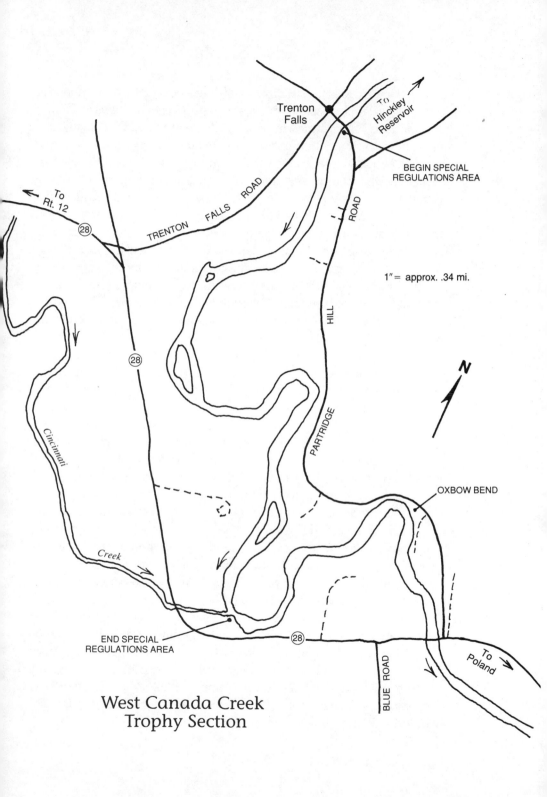

Trenton
Falls

To
Hinckley
Reservoir

BEGIN SPECIAL
REGULATIONS AREA

To
Rt. 12

TRENTON FALLS ROAD

HILL ROAD

1″ = approx. .34 mi.

28

28

Cincinnati

PARTRIDGE

N

OXBOW BEND

Creek

END SPECIAL
REGULATIONS AREA

28

BLUE ROAD

To
Poland

West Canada Creek
Trophy Section

The New York State Department of Environmental Conservation has established a Trophy Section on West Canada Creek. It begins at Trenton Falls and runs 2.2 miles downstream to the point where Cincinnati Creek enters the main river. Special regulations limit the angling to artificial lure or fly. Only three trout may be kept and they must be twelve inches or longer. From somewhat meager beginnings, the quality of fishing in the Trophy Section has steadily improved. Today it compares very favorably with similar sections of the Ausable, Battenkill, and Beaver Kill. Although insect activity is not as great as on those more famous streams, the number and size of the fish are impressive. As many of the fishermen who frequent this area practice catch-and-release, the quality of fishing continues to improve.

The Trophy Section is braced by New York State Route 28, Trenton Falls Road, and Partridge Hill Road. Although one may encounter some posted land along these roads, there are a number of access points and the entire 2.2 miles are fishable.

Below the confluence of Cincinnati Creek, West Canada Creek makes a long sweep away from the road and then returns to cross Route 28 at the Gravesville Bridge. From this point downstream it flows through the area known as the Kuyahoora Valley. It passes through the villages of Poland, Newport, and Middleville, and finally enters the Mohawk River at Herkimer. Over this entire distance of about twenty miles the stream is roughly paralleled by State Route 28. There are some access points in between these villages and virtually every inch of the stream is accessible to fishermen. At some points it may meander a quarter or half mile away from the highway before returning. Thus, fishermen are afforded a privacy and solitude which is often not present on some of the better known streams.

West Canada Creek is a relatively large stream as northeastern rivers go. It's very comparable in size to the lower reaches of the Catskill's famous Beaver Kill, and provides a wide variety of water types. White water rapids, boulders, and slow-flowing pools can all be found on West Canada Creek.

The water level of the creek is controlled by Niagara Mohawk Power Corporation. There are dams and hydroelectric facilities at Hinckley, Trenton Falls, Newport, and just north of Herkimer. Since the power company produces electricity on a demand basis, the water level of the stream may rise or drop rather rapidly and with very little warning. Several years ago, the Power Corporation placed signs at close intervals along the stream, warning, "Danger--Fast Rising Water."

Low water conditions expose a long gravel bar below the bridge in Mid-dleville. The combination of long pools and broken water is typical of West Canada Creek.

The average flow rate for West Canada Creek is about 1,320 cubic feet per second, but it can be much more than that during periods of peak release. Fishermen should be ever-mindful of this situation because there is no available warning except for a whistle that sounds at Trenton Falls and can only be heard in the upper part of the Trophy Section. Veteran fishermen seem to be able to sense the release, probably feeling the increase in the water pressure against their waders. Visitors who are new to the stream should watch nearby rocks or boulders for a rise in the water level. Once the water begins to rise, it will take only about fifteen minutes for it to reach its high point. During that time, the water level will rise 15-20 inches. Not only does this make the river difficult to fish by any method, but the swiftness of the current makes wading prohibitive in some sections. Although most fishermen, myself included, prefer to fish during the low water phase, the stream does have areas that are fishable in high water and some fine fish are taken during high water. Because of the length of West Canada below Trenton Falls, it is possible for a fisherman to leap-frog downstream and thus stay ahead of the rising water until evening. Although it's not etched in stone, once the spring run-off has dissipated the usual schedule calls for water to be released at Trenton Falls at 8:00 a.m. and throughout the day until 12:00 midnight when the gates are closed. They are then re-opened at 8:00 a.m. the next morning. Occasionally, during the summer, the gates at Trenton may be closed at 2:00 p.m. or 4:00 p.m. and re-opened at 8:00 p.m. and then closed again at midnight. This delights local fishermen who then have an opportunity to fish the upper areas in low water conditions during late afternoon and early evening hatch conditions. This, however, is not usual and is viewed as an unexpected bonus.

If the gates are opened at Trenton Falls at 8:00 a.m., the water level will rise at Poland around 10:30 a.m., Newport at 12:30 p.m., Middleville at 3:30 p.m., and Herkimer at 6:30 p.m. As previously stated, this schedule makes it possible for a fisherman to move downstream and stay ahead of the rising waters until evening.

Local chapters of Trout Unlimited have been attempting to reach some agreement with the Niagara Mohawk Power Company on stream flow and hours of regulation but there is no resolution at the present time.

The other major factor affecting water level is melting snow and rain. Since West Canada Creek is about 75 miles long, it drains a huge watershed, much of which is in the Adirondack Mountains. Because of this, the spring water level is usually high with water running over Hinckley Dam. High water is likely to continue through April and much of May. In a normal year, water levels should dissipate and daily regulation should begin around Memorial Day.

While the release of water for hydro-electric purposes creates some problems relating to water level, it has been significantly beneficial to water temperatures. The stream remains generally cool throughout the summer months with temperatures mostly in the 50's and 60's below Trenton Falls. Of course, the water temperature increases as cool water from Hinckley and Trenton Falls is warmed by the sun. Consequently, temperatures from Kast Bridge to Herkimer will be higher than in the Trophy Section or near Poland. Unless the flow is cut back drastically, the temperature of the water will remain high enough, even during the heat of the summer, to support a healthy and active supply of trout. Here again, local chapters of Trout Unlimited are working with Niagara Mohawk Power Corporation to ensure that water flow does not become deficient.

One of the contemporary environmental problems that has plagued many northeastern water systems is acid rain. Fortunately, West Canada Creek has held up quite well in the face of increasing acid rain problems throughout the Adirondacks. Tests of the stream in the spring of 1990 have shown a relatively stable pH of 7. Hopefully, this level will continue.

A FISHING SEASON ON WEST CANADA CREEK

Opening day on West Canada Creek is looked to with great anticipation by its following, just as on other streams throughout the state. The Opening Day ritual must be performed, even though the water level will be high and water temperatures will be in the upper 30's. Unless it has been extremely cold and the spring run-off has not yet occurred, these early conditions are difficult. The most successful fishermen at this time are bait fishermen using worms and minnows and spin-casters with Phoebes, spinners, etc. Since the stream will not have been stocked yet, all fish taken are holdovers. Many are from the previous year's class, but teenagers sitting by fires along the bank and bouncing a gob of worms along the bottom of a deep hole will inevitably pick up some trout in the 14 to 20 inch category.

In recent years the DEC has delayed stocking each year until stream temperatures approximate the hatchery water temperature. This has translated, roughly, into the third week of April. From that time until early summer, West Canada Creek will receive some 20,000-30,000 fish. The size and quality of the stockers is a matter of serious concern to local fishermen and constant efforts are made to ensure that West Canada Creek will receive "good fish."

April and May, while often difficult, are the months of greatest fishing pressure on the creek. This is the time when everyone has a chance. The bait fisherman, spincaster and fly rodder are equally at home during this period. Once the water temperatures begin to rise toward the end of May and early June and daily regulation of water occurs, bait and spin fisherman tend to be less successful and fish are more likely to be taken on flies. This is, of course, a generalization and some fish are taken on bait and lures throughout the season. In September of 1989, a 9lb. 8oz. brown trout was taken above Poland by a young man using a live grasshopper as bait. This fish ranks as one of the better trophy-size trout taken in recent years. Several years ago a fish in the 13 pound category was taken from the tailwater below Hinckley Dam.

For the fly fisherman, the early season on West Canada centers around "fishing the water" through most of April. There is very little visible insect activity. Streamer flies to use include the Muddler Minnow, Black Ghost, Olive Matuka, Llama Fly, and Brown Marabou Muddler. These flies fished dead drift or across and downstream will take fish during the early season.

During the second and third weeks of April many trout will be gorged with hellgramites. In the area of smaller rocks and riffles, a weighted black hellgramite imitation fished across and downstream will take fish.

The fourth week in April brings some of the first significant insect activity in the form of *Epeorus pluralis* or quill gordon. The Quill Gordon dry in a size 14 or 16, the same fly in a thorax tie and the Quill Gordon Nymph are likely to take some nice fish. While the hatch is generally light and sporadic, trout will be looking for it and be susceptible to the flies mentioned.

Insect activity increases significantly during the month of May. As the water temperatures warm, fish also become more active and the latter half of May can be excellent.

In early May, usually around the beginning of the second week, the little brown stonefly begins to appear. A brown stonefly nymph in size 14 and weighted works very well and is responsible for good catches at this time.

The middle of May produces the beginning of the caddis hatches. While caddisflies hatch all season long, the fish seem to be more impressed with some of these early appearances. Although substantial progress has been made in the past ten years in recognizing and categorizing the caddisfly, most fishermen still tend to describe them by color and size rather than scientific name. Caddisflies you will see in May on West Canada Creek are: gray body/mottled brown wing; olive body/gray wing; gray body/gray wing. They are all about a size 16, or at least size 16 is a good common denominator since there is some size fluctuation in each group. Over a period of time the following flies have proven to be effective imitations of the caddis described above: Deer and Elk Hair Caddis with both gray and olive bodies; Hare's Ear Wulff; Blond Caddis (gray body with reddish-blond mink tail wings and ginger hackle); Adams; and Quad-Wing Caddis. Size 16 is the best all around size for these although in some instances a 14 or 18 may work better.

Another hatch that appears in the middle part of May is the cranefly. Although some craneflies are as large as a size 10, the West Canada variety is a diminutive version. Imitations of this mosquito-like insect in sizes 18 and 20 are effective.

Anywhere from May 20 on the *Ephemeralla subvaria* or hendrickson may appear. The subvaria is a mid-day hatch on most streams, but on the West Canada, it will often hatch before the water rises. In the Trophy Section and down to Poland, this means the hatch may come off between 9:00 a.m. and noon. When this fly is on the water, some excellent fishing is available. The Hendrickson dry fly in both the Catskill and thorax ties as well as the Red Quill and the Red Compara-dun will produce fish. Size 14 is usual, but there are times when a #16 works better. This hatch usually goes on for about a week to ten days. As previously indicated, it may come off as early as May 20, but it is most always present on Memorial Day and continues into the first week of June.

Memorial Day is one of the more anticipated holidays in that fishermen guage certain entomological activity by it. In the Catskills and many of the legendary waters of Pennsylvania, this holiday has become synonymous with the appearance of the green drake. Because of the more northerly location, hatches on West Canada Creek are usually two to three weeks behind the corresponding hatches on Catskill and Pennsylvania streams. This includes the green drakes. Nonetheless, Memorial Day marks the beginning of the very best fishing on the Creek.

In early June, *Stenonema fuscum,* the gray fox, begins hatching. This is followed by *Stenonema canadensis,* the light cahill, in mid-June. Although they are not heavy hatches, they are very consistent with duns emerging sporadically throughout the day. At dusk there are some mating flights and some fishing to spinner falls. These are hatches that trout expect and cream and light tan Compara-duns will produce even when no flies are actually on the water. Also, a Hares Ear Nymph is a good producer at this time.

The green drake hatch on West Canada Creek is not legendary. *E. gut-*

The popular Eastern Rock Pool located northwest of Middleville on Rt. 28. Public access is available here and some very educated trout will test your ability.

139

tulata almost disappeared in the 1970's but has made a significant comeback in recent years. On those silty runs where it does hatch, it will bring up some of the biggest fish of the year. The March brown (*S. vicarium*) and the green drake hatch simultaneously, and, being the largest mayflies of the year, they do entice the largest fish. As on other streams, these are sometimes frustrating hatches to fish, but the reward is often a trophy size trout. Best imitations include: Long-tailed March Brown Nymph, Green Drake Nymph, Green Drake and March Brown Compara-duns, and Green Drake Emerger with trailing shuck.

At dusk, mating flights may be over the water, undulating lower and lower as darkness approaches. This can provide some unbelievable action and coffin fly imitations—especially the old Catskill version—have proven effective.

Throughout the month of June a caddisfly with gray body and mottled brown wing emerges. It is size 16, and a #16 Adams is very effective and accounts for some good catches.

Two other flies that make their appearance in June are *Isonychia* (dun variant) and *E. dorothea* (pale evening dun). These hatches are not as prolific as they are on some streams, but can produce some nice action when they do appear.

July is a month for hatches of caddisflies during the day. These flies usually hatch from 6 a.m. to noon with some ovipositing in the afternoon until dark. Gray/mottled, tan/gray, and olive/gray in sizes 14, 16, and 18 are prevalent on most days throughout July.

In the evening, the cream variant (*P. distinctus*) will appear. This fly provides some very good catches right at dark. The caddis and cream variant hatches continue well into the month of August.

The second and third weeks in August present some new and interesting appearances. *Pseudocloeon* in sizes 18, 20, and 22 and red and black flying ants in sizes 20, 22, 24 offer an opportunity to perfect midging techniques using fine tippets and very small dry flies. The trout are usually sipping these insects from the surface film and small dimples are often made by very respectable fish. The *Pseudocloeon* hatches in the morning while the flying ants tend to appear in the afternoon.

Just when it seems like most of the major hatches are over, a hatch which is probably the most prolific of all appears. This is the *Ephoron leukon*. Locally, it is called the eel fly. To most fishermen it is just "the white fly." I've seen local businessmen sweeping and shoveling literally thousands of these flies "the

Summary of Significant Insect Activity—West Canada Creek

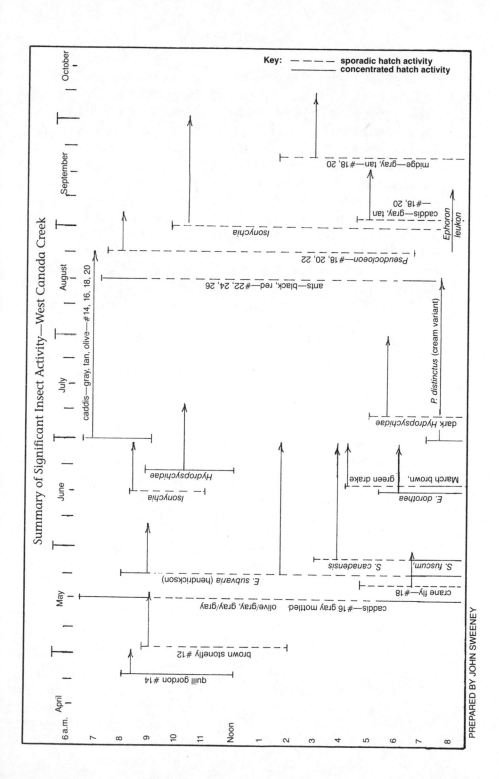

Key: – – – – sporadic hatch activity
——— concentrated hatch activity

PREPARED BY JOHN SWEENEY

morning after" to clean their sidewalk before customers arrive.

E. leukon will hatch around 7:00 p.m. starting around the 25th of August and lasting for about two weeks. Fish response to the hatch will range from aggressive attacks to complete neglect. As with many blizzard-type hatches, it is difficult to fish, but there are large fish to be taken.

The last segment of the fishing season, from mid-September to November 30 (the legal closing), is a pleasant time to be astream here. Reduced pressure, the beautiful colors of Autumn, and a chance at some large fish make this a propitious time to fish. There is a fairly good hatch of *Isonychia* in September and a good hatch of cinnamon caddis in October. Along with the continuation of *Pseudocloeon*, this insect activity provides a good opportunity for late season action. In addition to the hatches mentioned, streamer flies are effective. A Brown Marabou Muddler is one of the better patterns.

If you come to visit West Canada, the New York Thruway (Exit 30, Herkimer), and State Routes 28 and 8 will put you on the Creek. There are motel accommodations in Herkimer and campgrounds with trailer hook-ups near Middleville and Poland. Route 28, which parallels the Creek from Herkimer to Trenton, joins Route 12 at Barneveld. There are additional motels, restaurants and camping facilities in that area which is only a ten minute drive from the stream.

The Kuyahoora Valley is a picturesque area of New York State often called the "foothills of the Adirondacks." Dotted by small farms, woodlands and small communities, there are tourist attractions such as Middleville Diamond Mines and the Enchanted Forest which may be of interest to family members who do not want to fish.

John Sweeney is an avid fly fisherman, fly tyer and teacher of fly tying. He lives in Fairfield, NY, just minutes from the banks of West Canada Creek. He is a member of the Federation of Fly Fishers and a Director of the General Herkimer Chapter of Trout Unlimited. Fishing West Canada Creek almost daily for nearly thirty years, he has chronicled its hatches and learned the river in its every mood.

Thirteen

The Esopus
by Ed Ostapczuk

The Esopus Creek is located in the heart of the Catskill Mountains in New York's Ulster County. Its source is Winnisook Lake on Slide Mountain, the highest mountain in the Catskills. It runs through the Towns of Shandaken and Olive before reaching the Ashokan Reservoir. Flowing from Winnisook, the Esopus is flanked by mountainous terrain and well forested slopes. It is joined by numerous spring-fed tributaries and is home to the brook trout in these upper reaches. The headwater stream is small with a steep gradient of 172 feet per mile. With the exception of a short section in the Catskill Forest Preserve, this 8.5 mile length between Winnisook and Route 28 is generally posted.

Between Big Indian and Ashokan Reservoir, a distance of 17 miles, the stream grows quickly in both size and stature to challenge the wading ability of even the most skillful angler. Here a fisherman would find a wading staff a useful accessory. This section of stream includes deep pools, fast rapids, and productive riffles with such famous names as Greeny Deep, Railroad Rapids, Mothers Pool and finally, the Chimney Hole. Here, brown and rainbow trout are the predominant species and much of this section of stream parallels NYS Route 28 providing easy access for fishermen.

Some 25 miles from its source at Winnisook Lake, the Esopus empties into the Ashokan Reservoir. Ashokan is a man-made reservoir and is part of New York City's water supply system. Its completion in 1915 created a mini-ocean of over 8,000 acres which offers excellent fishing for both rainbow and brown trout as well as smallmouth bass and walleyes. It also is the nurturing ground for trophy Esopus Creek trout which make their annual spawning run into the stream every spring and fall. The spring spawning run of rainbows has made the Esopus famous. This can occur anytime from prior to the start of trout season, April 1st, through early May. To a lesser extent, there is a fall run of browns and some rainbows.

That section of stream between Big Indian and Ashokan Reservoir is one of the most productive wild trout streams in the Northeast. It has a moderate gradient of 36 feet per mile, and while it's still a small creek at Big Indian, it's a full-blown river by the time it reaches the Ashokan. I like to visualize this length of the creek as being in three distinct sections based upon stream size. Looking at the river this way will help convey the fishing strategies discussed below.

The upper section, or what is known as the Upper Esopus, flows from Big Indian downstream to the Portal at Allaben and is approximately five miles in length. This section of stream consists of natural run-off and is subject to the same seasonal fluctuations as other Catskill streams. It varies in width from twenty to forty feet and has an average depth of two feet during normal spring flows. This section is easy to wade and fish and contains a rich mayfly population. Much of this section parallels NYS Route 28 and Old Route 28.

The middle section extends from the "Portal" (discussed below) downstream to Phoenicia, a distance of five miles. In addition to the Portal, several of the larger Esopus Creek tributaries enter this section of the stream. The stream's width varies here from forty to sixty feet and its depth is a function of both Portal releases and natural run-off. Access to this section of stream can be gained from NYS Route 28 and Herdman Road located just northwest of Phoenicia. Look for signs leading to Woodland Valley. This section of stream is also the most affected by the notorious "rubber hatch." Tubing is a very popular weekend recreational pastime on the Esopus between Memorial Day and Labor Day, and much of it occurs on this section of the stream. During the summer months plan to fish when the trout are most active, prior to 10 a.m. or after 6 p.m., and your encounter with tubers should be minimal. Rainy or stormy days also tend to hold tubers at bay.

The lower section extends from Phoenicia downstream to the reservoir. This long run harbors the deepest pools and plenty of casting room. Its width varies from sixty to over one hundred feet and, since only two tributaries enter this section, it is capable of carrying and distributing upstream flows very well. All of this beat of river is paralleled by NYS Route 28 and/or portions of Old

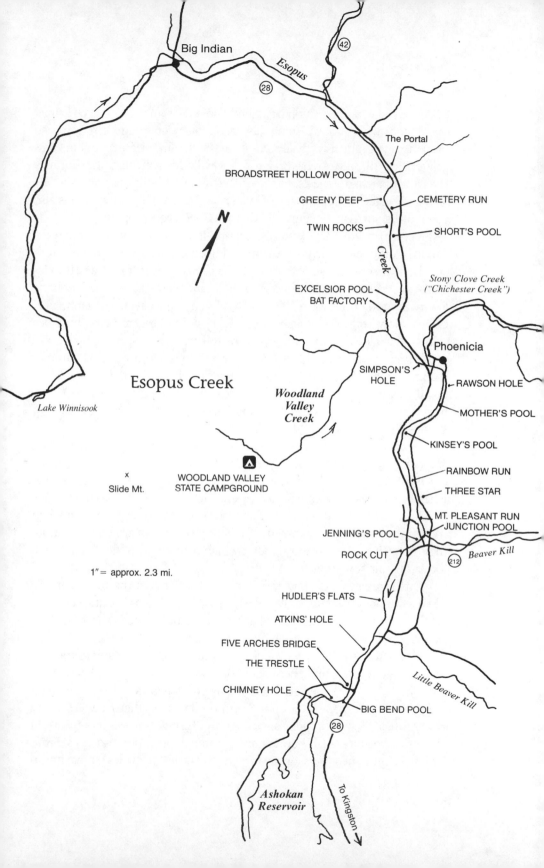

Route 28. As with the section described above, stream access can be gained to stretches with Public Fishing Easements or by entering from unposted property. Here, and as with all sections of the stream, please do not trespass or litter. From the Five Arches Bridge in Boiceville downstream to the Chimney Hole, the final mile of the Esopus, you need a special fishing permit issued by the New York City Department of Water Resources. This free permit is also good for fishing Ashokan and all other NYC reservoir properties.

As mentioned above, water is diverted into Esopus Creek through the famous Portal at Allaben, upstream of Phoenicia. The water comes from Schoharie Reservoir, also part of the NYC water supply, through an 18-mile-long subterranean aqueduct known as the Shandaken Tunnel. The Schoharie Reservoir was completed in 1926 when the Schoharie Creek was dammed at Gilboa, New York. An intake valve at the bottom of this reservoir provides cold water releases into the Esopus. At full reservoir capacity, up to 650 million gallons a day can be diverted to the Esopus. During the dry summer months, as much as 90% of the Esopus flow from the Portal at Allaben downstream 11.9 miles to the Ashokan can consist of this diversion. As you might guess, the Portal has a profound affect upon those nearly 12 miles of Esopus Creek and its trout fishing.

Over the years the Shandaken Tunnel has been viewed as both blessing and curse by Esopus Creek anglers. On the positive side of the ledger, the diversions keep the Esopus full of cold water during dry, hot, summer months when other Catskill streams wilt to mere trickles. Seldom does the Esopus Creek water temperature (below the portal) exceed 70 degrees, even when some nearby streams are as much as 10 or more degrees warmer. In addition, these diversions contain zooplankton which serves as an added food source for young rainbow trout.

On the negative side, water released from the Portal can be turbid at times. This is especially true after heavy rainstorms or when the Schoharie Reservoir is low and water drawn into the Shandaken Tunnel creates a shearing of silt from the reservoir bottom as it enters the intake.

Flows from the Portal were not always subject to regulations as they are today. After years of battle between various outdoor groups and New York City, the New York State Legislature finally enacted laws in 1977 governing the flows of the Shandaken Tunnel and outflows of other New York City reservoirs. This was brought about mainly through the efforts of Catskill Waters, a coalition of fishermen and conservation groups such as Trout Unlimited and Theodore Gordon Flyfishers. The law provides for maximum and minimum flows in the Esopus Creek depending upon the time of year and water conditions in the Ashokan and Schoharie Reservoirs. In addition, it allows for up to four "recreational releases" per year; these are high water events for kayaking and canoeing. You might want to contact the NYS Department of Environmental Conservation (DEC) in New Paltz, New York for more information about specific dates. Usually the events occur one weekend per month between June and September. Fishermen will generally want to avoid the Esopus below the Portal during these releases.

All in all, the Portal has had a very positive impact on the Esopus Creek

Top: A typical rock- and boulder-strewn stretch of the Esopus.
Bottom: Stonefly and Isonychia *nymph shucks tell of good hatching activity.*

147

trout fishery, helping to create a truly great wild trout stream. It is interesting to note just how productive.

Natural reproduction of rainbow, brown, and brook trout occurs throughout the entire Esopus Creek system upstream from the Ashokan Reservoir, although brookies are generally limited to the tributaries and to the headwater Esopus above Big Indian. In addition, the stream receives a yearly supplemental stocking of hatchery brown trout. Few hatchery holdover browns are caught from year to year, leading DEC officials to conclude that they are taken out of the stream shortly after each stocking.

Based upon DEC fishery studies conducted between 1975 and 1978, some amazing population estimates were calculated. In the 11.9 mile length of stream between the Portal and Ashokan Reservoir, DEC estimated the standing crop of wild trout to be in excess of 100,000 at the end of trout season. This averaged out to more than 9,400 trout per stream mile in this area! More than 75% of these trout were wild rainbows with the remainder being wild browns.

Above the Portal, the DEC estimate was much lower; this section of stream averaged 1,700 trout per mile. While these are point-in-time estimates subject to a certain amount of statistical error, the DEC sampling techniques are similar for all NYS streams. Hence the data supports the conclusion that the Esopus Creek is one of the most productive wild trout streams in the Northeast.

Now before you drop this book and head out for the Esopus, you should know that the size of most of these wild trout was between the fingerling stage and ten inches. The Esopus Creek system is an outstanding producer of wild trout, but they average on the small size. Except during the spawning runs, many of the trout caught in the Esopus are wild rainbows between eight and 10 inches. It appears that at about this size, the rainbows drop out of the Esopus Creek down into the Ashokan Reservoir. However, the Esopus contains larger trout from Opening Day until sometime into June or early July. Also, the closer that you fish to the Ashokan, as trout season progresses, the larger the trout tend to be. This is not to say that large rainbows and browns are not caught throughout the entire system all season; in fact, some are. Spawning trout utilize the Esopus Creek even above Big Indian, and they also enter all of its tributaries. Some of these larger trout remain in the Esopus Creek system through the entire trout season.

Another interesting statistic worthy of mention is that growth rates of trout were better below the Portal than above it. This would be expected given the favorable volumes of flow and cooler water temperatures. Also, the ratio of wild rainbows to wild browns below the Portal was 4 to 1, or stated another way, 80% of the wild trout were rainbows.

Armed with this inspiring information about the Esopus Creek, it's time to go fishing. I hope that it's evident from DEC's studies that any of the open sections of the Esopus Creek discussed above can be productive. You don't need to worry about secret spots. You should give some thought to a fishing strategy though, and that's what we'll discuss next.

While I am a fly fisherman, I have observed bait and spinner fishermen for many years, and have taught both my sons how to catch trout using these time honored methods. For the most part, bait is fished successfully throughout the entire length of the Esopus Creek all season long. Favorite baits include single salmon eggs, egg sacks, worms and minnows. Experienced minnow fishermen consistently catch the largest trout, as evidenced by a 9½ pound rainbow taken in the fall of 1990. Worms provide the steadiest action throughout the season for all species of trout while salmon eggs are a favorite of rainbow fanciers. Using either bait, you want to roll your worm or egg along the bottom of the stream; usually you will need the help of a couple of split shots to get down. Fish the pools, runs, and mouths of all the tributaries for best action. For equipment I would recommend an open faced spinning reel lined with four or six pound test monofilament attached to a rod of six feet or longer. Bait fishermen tend to be most successful early and late in the season, and during times of high water. As trout start feeding on hatching insects, bait fishing action tapers off slightly.

A spin fisherman equipped with the same outfit and an assortment of Rooster Tails, Mepps, and small Rapalas, or his favorite lure, should do equally well throughout the entire length of the Esopus. Utilizing either approach, I would recommend fishing the stream with felt-soled waders.

As a fly fisherman, I approach Esopus Creek fishing by considering several interrelated factors: (1) time of year, (2) stream height and color, and (3) water temperature. A closely related consideration that affects both stream height and temperature is the Portal flow.

Let's review the first consideration, time of year.

In general, I divide the time of year into three segments: (1) Early and late season, (2) Prior experiences, and (3) The remainder of the trout season. By early season I mean the month of April when natural run-off is high and

A 19-inch male spawning rainbow, taken by author in April on an Epeorus nymph.

stream temperatures are very cold. During these conditions trout are extremely sluggish and do not readily move to either fly or bait. If there's a secret to success under these circumstances, it's to make sure that your fly gets down to the lethargic trout in a natural manner. I try to locate and fish the bottom of well defined trout holding lies with weighted nymphs. For this reason, I fish the Upper Esopus and mainstream tributaries. Since spawning rainbows are spread throughout the Esopus Creek system this time of year, I'm confident about trout being present where I am fishing. I do concentrate on getting down and presenting my fly in a natural manner. I seek shallower pools, runs, and pockets where I can fish bottom and where the water temperatures warm fastest. If Portal flows are low or non-existent, then I also fish the mid-section of the stream between the Portal and Phoenicia, above the confluence of Woodland Valley Creek. Again, trout lies will be well defined and you can get down easily with weighted nymphs.

Other considerations for this time of year include fishing at first light when stream banks are snow covered. Daytime air temperatures generate snow run-off causing the already low stream temperatures to drop even further. When the mountains and stream banks are covered with snow, trout tend to be most active very early in the day. Fish with weighted nymphs, split shot if necessary, a strike indicator, and a leader no longer than nine feet. Trout strikes this time of year are barely detectable and you never know if the "bump" on the end of your line is a six inch or a three pound rainbow. When in doubt, raise your rod tip sharply.

For late season, after mid-October, the above approach is also a good strategy. Now, though, the best time of day to fish is from noon on when the sun has warmed the stream. For the past several years the Esopus has had an extended trout fishing season ending November 30th. This excludes the tributaries which close on September 30th to protect spawning brown and brook trout.

Prior fishing experiences have taught me to look for some outstanding dry fly fishing from late May through early July from the Ashokan Reservoir upstream to Mt. Tremper. The closer the calendar gets to July, the closer I fish to the Ashokan. During this time of year, spawning rainbows are dropping back to the reservoir and you may experience some movement of trout in and out of the Ashokan into Esopus Creek. On occasion you can catch rainbows up to 19 inches on dry flies below the Five Arches Bridge in Boiceville. This phenomenon can occur anytime up through very early July and appears to be a function of stream temperatures and flow. My favorite dry for this fishing is an Ausable Wulff (10-12) to simulate the numerous stoneflies that hatch in this area of the stream. Sometimes, even larger flies are needed to imitate these big Plecoptera.

For the rest of the season, I choose my fishing location based upon the other two factors.

The first of those is stream height/water coloration. Generally speaking, spring flows in the Esopus are a function of natural run-off from the tributaries. As the fishing season progresses, Portal discharges take on greater importance. As noted above, the stream width is much greater below Phoenicia and therefore the river bed is capable of carrying more water while still providing a pleasant fishing experience. Stream coloration can be affected by the Portal and/or Esopus Creek tributaries. It is possible for the Esopus to be off-color below Allaben, if Portal discharges are turbid, yet be clear above this point. If you made a long trip to fish this stream, take the time to check this possibility out. It is also possible for the Esopus to be off color immediately downstream of the Portal yet clear below Mt. Tremper as the turbidity settles out. Sometimes any coloration is the result of natural run-off from the tributaries. The Stony Clove, which joins the Esopus in Phoenicia, is a major contributor of natural turbidity. For the most part, turbidity is not a deterrent; the Esopus Creek is one of the most heavily fished trout streams in the state every year.

The final consideration for an Esopus Creek fishing strategy is stream temperature. In early and late season it's the Upper Esopus and tributaries which warm up the fastest, spurring on insect activity. However, as spring fades into summer, the best bet is fishing downstream from the Portal.

One evening in late July I was fishing the Esopus upstream from the junction of the Stony Clove Creek in Phoenicia. In an hour's time I quickly caught and released two dozen small rainbows on dries. Then I came upon two other trout fishermen above me, so I gave way to them and moved downstream several miles to Mt. Tremper. In the next two hours, I struggled to catch two more small rainbows. I was so intrigued by this experience that I decided to measure the stream temperature at several locations. I drove upstream to the Portal and recorded a reading of 59 degrees F. from water discharging into the Esopus. Then I returned to my first location in Phoenicia and measured the stream at 64 degrees F. At Mt. Tremper, my second fishing location, the stream temperature measured 67 degrees F. The last location that I measured was at the Five Arches Bridge in Boiceville; here the stream gave a reading of 69 degrees F. In the ten mile section of the Esopus between the Portal and Five Arches, the stream rose 10 degrees, but it took only the

Below the Five Arches Bridge is big water. Upstream is The Trestle and just below is the legendary Chimney Hole.

three degree difference between Phoenicia and Mt. Tremper to play a major role in my fishing success.

This was not the only experience I had like this. I have become a firm believer in the use of a stream thermometer even though I know the Esopus Creek quite well. I find a thermometer even more valuable when I fish trout streams away from my home river. During the first days of a new trout season I use the thermometer to locate the exact opposite effects that I have described above; again, the warmer the water, the greater the insect and trout activity.

Speaking of insects, the Esopus supports the traditional Catskill hatches. It has excellent hatches of sulphur duns starting in late May and *Isonychia* which last most of the summer. It also supports excellent stonefly hatches in its lower section. Except for green drakes, which are almost nonexistent, the other traditional Catskill mayfly and caddis hatches are present. For weighted nymphs I prefer the Hare's Ear (14), March Brown (10), Golden Stone Fly (6-8), Hare's Ear Stone (6-8), and the *Epeorus* Nymph (12) as described in Ernest Schwiebert's *Matching the Hatch*. Two excellent unweighted nymphs are the Cooper Bug (14) and the Zug Bug (12-14), which I use to represent *Isonychia* nymphs and caddis pupae. My favorite two dry fly patterns are the Adams (10-20) and Ausable Wulff (6-18). I feel very comfortable with just these two patterns but would also recommend a few Henryville Specials (12-14), Badger Spiders (14), and the Hairwing Royal Coachman (10-14) which is an excellent fast water fall pattern. I fish both weighted nymphs and dries using a textbook upstream approach.

With all its riffles and rapids, fishing three wet flies downstream is not only a classic Catskill tradition but also a very effective method of catching trout. Fishing them either dead drift or working them with some form of motion or twitch can be very productive. Patterns that I would not be without include: Leadwing Coachman, Dark and Light Cahill, Gold Ribbed Hare's Ear, Royal Coachman and the Brown Hackle. You should carry these in sizes 10 through 14. The Light Cahill is an effective wet to fish just under the surface film during sulphur dun hatches. Finally, I would recommend two streamer patterns, the Muddler Minnow (6) and White Marabou (6). I also tie Muddlers (8-10) on nymph hooks and fish them as nymphs or dries effectively. As far as fly fishing equipment goes, I would recommend using your favorite eight-foot rod with matching six-weight fly line and backing.

Trout fishing history and angling lore run deep on this stream. Former DEC Deputy Commissioner Cecil Heacox dubbed several geographically related streams in the Catskill the "Charmed Circle." The Esopus is one of those, and has contributed more than its share to American angling history.

In 1918, bamboo rod maker Jim Payne conceived a dry fly rod prototype while fishing the Esopus Creek. Five years later in 1923, T.E. Spencer caught a 19 pound 14 ounce brown trout from the Chimney Hole, and this fish remained the state record for 31 years! Preston Jennings did much of his research for the classic *A Book of Trout Flies* which helped lay a foundation for American angling entomology. Phoenicia was the "Capital of the Charmed Circle" in those early days of American trout fishing and through the years an army of angling luminaries wet a line in this Catskill jewel. These included Theodore Gordon, George LaBranche, A.J. McClane, Art Flick, Larry Koller, Ernest Schwiebert, and a host of others. Perhaps the best short story ever written of one man's love of a trout stream was authored by Paul O'Neil and titled "In Praise of Trout and Also Me." This first appeared in *Life* Magazine in 1964 and the Esopus was the center of this angler's affliction. The late Ray Smith is legendary in Esopus Creek history. He was *the* Esopus fly tier and fisherman during his time, and his patterns, such as the Red Fox and the Wild Turkey, live on.

In May of 1913 Theodore Gordon, the father of American fly fishing, wrote the following about Esopus Creek:

> By the way, the new Shokan dam, in the Catskills, will afford the finest trout fishing in America, if properly treated, and not spoiled by the introduction of other predatory fish. It will be stocked naturally from the Esopus with the rainbow and European trout of good size and quality.

By any measure, the Esopus has lived up well to his prediction over the last eighty years.

Ed is President of the Ashokan-Pepacton Watershed Chapter of Trout Unlimited. He has been active in TU on a local, state, and national level since 1969, and was a leader in the twelve year battle against the Prattsville Pumped Storage Project. His writing credits include articles in *Trout*. Ed lives in Shokan, New York with his wife, Lois, and their four children. He fishes the Esopus and waters of the central Adirondacks regularly.

Fourteen

The Beaver Kill
by Jim Capossela

In any book on great trout rivers of the world, the Beaver Kill would be an important chapter. But of all those rivers, it is of this one most of all that it would have to be asked: Who is author and who is subject?

The Beaver Kill flows as much through time as through space. It nears, soon enough, the spot where A.J. McClane and Arnold Gingrich passed their euphoric "Turnwood Years." It passes the home of Lee and Joan Wulff, even close enough to wind the morning coffee. It surely spies John Burroughs, who has come over from Big Indian to fish. It sees Sparse Grey and his outrageous lotus eaters stripping down to just their "pelts" behind their clubhouse. At Roscoe, "Big Flats," it veers dangerously close to Keener's Pool, the Antrim Lodge, where Dana Lamb and Red Smith and a hundred other ghosts are hoisting Whiskey Sours the snowy April afternoon. The Beaver Kill glides by the old Hillside Summer House where Charles Ritz and George LaBranche are registered. It sees Schwiebert try for that second twenty-incher at Hendrickson's Pool; watches Harry Darbee sneaking down to a secret spring hole near Wagon Tracks; takes in Ernie Maltz floating a caddis at the Acid Factory; and pays witness to ordinary people like you and me fishing to March browns at Peakville.

The Beaver Kill is located in New York's Catskill Mountains. It drips off of Double Top Mountain and 43 miles later joins the East Branch Delaware River at East Branch. It begins at about 3,400 feet of elevation and ends exactly 995 feet above sea level. Its average drop is thus 55.9 feet per mile but its average drop below Roscoe is only about 14 feet per mile.

Until about 1790, it saw only transient Indians, deer, bear, mink, beaver. Since that time, people have farmed its banks, polluted it, paved over and around it, fought for it, loved it—at times nearly to death, and of course fished it. My records show that the intensity of its hatches has slowly waned in the past twenty five years, but they remain good, although fluctuating. The greatest blow to the river was the construction of the Rt. 17 Quickway, which was built in the 1960's and which now crosses the Beaver Kill and Willowemoc Rivers 13 times. The wounds of the road building have partially healed but the noise of heavy truck traffic on Rt. 17 is audible miles into the mountains, and the highway is visible from the stream, below Roscoe, perhaps half the time. The entire public stretch of the Beaver Kill is fished heavily from April 25 to July 4; weekdays offer but little relief during these prime hatching weeks. Before April 25 and from Independence Day to Labor Day, the river receives moderate fishing pressure. At these times, a pool to yourself is a real possibility on weekdays. In September and October, the river sees moderate to light-moderate use. After Labor Day, weekdays can actually be quite pleasant, elbow room-wise, especially if the weather is gloomy.

What is usually called the upper Beaver Kill, upstream of Roscoe, encompasses about 28 of the river's total miles. It is achingly beautiful water, and in the Catskills it is rivalled aesthetically only by the upper Neversink. In truth, most of the early angling history that was made on the Beaver Kill was made on this upper part. That's largely because brook trout dominated the picture back then and the brookie never fared well in that warmer water below Roscoe. While brown trout became firmly established in the Beaver Kill between 1900 and 1920, brook trout continue to be an important component of the trout fishery upstream of Roscoe, but especially upstream of Lew Beach. Below Roscoe, it is almost completely browns until you reach Horton where rainbows start to mix in. From Horton on down, rainbows are increasingly numerous.

It should be said that there are a few pieces of public water above Roscoe. There is a short mile or so at the Covered Bridge State Campground at the hamlet of Beaverkill. There are also several miles of tiny headwater stream that flow through state land. This would be fishing for tiny brook trout on very small water. Other than that, unless you're a member or guest at one of the private clubs along the upper Beaver Kill you'll have to stick to that section from the Rt. 206 Bridge, just north of Roscoe, down to the river's terminus at East Branch.

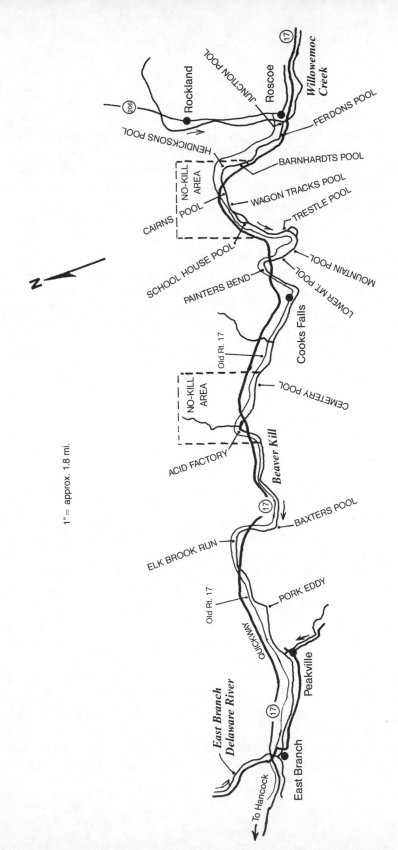

1" = approx. 1.8 mi.

The Lower Beaver Kill

There are two no-kill areas on the Beaver Kill. The first is from the Sullivan County line a short ways below Roscoe downstream for 2.5 miles. The second and newer one is from one mile upstream to 1.6 miles downstream of the iron bridge at Horton. On both sections, fishing is permitted year-round but only artificial lures may be used and all trout must be immediately returned. Streamside signs delineate the extent of these trophy sections. On the rest of the stream below the Rt. 206 bridge, the season runs from 4/1 to 11/30 and the daily limit is five trout nine inches or larger.

The no-kill rules have significantly increased the average size and number of trout present. Of the average 27,000 trout (mostly browns) that are annually stocked in the Beaver Kill, a good many now make it to 14 inches or better; 14-18 inch fish are relatively common, while 19-22 inch fish are very much present. Over the past ten years, I have gotten very few reports of fish larger than 22 inches. I believe trout of more than four pounds to be rare in the Beaver Kill.

The distinct majority of trout taken in the public section of the Beaver Kill are from stockings. It is believed that only some 10% are wild fish. In recent years, reports have come my way that in certain sections of the lower river, the percentage climbs to about 30%. Based on the opinion of certain experts, I believe 10% is pretty close to the accurate figure.

Probably the major reason why there are not more wild fish is the fact that the lower Beaver Kill is tributary-poor. If stocking ceased, there would be relatively few trout in the lower Beaver Kill, fishermen or no fishermen, in the opinion of one prominent state fish biologist. In the stream's headwaters, wild trout are very numerous. Also, the rainbows found in the lower Beaver Kill are virtually all wild fish.

The no-kill sections with their excellent head of oversized brownies are understandably busy, and getting busier. As I've often joked to my friends, there seems to be someone with his feet nailed to the bottom of the stream at the top of Cairn's Pool. Between the no-kill sections there is some interesting water, and this piece is cast to by both fly and spin fishermen. One popular bait pool is at the Cooks Falls Bridge; the water for a mile downstream is also nice in places. Below the lower no-kill, from Elk Brook downstream, the Beaver Kill carves an increasingly deep valley, and it runs wider and in some places deeper. Until recent years, the lower end was much more lightly fished. That is no longer the case.

With the advent of no-kill and year-round trout fishing, anglers have discovered that Beaver Kill trout can be taken in the off months. Catskill winters are normally rough, so the earliest you'll usually seen anyone astream is March. From the middle of that month through most of April comparatively few trout will be seen rising to naturals on the surface. Sport shops and taverns in the area are fond of scribbling "what's hatching" on their blackboards, and in early season you'll usually see early brown or early black stoneflies posted. You may see a few of these, you may see a few small blue-winged olives, often size 16 and smaller, and you will probably see a few caddis. But rarely will you see a good rise of fish before April 25. Better to probe the depths with nymphs or caddis larva imitations.

May 1 is when things usually start to happen. Though I have encountered relatively few good quill gordon hatches, when I have it's been between April 28 and May 7. The first week of May may also see the appearance of blue-winged olives (*Paraleptophlebia*, and/or two *Baetis* species). I have found that this can be one of the best hatches on both the Beaver Kill and the Willowemoc, and one that can elicit a very active rise of fish. The little size 16 and 18 sailboat

duns seem to have difficulty rising in the cold water, and the trout sip away steadily and methodically. A well-tied hackle-tip olive is deadly for the *Paraleptophlebia hatch,* although the more pragmatic contemporary angler is apt to be seen floating a Compara-dun.

The hendrickson *(E. subvaria)* seems to be a durable hatch that holds up well on rivers where other, perhaps more sensitive mayflies have disappeared. The first two weeks of May is prime time on the Beaver Kill, but the past two seasons the action started a good week earlier, probably due to warmer than average weather. The large, #12 hendricksons normally evoke a very good rise of fish, but this hatch has been so stupendous on the Delaware the past few years that I've driven right by the Beaver Kill.

Also in early May, the celebrated "shadfly"—also called "grannom" but scientifically *Brachycentrus numerosus*—appears. This often blizzard-like hatch of caddisflies is something to witness. One year, I brought my girlfriend up to the Beaver Kill to show her how to fly fish. Well, the shadflies were so thick that they were getting in her ears and hair, and they actually scared her off the river. Fly fishing cancelled on account of too many bugs! Nonetheless, this spectacular hatch rarely prompts much of a surface rise, and during it you'd be best off with pupal imitations.

The last two weeks of May can be a strange time on the Beaver Kill. The more or less predictable early season hatches have largely passed, and the very dependable early June hatches haven't quite begun. These two weeks mark the transition between spring and summer in the Catskills. If low pressure prevails, it will be wet, windy and often surprisingly chilly. One year on May 24th a friend and I arrived to float the East Branch Delaware and heard of frost and snow flurries the night before! On the other hand, it can also be blazing hot if high pressure dominates the weather picture. If it's somewhere in between, with moderate temps, average rain and lots of cloudy, drizzly, misty days you can expect some excellent hatching and fly fishing.

In late May, you will often see some of those "other hendricksons," *E. rotunda* and *E. invaria,* plus small blue-winged olives and various caddis. Grey foxes and March browns may be present, especially the last week of May, and these big juicy mayflies can put big trout on the prowl. March browns have good years and bad years. The last two have been very good indeed. The grey foxes, by the way, linger well into June. They're normally even more sporadic than the March browns.

One prominent expert, in a recent article, stated flatly that there are no rainbows in the Beaver Kill. I suggest that he hunker himself down to the lower

Beaver Kill where he may be very surprised at what he now catches.

On June 3rd two seasons ago, I got to the Catskills for a two-day trip. I drove down to the lower Beaver Kill at about 3:30 p.m. and when I got to the stream's edge I saw large stoneflies crawling all around the rocks. In the river there were only sporadic rises, but they were heavy ones. I knotted on a Humpy, a high-riding western fly that I had used in the past during stonefly hatches. Its buoyancy lets me really twitch it in the riffles. After taking four good browns, I finally located what I was looking for: An eye-popping riseform in midstream. The fish took without hesitation and fifteen minutes later I slid a very beautiful, 17-inch rainbow into the shallows.

The stonefly hatch waned and so I decided to drive down to the West Branch Delaware to see if any sulphurs had started yet. But the river was very high and rough so I gave up and drove to Fish's Eddy on the East Branch. From the old steel bridge, rises were visible up and down as far as you could see. It was a superb fall of coffin flies, but the fishing was very tough.

The next day at about 3:00 p.m. I headed on down to that same stretch of the lower Beaver Kill. All hell was breaking loose! The stoneflies were not to be seen, but there was a flotilla of *Isonychias* on the water and other flies were present too. Best of all, very large fish could be seen and heard splashing against the deep, farstream channel. I worked over a brown of three to four pounds for a good forty-five minutes but could not raise him. Now, green drake duns were floating down the river, and there were also grey foxes and a few other flies I couldn't identify. I believe some of the big fish working were taking emerging green drake nymphs and the fish were extremely selective. Working upstream into the faster, more forgiving water, I watched a man above me land a rainbow of about 16 inches plus a smaller rainbow and a brown. All I could manage that afternoon, though, were two smallish browns. The big fish were just too tough for me.

I feel quite certain that rainbows are increasing in number and size in the lower Beaver Kill, and I also believe they are extending their domain upstream. These are probably all wild fish. One biologist told me that the rainbows in the lower Beaver Kill are due to the presence of Trout Brook, a significant tributary from which naturally spawned 'bows recruit back down to the main river. The rainbows may also be a natural extension of the rainbow fishery in the East Branch Delaware. As in the East Branch, the rainbows seem to be largely but not totally oriented to the faster riffles. The browns in the lower Beaver Kill seem to be found in both the riffles and in the pools, with the biggest fish in the pools for sure.

To get back to Beaver Kill hatches, the celebrated green drake hatch seems to be heavier on the lower Beaver Kill, and especially on the East Branch Delaware and Main Stem Delaware. This may be because there is more of the silty bottom that the burrowing green drake nymphs require. On the East Branch, the hatch may arrive as early as about May 24, but on the lower Beaver Kill it will usually start five or six days later. When the duns are especially numerous on the surface the fishing can be exasperating, as large, selective trout will be choosey in the extreme. When the duns are coming off sporadically, you can expect much better cooperation. Imitations for the spinner or coffin fly should be thoughtfully tied. I advise that you carry some fully spent and some fully hackled because at times the spinners are really bouncing around and the full-hackled pattern works best. A good trick, if you're being frustrated during this hatch, is to move into slightly faster water where your large imitation cannot be studied as well by the trout.

I believe the best big fish hatches on the Beaver Kill are the green drake and the March brown. Like the March browns, the drakes have hatched in strong numbers the past few years. Obviously, neither fly is much of a factor in those years when it is very scarce.

The first ten days of June can be a magical time on the Beaver Kill, but not as magical as twenty years ago when hatches were more intense. Prime fishing time now splits, with both good morning and evening hatches possible. The water will have reached the optimal level for brown trout, around 59-63 degrees, and I believe that at this time the trout are the most active of the entire year.

Actively fished caddis pupae can be deadly at this time, even if relatively few flies are present on the surface. Early in the morning in June you may also see some hatching stoneflies. Good stonefly hatching is oriented to specific sections of the Beaver Kill. It pays to learn these by keeping notes. Generally, there are better stonefly hatches on the lower Beaver Kill.

A very good and very interesting hatch on the Beaver Kill-Delaware system is the #14 *Ephemerella cornuta,* a blue-winged olive with a fairly bright green body. Normally a morning hatch during the first three weeks of June, the duns can also be seen during the afternoon hours. Before the *cornutas* were brought to light by the Caucci-Nastasi team, Beaver Kill anglers would anticipate *E. attenuata* (a small blue-winged olive) hatches in the morning during early June. It's hard for me to identify most of those small blue-winged olives, a category which includes *attenuata,* but those *cornutas* are unmistakable and the trout love 'em.

Sometimes there is a mid to late afternoon lull in early June, but other times the fishing can be excellent all day long. This is especially true on cloudy, misty, windless days. But whatever happens during the day, a June evening on the Beaver Kill can be dramatic.

A pattern I have seen often develops as follows. At about 5:30 to 6 p.m., a very dark, size 12-14 caddis appears. I call it the black lady, but it is apparently *Psilotreta labida*. I've had great luck fishing this hatch while working an Adams at the bubbly heads of pools. In the flatter water, trout can be extremely choosey with this particular sedge. In some years, jumbo *Isonychia* duns will start floating by and you may also see a terrific fall of coffin flies. Fish will be very selective. Sometime around 7:30 or 8 p.m. sulphurs may appear, and my experience is that trout will almost always switch to the sulphurs. Trout are ultra choosey here. If a #16 doesn't work, try an 18. There is often a fine line, time wise, between when the trout are taking the sulphur duns and spinners. Have both spent and semi-spent sulphur patterns, and observe carefully what's happening. To further complicate things, there may be other flies, such as *Isonychia* spinners on the water. Yes, an early June evening on the Beaver Kill is magical, but it is sometimes very demanding. By the way, I always stay past 9 p.m. and finish up with a pure white, loop-wing fly that I can see well past dark. This is usually good for a few more fish until, in total darkness, I reluctantly clamber back up the bank.

Through the month of June, the *Isonychia* hatch can be quite important. Nymph, dun, spinner—all have their place at certain times. The experts claim that the Beaver Kill sees two important species of this genus: *bicolor* and *sadleri*. I do know that on the Beaver Kill-Delaware system, this renowned "lead wing" hatch either continues sporadically all summer or else starts up again in September. That's because we've seen this fly on those cool September days. Nonetheless, on the Beaver Kill, June is the month I am most on the watch for *Isonychias*. They especially can make things happen in that period from June 15 to July 1 when many of the other important hatches have tapered down.

From mid-June to early July, the morning activity gradually diminishes, and the duration of the evening hatch shrinks. The later in this period you go, the later the evening hatch. Yet I still like the period up to July 7th or so, when I can almost always count on some kind of evening activity. For example, very light, large flies often lumped together under the heading "cahills" can come off just before dark. Beyond that, there can be some on-and-off daytime activity to small blue-winged olives (*E. attenuata* and two *Pseudocloeon* species), caddis, and a few other infrequent and lesser known mayflies. As discussed in the next chapter, cloudy cool days can prompt some unexpected mid-summer hatching activity on Catskill rivers.

After about the first week of July and sometimes even sooner, the Beaver Kill normally becomes very low, and to me, at least, unappealing. There is no question, though, that the serious fly fisher can find delightful challenge and more elbow room during the summer doldrums. Part of that challenge arrives in the form of the eye-straining "trico," a tiny size #22-26 mayfly that hatches in very early morning. This hatch can go on for weeks, from the tail end of June to about mid-September or later, and although the insect is tiny, big fish can be drawn up. Tips for fishing this, the meat n'potatoes hatch of summer, can be found throughout the fly fishing literature.

The primary hatching period for caddis is much longer than with mayflies, so these downwings are something to watch for in high summer when mayflies can be quite scarce.

Beaver Kill trout perk up dramatically in mid-September, though hatching will be minimal. Trout—and trout fishermen—look to the land-borne insects during the early autumn period. Imitations of ants, hoppers, crickets, etc., can all be fished with success at certain times if you are stealthy enough to deal with the low water and you can find the right spot. Remember, too, that caddis and microcaddis can make appearances in Autumn. It's almost impossible to predict when, where and in what size. Just have a good selection with you.

With the onset of autumn rains, and the continuing drop in water temperature, Beaver Kill trout can be extraordinarily active during the first two weeks of October. Fly fishermen should experiment with bucktails, balsa-bodied ants and various searching patterns, if no hatches are to be seen. This is a time of year to forget the shackles of printed theory and stretch out with your own creativity.

Most anglers coming to fish the Beaver Kill or its equally famous tributary, the Willowemoc, find the services they need in Roscoe or Livingston Manor. There are three or four well-stocked tackle shops in or between these two villages. Motels and campgrounds are numerous in the area. Fancier accommodations can be found in Liberty, 18 miles away.

The entire lower Beaver Kill downstream of the earlier referenced Rt. 206 bridge is public water. Decades ago, permanent easements were purchased by the state for fishermen. There are several parking lots designated for fishermen. Head down (downstream) from Roscoe on old Rt. 17 and where to park will be more or less obvious to you.

Jim Capossela is the founder and president of Northeast Sportsman's Press. A professional writer his entire career, his articles have appeared in *Field & Stream, Outdoor Life, Sports Afield* and many other magazines. He is the author of 10 books on the outdoors, including *Good Fishing in the Catskills*. Jim has fished the Beaver Kill every season for more than 20 years.

Fifteen

The Delaware
by Jim Capossela

When I first set eyes on the Delaware River there were elk and antelope grazing peacefully on the big flood plain just below the junction of the two branches. Cactus and fireweed were growing in profusion, and there were grayling here and there in pockets of faster water. Looking down off a bridge you could see dozens of cutthroats, mostly between 16 and 18 inches; in the flatter pools gulper browns of better than six pounds were sipping softly. The salmon fly hatch was awesome, and the streamside willows were awash with the big Plecoptera. Even the greenest duffers riding the drift boats were nailing two and three pounders, and some better than that. In backwater sloughs there were curlews and kingfishers, and soaring over the prairie were three eagles eying some creature that had recently bitten the dust. The sky was big, the water was broad, and there were places where you could backcast your whole fly line...

This, of course, was not the log book entry of my first day on the Delaware. It's just that it's very easy to daydream on this, the great western trout river of the east.

The entire Delaware River trout fishery, below the dams, is phoney. It's a phoniness we can live with. There'd be no trout here at all, or few, were it not for the tailwater releases from the only two large dams ever built on this otherwise great, free-flowing river. Those tailwater releases, from Pepacton and Cannonsville Dams, have created about 70 miles of some of the best wild trout fishing in the east. Yes, there are stocked fish, but there are also excellent numbers of wild rainbows that grow to about 22 inches, and some wild browns. Tradition on the river is paltry; the whole thing didn't start until about 1960.

THE EAST BRANCH

Before Pepacton Reservoir came along in the 1950's, the East Branch of the Delaware was an excellent and beautiful river, its primary trout water extending from its headwaters near Roxbury down to about Downsville, but its marginal trout water extending much farther downstream. Almost every year, it would seem, someone would nail a ten pound or better brown. Pepacton wiped out about 25 prime miles of the East Branch, but now, with cold water releases from the reservoir, and through the courtesy of many cold, feeder streams, trout habitat extends all the way from the dam at Downsville down to Hancock. There are brown trout both stocked and wild, wild rainbows, and at least a few native brook trout. The odd brookies are transients from cold tributaries that enter nearby.

There are two quite distinct segments to the East Branch: The upper section from Pepacton down to East Branch village, and the lower section from that point down to Hancock. That's how we'll refer to them in this chapter.

The upper section is closer to the reservoir and thus runs colder. It is mostly browns here, but the extreme upper end, near Downsville, produces a few chunky brook trout.

Proceeding downstream, the water gets warmer and at East Branch Village the Beaver Kill enters and warms up the Delaware even more. For nine months a year this matters not, because the river is always cold enough. But during summer, high temps in the lower East Branch are a major reason why trout are just not that abundant. The trout that are present survive the hot spells by finding spring holes or cold tributaries or mountain seeps. Either that or they migrate, but I favor the former theory.

East Branch rainbows seem to peak out at about 18-19 inches, or at least that is the largest I've either caught or seen them. This is several inches smaller than the largest ones taken from the main stem. I have caught rainbows all the way up to East Branch, and in fact on up into the lower Beaver Kill. I believe that rainbows now dominate the entire stretch of the

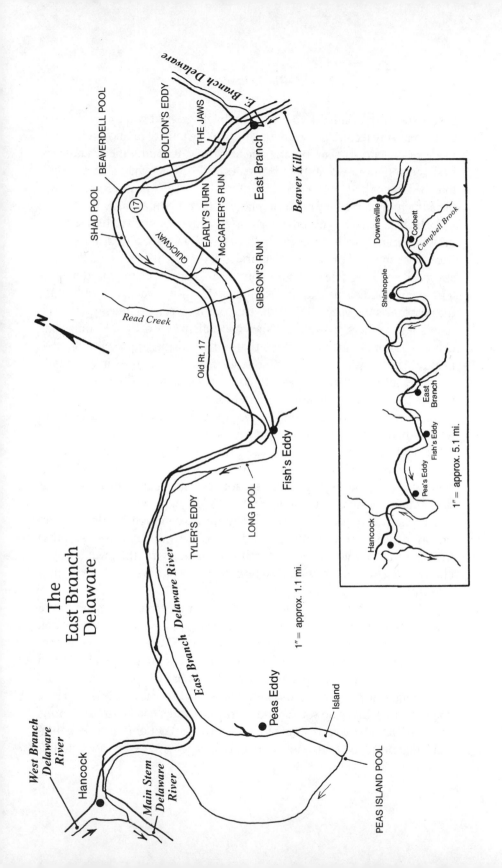

East Branch from Hancock to East Branch village. And while over the past seven years my records show about a one to one ratio of rainbow to brown, I believe the rainbows are pulling ahead. Surely, if you hit the river after a fresh stocking, those drab little brownies will be everywhere. And surely, too, the largest trout in the river are browns. But there is no question that the big attraction on the lower east branch is the wild rainbows.

The East Branch is never an easy stream. In the upper section stocked brownies mingle with some wild browns, and both grow to healthy sizes. Because so much of the water is flat up here, though, the fish are difficult to approach and long, fine leaders are often necessary. Also, their feeding patterns are unpredictable and the fish just aren't easy to catch. Complicating the problem is the busy water traffic that occurs at certain times. Canoeists, tubers and bathers, as well as fishermen, all spawned by the numerous cottages, campgrounds and clubs that surround the upper East Branch, help to rile things up. Finally, in spite of mandated summertime releases, the water level is often unpleasantly low after June first. The releases keep the fish alive but are certainly not generous.

I have not logged too many hours on the upper East Branch but contacts tell me there can be a real good hendrickson hatch up here.

Below East Branch Village the fishing is also tough, even though there is more of that forgiving riffle water. First, as I stated, I believe the absolute population of trout in this lower section is just not that great—without doubt, much less than the now heralded West Branch. Then there is the two-horned dilemma of fly hatches: They are less common and diverse than on, say, the Beaver Kill, meaning that rising fish are even more the exception than the rule. Yet when a good hatch does materialize, the trout are very choosey. The wild rainbows throughout the Delaware system are extremely selective.

I have fished the lower East Branch many times in every open month. The best hatches I've seen have been stoneflies (one 2¾ pound brown I took had a hundred nymphs in its stomach); green drakes; sulphurs and other small cream-colored flies the identity of which I am uncertain about; and *Isonychia*. March browns and grey foxes appear in their proper season, but very sporadically by my records. Some late season *Stenonema* flies hatch here (big—size 10-12) as do some good grannom caddis hatches in the spring. Near Fish's Eddy, one angling buddy experienced not only a thick, grannom hatch but a good rise of trout to it. This is not always the case with this early season Catskill hatch. Just above that spot, I encountered a heavy 8 p.m. hatch of a large, size #10 yellowish mayfly. It was June 20th.

One time while walking downstream I noticed a kind of dust on the banks and at the edge of the river. Closer inspection revealed that it was not dust at all but green drake nymph shucks. Millions of them! To hit this hatch, try May 25-June 3 in particular (a little earlier than the Beaver Kill) and look to the slower, siltier sections. The coffin fly spinners come down a few days later, but often in somewhat faster water. Sometimes the trout come up to these big, tempting imagoes and sometimes they don't. When they do, it will be the best dry fly action that you'll ever see on the lower East Branch. By the way, if you spy the kind of "dust" just mentioned, pay close attention to where you saw it. Just upstream there is probably a silty pool with fine guttulata hatching activity.

This past season, I experienced two interesting hatches on the lower East Branch, both quite humbling.

On June 15, I ran into a fantastic spinner fall of *cornuta* mayflies. Big, gold- and crimson-sided rainbows were feeding but I didn't quite have the right pattern and the trout were phenomenally selective. The spinners were riding downcurrent sort of semi-spent. That evening, between 7:30-8:00 p.m., I also saw some very small cream spinners about size 16.

On July 12, I returned to this pool and was perplexed by the appearance of a large, size #14 blue-winged olive mayfly dun. There was also a tiny olive size #22. On this cool, rainy day, trout were rising—but not being fooled—between 5-8:30 p.m. It proves good action can occur in mid-summer. Cool, rainy weather is often the catalyst.

Access to the East Branch of the Delaware is still quite good. There is admittedly much human activity and some posting on the upper section, but by driving along Rt. 30 you'll find your places to fish. If you are not so gregarious, the lower East Branch will probably suit you better. Almost this entire 13-mile stretch is open to the public, partially via a few short state easements but mainly through the generosity of private landowners who have not posted as yet. And while there are no campgrounds and very little human activity, there are also fewer fishermen.

THE WEST BRANCH

The West Branch, for all its fine fishing, is now all too often too crowded for my tastes. In addition, I don't like the shape of the river as well as I do that of, for example, the East Branch or the Beaver Kill or even parts of the Main Stem. But I still come here often, and who wouldn't. No less than the Caucci-Nastasi fishing team made this statement in a magazine article: "The upper Delaware River System is one of the best wild trout fisheries in this country, and its West Branch is the crown jewel of that system."

Before Cannonsville Dam, West Branch trout ran down only about as far as Deposit. Thus the section we're discussing here was once primarily a warm-water fishery, mostly smallmouth. Cold water now released from the bottom of Cannonsville has changed all that.

From Cannonsville dam downstream about a mile to the low Stilesville Dam, New York City has enacted a no-fishing, no-entrance policy. Thus the West Branch for anglers runs about 16 miles from Stilesville down to Hancock.

The New York State easements that exist on much of the Beaver Kill and on some of the East Branch are not found on the West Branch. The banks on both sides are mainly in private hands, and posting is moderate. The water

The West Branch Delaware, an erstwhile bass river made great by the cold releases from Cannonsville Reservoir. The mist is born of very cold water making contact with the warmer air.

right around Deposit, good water, is mostly unposted and provides fine opportunity. There is free water, too, at the Stilesville dam, where I saw a worm fisherman take a 20-inch brown recently (this is probably the best place in the river to try for a really big brown) and for a ways downstream. A fine place to fish is just below the Quickway Bridge at Deposit, where there is a long, productive pool and some mini-pools and runs created by a small island there. Two seasons ago I fished to an unbelievable hendrickson hatch at this pool. The April 27th hatch started in early afternoon and seemed to go on forever, with heavy hatching continuing well into the evening.

Below this the access gets tougher. From Deposit downstream to a point about one mile below Hale Eddy, it is still New York State property on both sides of the river. On the west side, there is a local road (River Road) that can be accessed from the business district in Deposit. This section has some posting, but there are unposted sections as well as a number of pull-offs for parking. The bank here can be quite steep, though, and overall the parking situation is poor. On the east side of this stretch, the Quickway borders the river, sometimes close and sometimes just out of sight. Some anglers do park along the Quickway, but try to use the established pull-offs.

One popular access point is right at the Hale Eddy bridge, which can be accessed from either the west or eastbound lanes of the Quickway. There is enough parking here for a number of cars in a small lot just east of the bridge by the still active railroad tracks. There is excellent water right at the bridge and for a good ways both upstream and downstream.

From the Hale Eddy bridge down to Hancock, on the east side of the river, you again have a situation where the river is bordered by the Rt. 17 Quickway with the train tracks sandwiched in between the two. The advice is the same as above: Look for the unposted sections, ask permission before crossing private lands, and stick to the established pull-offs if you're going to try and park along the Quickway.

Still on the subject of access, let's now cross back over to the west bank of the river. Not far below Hale Eddy, the Pennsylvania border first touches the river, and it is Pennsy turf on the west bank from here down to Hancock. Happily, along this stretch the State of Pennsylvania has acquired a couple of miles of river bank. Although it is PA Game Commission property, fishing in the river with either a NY or PA fishing license is allowed. Signs clearly define the extent of this now public water.

In addition, the Pennsylvania Fish Commission has a nice access point at Balls Eddy, downstream of the State Game Land. There is a very good launch ramp here for (primarily) canoes, and there is some very nice water upstream, downstream and right at this ramp. There is plenty of parking, restrooms and once again either a PA or a NY fishing license is acceptable.

Outside of this public water on the west bank, the river is intermittently posted. Camping anglers can get at the West Branch by staying at the Delaware River Campground just a short ways below the Hale Eddy bridge.

Because of the way water is released from the reservoir, water conditions on the West Branch are somewhat strange, not to mention very unpredictable. Since summer is when the releases are necessary to protect the trout, these releases are not normally made in spring. The city "saves them up" you might say. Thus from the opener on April first to June 15th, the West Branch can run surprisingly low and clear for that time of year. An exception would be when there have been heavy rains, and water is spilling over the dam. By early June, again barring heavy rains, the river can be very low and uninviting, as well as very weedy. From June 15th to August 15th, though, the heavy releases usually keep the West Branch quite high and cold. When those sticky weeds take hold, you can just about forget any lure or fly that sinks to the bottom.

But to get back to spring for a moment, the April-May reduced releases are usually not a problem. In fact, it's nice to see a stream at clear, normal (if still cold) conditions at a time when excessively high, turbid water is the rule. Right from the gun in April, bait and lure fishermen do well on browns that run up to 20 inches and better. In fact, one April 20th I fished the West Branch when the air temperature had hit an amazing 90 degrees. With the low water and intense heat, it felt like mid-summer, but twenty or so chunky browns were fooled by my spinning tactics. The limit, by the way, is five fish nine inches or better on the West Branch.

The West Branch is a very fertile river. As I mentioned earlier, I have timed some truly fine hendrickson hatches here over the years. The *Ephemerella subvaria* duns ordinarily promote excellent surface activity, but the bigger fish will not be easy. One effective pattern is the Haystack or the similar Compara-dun in an appropriate shade and size. Also in fairly early spring, there will be some caddis and some stoneflies hatching, and you may even see some of the quill gordons (*Epeorus pleuralis*) that seem to have regrettably dwindled on many other Catskill Rivers. Then after the early season flies, the gap is often filled by the little blue-winged olives (18-24) that are so pervasive and so important on so many Catskill Rivers. From June into early July, two species of "Drakes" may appear. These are the green

(*Ephemera guttulata*) and the brown (*E. simulans*). Then, too, from mid June through early July the sulphur hatch can provide superb, late day and evening fishing (occasionally mid-day, too). Two lesser touted mayflies, *Ephemerella deficiens* and *Heptagenia hebe* appear on the West Branch in mid-July and may persist right through October.

While stoneflies can be quite important on the East Branch, caddis flies are very significant on the West Branch. Even sporadic caddis hatches have saved the day here more than once. In the lower water periods, microcaddis in size 18-22 is something to watch for.

From the Stilesville dam down to below Deposit, mostly brown trout will be encountered. They will average a very healthy 11-13 inches and many 14-18 inch fish will be seen. The fish are cold, firm, trim and hard fighting. I've never caught a rainbow in this upper end, though I have pulled in a few smartly-colored brookies. Near Hale Eddy, rainbows start to mix in and become increasingly numerous as you proceed downstream to Hancock.

THE MAIN STEM

When the East and West Branches meet at Hancock, one of the America's great rivers is born. But here on the Delaware proper, an angler used to 30-foot-wide streams can easily feel overwhelmed. There are pools (eddies in the Delaware vernacular) that can stretch to a thousand yards. There are places where the river itself is hundreds of yards wide. There are also steep embankments where one has to gingerly clamber down over rocks that are foot-loose and reported to harbor Eastern rattlesnakes. The main stem of the Delaware is not for everyone.

In spite of these obstacles, though, and also in spite of occasionally lethal water temperatures and parades of canoeists, there are trout here, trout that average an honest 14-15 inches.

A long time ago, the Delaware held only natural populations of smallmouth bass, shad (in season), eel, and some panfish. The rainbow trout was brought up by train in the late 1800's to several feeders of the Delaware, among them Callicoon Creek. The 'bows thrived in these New York and Pennsylvania streams for eighty odd years though all the while most of the main river remained too warm. Those initial plantings provided the seed stock for today's Delaware rainbow fishery. Contrary to what many think, the walleye was also introduced, sometime around 1930.

Right now the upper part of the Main Stem Delaware would still be a warm water river were it not for the cold water releases from Cannonsville

Reservoir. Thanks to the tailwater effect, trout are now found in good numbers from Hancock all the way down to Callicoon, a stretch of 25 miles. Unquestionably, some trout are taken even well downstream of Callicoon, especially at tributary mouths.

There is one very happy coincidence on the main Delaware: The best canoe water is below Callicoon. This lessens river traffic in the trout zone. Of course canoeists can and do float from Hancock down, and even in the east and west branches. But below average rainfall can make this upstream mileage really bony, and so canoe activity is concentrated below Hankins. Before June 15th, canoe traffic on the upper part of the main stem is extremely light, even on weekends...this in spite of normally excellent water levels at this time. Between then and Labor day, there still is little traffic on weekdays, though weekends can be busy. River traffic is extremely heavy on the Fourth of July weekend and also Memorial Day weekend.

In spite of this seemingly negative attitude towards canoeists, a canoe is a magnificent way to both learn and fish the main stem between Hancock and Callicoon, water levels permitting.

Overall in the main stem, rainbows outnumber browns by what I estimate to be eight to one. As one proceeds downstream, especially below Lordville, the figure seems to be 12 to 1 or more. Near Hancock, and for several miles downstream, browns are very numerous. Here the ratio may be about even.

Almost all the main stem trout (about 90%) are wild. There is no stocking. This could change, though, since New York's Dept. of Environmental Conservation has drafted a plan whereby brown trout would be stocked in the main stem. The plan also calls for no-kill trout fishing below Hancock and a promotional program that would actually seek to increase fishing pressure on the entire Delaware system fivefold. This ill-advised plan is being vigorously fought by certain chapters of Trout Unlimited.

Spin fishing for trout can be extremely fruitful on the big Delaware, but there are many days when it is fruitless. As far as bait fishing goes, a skilled bait angler will take fish anywhere, but the extreme rockiness of the Delaware makes bottom fishing with bait difficult.

In an earlier book I reported on the Main Stem of the Delaware and subsequently realized that the information I presented was incomplete.

Up to five years ago, most of the time I'd spent on the Big D was on the lower part of the trout zone...that water below Lordville. In that section, the fly hatches are modest and the incidence of rising fish is even more modest.

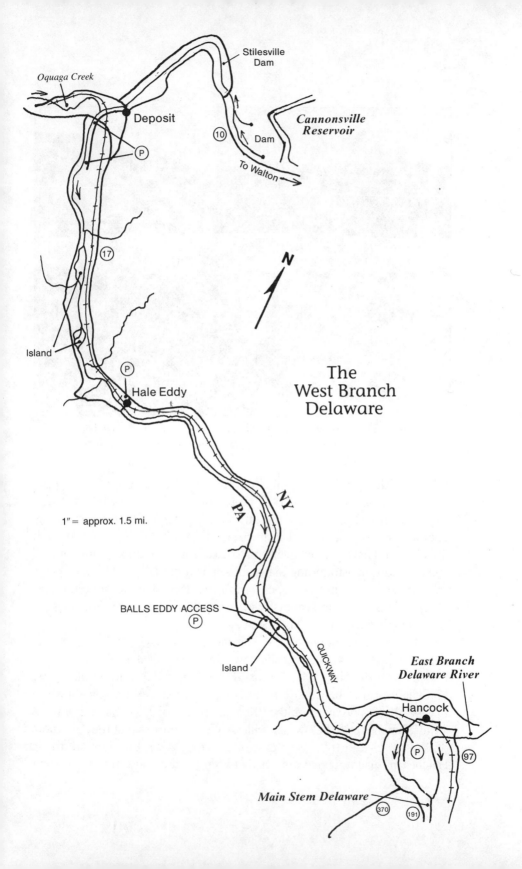

Oquaga Creek

Stilesville Dam

Cannonsville Reservoir

Deposit

(10)

Dam

To Walton

(P)

(17)

N

Island

(P)

Hale Eddy

The
West Branch
Delaware

1″ = approx. 1.5 mi.

PA

NY

BALLS EDDY ACCESS
(P)

Island

QUICKWAY

East Branch
Delaware River

Hancock

(P)

(97)

Main Stem Delaware

(370)   (191)

The entire Delaware system described in this chapter can be floated, but only when water levels permit. The Main Stem downstream of Hancock (shown here) is almost always canoeable.

When I finally drifted upstream closer to Hancock, I found that the upper part of the trout zone has not only more trout but better hatches. In truth, the hatches from Hancock downstream about eight miles can be outstanding. They are not only varied and at times very heavy, but they persist through the summer. I have personally fished to excellent green drake spinners falls, and once saw an astounding March brown spinner fall. The hendricksons are also very heavy in this upper part of the main stem, as are the tricos. Many other mayflies and caddisflies also hatch in abundance. Stoneflies are important throughout the Main Stem.

My best theory now is that the fertility lent by the West Branch peters out quite quickly as one proceeds downstream from Hancock. One expert I spoke with disagrees. He believes the river may be more fertile below Lordville because the water temperatures are higher. Whatever the truth may be, there is no question that there are plenty of catchable rainbows of 14 to 20 inches even below Lordville. My experience is that they are more difficult to take in this lower part of the trout zone, but they are there. Hatches in this lower part are best between April 23 and June 10th. Later season hatches are not as good as in the upper trout zone.

Big wet flies fished after dark is one ploy for the lower main stem. Local anglers with big nets (to land the fish) can be seen fishing after dark for both browns and rainbows that can better the 20-inch mark. Some use bait, but a great many use those oversize wets. You can also use a topwater bug or small popper and fish it in the slower pools. Keep casting and twitching it enticingly on the surface. This is a tactic that I've used with good success this past season on the bigger holes in the East Branch.

Both the weather and the water temperature cool very quickly after Labor Day, sometimes as early as late August. I have not fished the main stem after Labor Day too often, but I've heard that things can get interesting. There is one late season fly that comes off in August and September and is reported to evoke excellent feeding. It is called *Ephoron leukon,* a big, whitish fly.

You can take rainbows here even on extremely hot days and even in the middle of the day in summer. One Fourth Of July weekend I was with a group at Hankins, and we set out on a cooling, 5-mile tubing trip. I was floating along peacefully just below Basket Brook when I spied two fly casters below me (there are some real nice riffs below the brook). It was the hottest day I ever remember in the Catskill, with readings of 103 degrees in the sun next to my tent and readings of 96 degrees out of the sun. Yet the two diehard gents we floated past each hooked a nice rainbow while we were in sight. One was about 14 inches and the other about 16 inches. The water temperature had to be near the 75 degree mark.

If you wish to float-fish the Main Stem, there are several canoe rental places from Hankins downstream. Get helpful maps at the National Park Service heaquarters in Narrowsburg. There are also a few river guides who will take you down the river in Mackenzie drift boats.

Jim Capossela is the founder and president of Northeast Sportsmans Press. A professional writer his entire career, his articles have appeared in *Field & Stream, Outdoor Life, Sports Afield* and many other magazines. He is the author of 10 books on the outdoors, including *Good Fishing in the Catskills.* He has camped for weeks at a time along the Delaware.

Sixteen

Fishing Creek
by Barry Beck

The Indians called it "Namesesipong" or "water with fish," and the visiting angler of today would find it hard to believe that in the early 1780's its currents often ran red with blood. For Fishing Creek and its valley served as an important warpath for the fierce Iroquois nation of the north in frequent forays against other Indian tribes of the south. The early explorers, who would leave the Susquehanna River and venture north along her banks, often met their death by arrow or tomahawk.

Fishing Creek is born in the mountains of Pennsylvania's Sullivan County. North Mountain, a link of the Endless Mountain chain, gives birth to two branches, the East Branch and the West Branch. Both are essentially wild brook trout habitat areas. The West Branch drops quickly from the southern slopes and is joined by three tributaries: Painter Run, Bloody Run, and Elk Run. Traveling through the Villages of Elk Grove and Central, it eventually makes a rendezvous with the East Branch just below Rt. 118 in Columbia County. It should be pointed out here that a short section of the West Branch in the Village of Central will normally go dry and underground in the month of August. It resurfaces just above Rt. 118.

The most popular access to the West Branch lies one mile north of Elk Grove at the fire tower road. This dirt road leads into public game land owned by the Pennsylvania Game Commission. With the exception of hunting season, the Commission road is chained and closed to motor vehicles. A convenient parking lot is located at the gate. Here the West Branch is a short

40 yards away. Because the Game Commission road parallels most of the next three miles of stream, it makes sense to fish upstream as far as one wants to go and walk the road back to the parking lot. A bicycle can be a real advantage for easy access into the upper mileage.

Because of the steep decent from North Mountain, this wild section of stream is a blend of quick shoots and runs with good cover provided by undercut banks and boulders. The most productive time to fish this area is after spring runoff, starting in mid-April and on into the middle of June. The fall months of September and October often provide some excellent fishing and the wild brook trout are quite spectacular in spawning colors.

Attractor dry fly patterns like the Royal, Grizzly and Ausable Wulffs work best in sizes 12 and 14. Stonefly nymph imitations dressed in amber or black on sizes 10 and 12 work well for subsurface fishing. Natural aquatic insect populations lean toward the stonefly and caddis families, although there are a limited number of mayfly species in this upper section of Fishing Creek's West Branch.

The East Branch drops from hemlock and laurel dotted ridges through gorges and waterfalls traveling through the village of Jamison City and continuing downstream to its junction with the West Branch. Jamison City is now a summer retreat for sportsmen and their families, but served as the hub for large lumber and tanning industries in the early 1900's.

The East Branch has never been as productive as the West Branch for me. Although the scenery is spectacular, the water is at times on the borderline of being too acidic. High spring runoff from a mountain top swamp often pushes pH levels down to the danger level for fish. Nonetheless, some decent brook trout fishing can be found in the Jamison City area. Try starting at the metal bridge next to the Jamison City Hotel and fishing upstream 1½ miles to the White House Bed & Breakfast property line. This is a very easy section to fish and once more, a dirt road parallels the stream for convenient access. Wulffs and stoneflies in sizes 12 and 14 are again the key fly patterns.

Practical fly rods should be on the short side for both branches. Six and a half to seven foot rods that carry three- to five-weight lines are the most popular. Tapered leaders need not be longer than 7½ feet and tapered to a 4x or 5x tippet. Felt soled hip boots are more than adequate for wading both branches.

The Junction Pool serves to marry the two branches, and here begins a one mile section of stream set aside by the Pennsylvania Fish Commission as a Catch-and-Release area. Regulations mandate artificial barbless lures

and flies only. There is no closed season, and no fish may be killed or in possession. This special section is without doubt the most popular of Fishing Creek's 20+ miles available to the public. Besides having a healthy trout population, it is also bordered by the Grassmere Park Campground, convenient for anglers who like to camp.

The best way to access the Catch-and-Release section of Fishing Creek is to follow signs off Route 487, three miles north of Benton, to Grassmere Park Campground. The signs will take you past Camp Lavigne (a local boy scout camp) to Rt. 118 and then turn you right into Grassmere. Do not turn into the park entrance, but continue on the paved road marked "No Outlet" to a lower parking lot provided to the anglers by the Freestone Fly Fishers Club. This local club is responsible for most of the stream improvement devices on the project water, and for keeping the area litter-free.

We are, at this point, on the lower section of the Catch-and-Release water. Just upstream of the parking lot is one of the best pools in the project. One can almost always find a good number of feeding fish against the far bank. The late Vincent Marinaro, noted Pennsylvania author, would spend hour after hour on this pool casting tiny terrestrial imitations on ultra thin leaders to sipping, selective brown trout.

You may fish the Catch-and-Release water year-round, but the best times are from early March to mid-November. Early season stonefly hatches bring the first trout to the surface, followed by eagerly awaited little blue quills, the first major mayfly hatch of the season.

The project water is small by most standards, 40 to 50 feet wide and very easy to wade. Again, shorter rods 6½ to 7½ feet in length are the most popular although leader length should extend out to 9 or 10 feet. The trout in this section are accustomed to people and are not shy as to movement by the angler. On the other hand, as with most fish that have been caught and released a number of times, they are well educated in telling a natural from an imitation. Fishing to selective midging fish can often demand 7x and 8x tippets and flies tied on hook sizes 26 and 28.

There is little or no farming in this upper valley of Fishing Creek so even with spring runoff, the stream normally runs clear. The clarity makes it easy to spot fish and any angler will improve his or her odds of success by casting to individual fish rather than simply covering the water.

Lodging for the upper valley is available at two fishing and hunting hotels, one in the Village of Central, and one in Jamison City. There is also a Bed & Breakfast just north of Jamison City. All are within a 15 minute

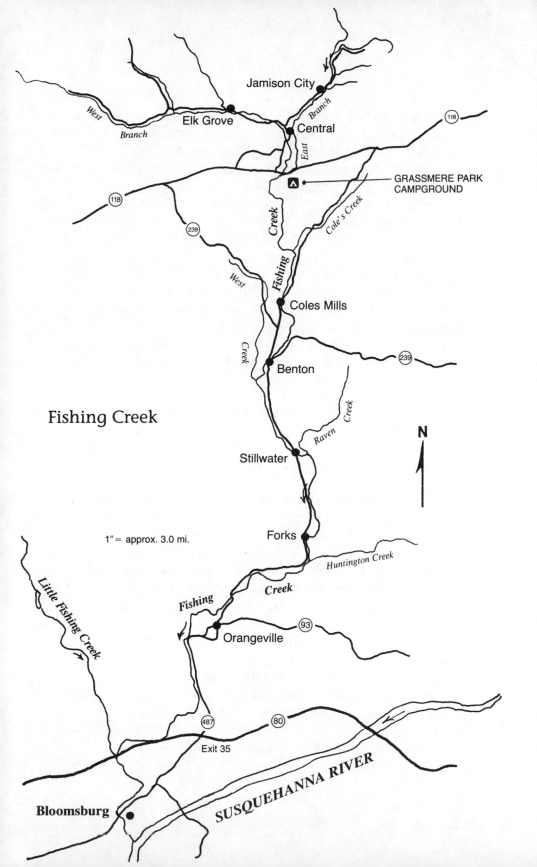

Fishing Creek

1" = approx. 3.0 mi.

drive from the Catch-and-Release project. Besides the Grassmere Park Campground, there is another well kept private campground four miles east on Rt. 118 and a large public camping area at Ricketts Glen State Park.

Ricketts Glen is one of the most scenic parks in Pennsylvania and has 120 tent and trailer campsites available year-round. Besides the campsites, there are also ten modern cabins available for rent with advanced reservations. I would be remiss not to mention the Glen's natural area, which is a registered national landmark. Kitchen Creek flows through the Glen dropping swiftly from Red Rock Mountain and creating 22 spectacular waterfalls. One, named Ganoga, is 94 feet high. A series of hiking trails parallel the stream as it works its way through the Glen. Many of the trees are over 500 years old. Diameters of almost five feet are common and many trees tower to 100 feet in height. The area represents the meeting ground of the southern and northern hardwood types so that the variety of trees is impressive. Kitchen Creek will find its way to Huntington, Fishing Creek's largest tributary.

Below the Catch-and-Release area, the stream leaves the road and anglers must walk in to fish the next 1½ miles of water. This particular section has not been stocked for the past ten years, but has a good number of resident brooks and browns. The stream emerges again at Long's Bridge and continues downstream through Camp Lavigne. The Camp provides parking and access, but is best fished in early spring or fall, before and after camp is in session.

One-half mile below Camp Lavigne a dirt road leaves Rt. 487 and leads to a bridge crossing. The dirt road is Hackett Road and below the bridge there once stood a dam which provided power to a grist mill. The pool created above played host to the best of the early Fishing Creek fly fishermen. Here, gentlemen like Parvin Young, Alan Beason and Charles Gregory would gracefully cast their offerings to the stream's selective trout. As a young boy, I would stand on the bridge watching and admiring their skills. It was a different era then. Across the bridge stood a stately white house where the fishermen would take tea in the afternoon while drying their freshly dressed silk lines on the lawn in anticipation of the evening's hatch. The dam is gone now, destroyed by a recent flood. The fishermen too are gone. Parvin Young moved on to a Pocono club, Beason died years ago, and Gregory disappeared from the area without a trace after selling an impressive tackle and book collection. Occasionally we will stop on that bridge and when the light is right, I can still see their elegant Leonards, light reflecting off the pale honey colored cane as they cast.

Below the old dam abutments, the stream once more parallels Rt. 487, its path obstructed now by a small impoundment referred to as Beishline's Dam. Across Rt. 487 is the Mill Race Golf and Camping Resort. The stream again leaves Rt. 487 and for the next mile runs south to the town of Benton. This walk-in-only area is open to public fishing and is certainly worth the walk. Access is from the bridge next to the Mill Race Resort, or at the other end, the elementary school building in the town of Benton. This is a classic piece of freestone trout water starting with a typical pool/riffle/pool configuration. The pools here are slate lined with overhanging banks of hemlock and pine with gin clear water. Because of the clarity, depth can often be deceiving. It also heightens the selectivity of Fishing Creek's trout. Solitude is not hard to find here! In recent months, there has been some interest at the local level in appealing to the Pennsylvania Fish Commission for special regulations for this stretch of water. If that should happen, the stream will be the better for it. Water as pristine as this should not be subjected to the current eight fish per day limit that is now the rule.

Below Benton, Fishing Creek is provided strength by two more tributaries: West Creek, a small freestone with some stocking by the Fish Commission, and Raven Creek, smaller yet with some occasional stocking by a local cooperative trout hatchery. As we travel downstream for the next four miles to the Village of Stillwater, Fishing Creek's character will begin to change. The pools will grow longer and deeper. And, because we are now going through farm country, the clarity can often be negatively affected by local rainfall.

In its upper reaches, Fishing Creek runs cold throughout the year. 58°-60° can be normal August afternoon water temperatures on the Catch-and-Release area. Throughout most of its mileage, Fishing Creek's temperatures are aided by numerous cold water springs that seep into the stream. Just below the town of Stillwater, there is a mile of posted club water. Below the club's lower boundary, the stream once again parallels Rt. 487 downstream two miles to the village of Forks. This is an excellent two-mile section with various roadside access areas with only one or two walk-in areas.

At Forks, Huntington Creek joins in, and becomes a major factor altering both the temperature and the size of the main stream. In its headwaters, Huntington is a coldwater stream with a good brook trout population. But by the time it reaches the village of Forks, it has traveled 15 odd miles and has warmed up to summer temperatures of 70° or higher. In the spring,

Huntington's warmer inflow is an asset, aiding Fishing Creek's colder water to get the hatches going and fish moving. By July and August, though, the asset turns into a liability with warmer temperatures now forcing the trout in Fishing Creek to seek out spring holes for survival until cooler fall temperatures prevail.

Rt. 487 continues to parallel Fishing Creek from the Village of Forks downstream some five miles to the Village of Orangeville. Streamside cottages and summer retreats line the banks throughout the area. Most of the water is open to public fishing with spring and fall being the most productive seasons.

Within this section, one mile north of the Village of Orangeville is a private 1½ mile stretch of water that is managed by the Freestone Fly Fishers. This beat of water had been closed by the landowners to public fishing for more than 12 years. The Freestone Club arranged a long term lease for the fishing rights as of January 1989, and now there is fishing by season permit or by a daily guest pass. The rates for the permit or the pass are very reasonable and the regulations are similar to the public Catch-and-Release area: artificial lures or flies only, no fish may be killed or had in possession, and fishing hours are from sunrise to one hour past sunset. A picnic area and parking lot are provided.

Public fishing access in the Orangeville section of Fishing Creek can be found at the Rt. 487 bridge crossing at the Hess Food Market, just north of Orangeville. The long riffle above the bridge gave up one of Fishing Creek's largest brown trout in the spring of 1987. Spin fisherman Mark Shelhammer hooked and landed a huge 14½lb. brown on ultra light tackle. This is also a popular section with local night fishermen. The long flat below the bridge has given up many 20-inch-plus fish.

Big water often demands heavier tackle. Pools in the Orangeville area are long and wide, and 50 to 60 foot casts are often necessary. Rods of 8½ to 9 feet in length for 5 and 6 weight lines are the most popular. In the upper sections of Fishing Creek, you can always get away with a floating line, but in the spring with high runoff, a sink-tip line is a real advantage on this lower water for subsurface fishing.

From the town of Orangeville south via Rt. 487 to the Village of Lightstreet, public fishing access is very limited to a few walk-in-only areas well marked by PA Fish Commission signs. This seven mile section is also lined with streamside cottages and one small private campground.

The Lightstreet bridge crossing on Fishing Creek provides the final public access as far as good trout fishing goes. From this point on downstream to its confluence with the Susquehanna River south of Bloomsburg, Fishing Creek is marginal trout water. A few locals who know the spring holes manage to take an occasional nice brown trout, but by and large, this section of stream is for smallmouth bass fanciers.

Most fishermen will first see Fishing Creek from Interstate 80, Exit 35 at Lightstreet (Bloomsburg University exit). This exit will put you on Rt. 487 north which parallels Fishing Creek for a good part of its mileage. Of the 25+ miles of stream, there are only four miles that áre private; the rest are available for public fishing. Other than the obvious bridge and roadside parking areas, look for Fish Commission "Walk in Only" areas well marked with PA Fish posters. P.A.L.S. is another posted sign that provides fishing permission through a cooperative program worked out between landowners and a local sportsmen's club. If you are unsure about fishing privileges, ask the nearest farm or house landowner. Don't take the chance of illegal trespass.

Aquatic and terrestrial insects play a major role in a trout's diet and it would behoove the visiting angler to become familiar with the seasonal hatches on Fishing Creek. Early spring stonefly hatches bring on the first real feeding activity followed by little blue quill, quill gordon and hendrickson mayflies. The heaviest hatches are from the Beishline Dam, just north of Benton, downstream to the Lightstreet area. Heavy hendrickson spinner falls in late April will bring up some very good fish, while a weighted Hendrickson Nymph fished dead drift on the bottom will provide subsurface activity.

Mid-season (May/June) hatches are a mixture of caddis and mayflies. March browns and gray foxes bring on the warmer weather followed by heavy grannom caddis hatches and our favorite, pale blue wing sulphurs. The sulphur is our most dependable hatch of the year. From mid-May to late June, this lovely insect makes its appearance almost every evening and the trout really key in on this hatch.

A rather large blue-winged olive (*E. Cornuta*) shows up around the end of May. The heaviest hatching of adult duns is mid-morning and it ends shortly after noon. Dark olive spinners will often join the sulphur spinners in the evening. The observant angler will have to decide which insect the trout are taking.

Smaller blue-winged olives (sizes 22/24) can show up on almost any overcast or rainy day from May through October. The duns will appear around 3:00 in the afternoon and last only for a brief hour or more. Light cahills and slate drakes bring in the summer season (July/August) and land-born or terrestrial insects such as beetles, hoppers, crickets and ants now play a major role in the trout's diet.

Normally, Fishing Creek will run low, clear and cold through the summer month of August, sometimes continuing into early September. The fish can become very shy and a careful approach is necessary by the angler. Camouflage or subdued colored clothing can help, as can keeping a low profile.

Mid and late September rains will bring water levels back to normal and by October, good fishing is in full swing. Fall in the Fishing Creek valleys is a glorious time of year, with crisp cool evenings and bright fresh days backdropped by a festival of fall foliage. Heavy *Baetis* hatches occur nearly every afternoon and last until mid-November, providing the last dry fly fishing of the year.

Because Fishing Creek remains 90% ice fee, there can be some excellent winter fishing for those hardy anglers who can brave the cold. Wooly Buggers and weighted Muddler Minnows work best fished deep and slow on sink-tip lines. On rare days, when afternoon temperatures of 45° or warmer show up, one can often find fish up and feeding on midges in the surface film.

Fishing Creek is a common name for a number of streams in Pennsylvania. The Pennsylvania Fish Commission, in the regulation booklet, refers to the one we've been discussing as Big Fishing Creek. But on their Trout Fishing in Pennsylvania brochure, they label it Fishing Creek. History tells us that the early settlers referred to it as Fishing Creek—as we who live near the stream do.

Barry Beck has fished and guided in the Fishing Creek valley for the past 30 years. A professional outdoor photographer and writer, Barry and his wife, Cathy, also own and operate Fishing Creek Outfitters: a fly fishing school, guide and fly shop operation. Although assignments often take them far away, the Becks are always glad to call Fishing Creek home. Barry and Cathy, and their daughter, Annie, live in a cabin one mile above the banks of Fishing Creek.

Seventeen

Kettle Creek
by Dave Wolf

The drive is long from whatever direction you might come. Even a trip from the next valley is a half hour in length, more or less depending on which route you choose. Dirt roads full of muffler-crunching boulders can be part of the trek. Kettle is not a "hit it for a couple of hours" type of stream. Rather, the travel time dictates that you spend awhile here, and that you be a serious pursuer of the trout.

I was first introduced to Kettle as a child. My grandfather, an avid fly fisherman, set out to build a cabin with a dual purpose: first as a fishing camp and second as a hunting cabin. Fishing was first and foremost, although deer hunting was a close second. He had finally decided on two sectors of the state into which to sink his hard earned money: The bluff overlooking Kettle; or Poe Valley, a short drive or long walk from Penns Creek. He loved both areas and we spent every weekend in one locale or the other. I believe that Kettle was his favorite, although I can't recall him ranking one above the other.

Kettle provides a perfect setting for trout fishing. In the stands of hardwood, mixed with pine and hemlock, you can watch wild turkey pick their way through a stand of beech. Etched in the moist earth along the stream's edge are the splayed hoof prints of the whitetail, an animal that outnumbers the people who live here. Black bear tracks are cause for excitement, but still not uncommon, in an area where the local merchants cannot, thankfully, gather enough political clout for a four-lane highway to bring tourists in by the busload.

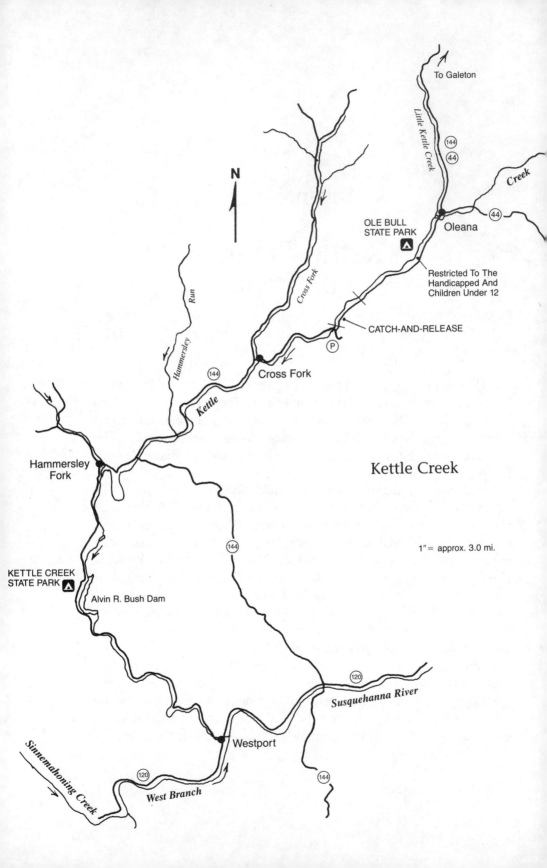

To Galeton

Little Kettle Creek

Creek

(144)
(44)

(44)

Oleana

OLE BULL
STATE PARK

Restricted To The
Handicapped And
Children Under 12

Cross Fork

CATCH-AND-RELEASE

(P)

Hammersley Run

(144)

Cross Fork

Kettle

Kettle Creek

Hammersley
Fork

(144)

KETTLE CREEK
STATE PARK

1" = approx. 3.0 mi.

Alvin R. Bush Dam

(120)

Susquehanna River

Sinnemahoning Creek

Westport

(120)

(144)

West Branch

N

The setting, in fact, is much like it was when my grandfather and I first visited, although more turkey are found in the hardwoods, and the brown trout has taken over popularity from the brook. I suspect that size is the reason here. Browns that often go over twenty inches make a seven inch brook trout look like perhaps it should be used for bait. But the brookie has its following still, and those who cast a trio of wet flies with a slightly bent bamboo rod still haunt the miniature streams in search of what they consider to be the finest fish that swims.

Tradition dies hard in a county where soda is still pop and a handshake is as good as a contract. Split bamboos and tandem wets are still seen along the banks of Kettle, even though fine graphite rods, expensive reels and parachute flies are to be seen in the local fly shop. Here mingles the old and the new: the bamboo and the boron, the brook trout and the brown (with a rainbow thrown in for good measure), the conservative local angler and the dapper out-of-towner.

The sleepy town of Cross Fork is the largest population center near the

stream. It boasts a population of fifty, give or take a few depending on the number of births or deaths in a given year. The population is aging in this economically depressed area and for the most part the young leave after graduation for the bright lights and promise of the cities, trading in their four wheel drives for Hyundais and Toyotas.

The stream originates in the southeastern sector of Potter county and flows through the northeast part of Clinton County before emptying into the West Branch of the Susquehanna some 35 miles from its source. But below the dam at Kettle Creek State Park the stream is no longer a trout stream. There are two reasons: mine acid drainage and water temperatures above the trout's tolerance level.

Kettle from the Kettle Creek dam upstream to the headwaters, nearly twenty miles, offers excellent fishing the better part of the year. The Pennsylvania Fish Commission stocks the stream from the Kettle Creek Dam to a point a few miles above Ole Bull State Park with a mixture of legal sized (over seven inch) brown, brook and rainbow trout reared at state hatcheries. Local sportsmen's groups in the area also raise trout for stocking purposes and many of these are trophy size.

Above the Village of Cross Fork upstream to the headwaters, wild brown trout do exist. On the Fish Commission specially regulated waters, beginning just below the 144 bridge and extending upstream 1.7 miles, a good mixture of wild and stocked trout coexist. Here, the special catch-and-release regulations that allow only artificial lures or flies and no killing of trout create some of the best fishing on Kettle. You can expect good populations of fish the season long, despite the fact that they can become quite selective. The regulated area is open year-round, which allows anglers to fish to the little black stonefly hatch. Imitated in size 16 and 18, this hatch often begins in mid to late March.

From Cross Fork downstream to the Kettle Creek State Park, you will find that the majority of the trout are stocked fish, although wild trout do exist near the mouth of the better feeder streams like Cross Fork Creek and the Hammersley. Depending on water temperatures and flow the section from Cross Fork Creek to the Dam can offer fishing into August, but in most years the trout have migrated from these areas by the end of June.

Both Ole Bull and Alvin Bush Dam are stocked with trout and offer both the fly angler and the bait and spin fisherman some interesting fishing, although it is short lived and often ends quickly after the last stocking at the end of May.

Above the catch-and-release area upstream to Oleona, the creek narrows and maintains quality water temperatures throughout most of the year. Here, wild browns and native brookies reside in good numbers. This section of stream does not get the attention the lower reaches receive, simply because it is not as large and has no specially regulated areas. Still, this beat of stream offers some of the better fishing for anglers in search of truly wild trout.

Kettle attracts all types of anglers. Bait fishermen and spin fishermen make up the majority during the early season. Bait fishing is done with ultra light spinning equipment and nightcrawlers, garden worms and minnows both salted and alive. Roostertails in white and yellow bring much success, as do copper colored C.P. Swings.

Fly fishermen often start the season by meeting up with little olives in sizes 18 to 20, followed quickly by blue quills in size 18 and quill gordons in size 14. Hendricksons begin hatching at the end of April and you should be finding some tan caddis in size 12 to 14 at this time.

About the first week in May large March browns often imitated in size 10 begin to emerge, followed by gray fox in size 14. My personal favorite, the sulphurs, come later in the month and overlap the most famous hatch here: the green drake. The brown drake usually occurs during the first week of June and offers sensational spinner falls after the hordes of green drake fanatics head home.

Bicolors and cahills come on the heels of the brown drakes and often you will find the cahills, in particular, overlapping the green drakes. Tricos begin at the end of June and are best imitated with a size 24 hook. Cream cahills in sizes 18 to 20 come at the tag end of July and are often found throughout the summer and again in early fall. Midge fishing and terrestrial fishing is something to try throughout the summer months, when trout find those bugs to their liking. This is especially true on the catch-and-release area where they feed throughout the day on the small offerings in the slower waters.

One of the major tributaries to Kettle is Cross Fork Creek, which has 5.4 miles set aside for fly fishing only. Regs here allow the taking of three trout per day nine inches or more in length. The stream offers excellent populations of wild browns and native brookies and has not been stocked in years. It is a small stream, rarely more than 30 feet wide, and has a good pool-riffle combination. The trout can be spooky and selective. Water temperatures on this freestone stream remain constantly cool and fishing here can sometimes be superb the season long. Cross Fork Creek enters Kettle downstream of the Village of Cross Fork within sight of the small gathering of homes and businesses.

Hammersley near Kettle Creek State Park is another good feeder stream, one that offers the wild brook trout fancier some excellent opportunity. Trout do not run large here. Anything over ten inches is a good one and one over 12 inches is a trophy. All brookies found here are natives and the stream has not been on the stocking list for years. The pristine setting is as sparkling as the wild fish given up by Hammersley.

Kettle, located in the northcentral sector of the state is a freestone stream by nature. Its flows fluctuate with snow melt-off and the amount of rainfall in any given week, month or year. The stream can be clear and low one day and cloudy and high the next; it is the nature of the beast, and a reality that freestone anglers must contend with. After the first of June water temperatures begin to warm. This goes hand in hand with low flows and the diminished oxygen levels that are so often associated with slow running water.

Trout under these stressful conditions begin to move upstream toward the headwaters and into the tributary streams. This does not mean that fishing is done for the season, but rather that anglers need to hunt up the trout. This is best done with a stream thermometer. During the doldrums, find water temperature in the mid to upper sixties and you will find trout.

Freestones also mean fishing the water. When a heavy hatch is not in progress you can spend days on end waiting for the ring of the rise to direct your cast. Anglers here use searching patterns, with one of the most popular being the Adams. I have found that the Mosquito and the Grizzly Caddis are also excellent searching patterns. You need to cover a lot of water and do a lot of casting, but good trout can be taken when no hatch is in progress.

Trout in this sector of the state begin to move into their spawning grounds around mid-October. I have personal objections to fishing over spawning fish, but September and early October are excellent times to be on the water here. Now you have few people, fish putting on the feed bag, the splendor of the changing hardwoods and, with luck, decent hatches.

One has to wonder what the Kettle Creek Valley would look like without the dual economies of fishing and hunting. It would be easy to picture the area nearly void of human habitation.

But the Kettle Creek Valley was not always so desolate. During the late 1800's the timber industry was a booming business and the forests a gold mine. When the final hemlock fell, though, the timber industry moved on, taking the money with it and leaving the residents to cater to sportsmen (and later to timber once again, but on a smaller scale).

Kettle has lived on its reputation for many a year. It began in the eighteen hundreds before the loggers took every tree and wildfires swept through the valley. The second growth of timber, comprised mostly of hardwoods is now being cut, and the valley is lush and green once more.

Kettle is a place to "get away from it all" if you wait until the mid-April to mid-May crowds disperse. It is laid back country with friendly folks inhabiting the valley. Keep in mind that only 18,000 people inhabit over a thousand square miles that constitute Potter County. The valley does have two excellent fly shops—one in Cross Fork, the other in Hammersly Fork—a general store, a filling station and of course a local tavern or two.

No one here seems to be in too much of hurry, as there is no need to be. Fishermen are welcomed, and wader donned anglers entering a store don't even rate a second look. Blue jeans and flannel shirts are the order of the day, and the cool nights make air conditioning an unsold product in these parts.

Fishing is important here; to the economy and to the people. Sportsmen gather great support in a community where there is little more to do than hunt or fish. Stream improvement devices have been placed in many sections of the stream in order to keep the ever changing waters in check and to assure a good pool to riffle ratio. The stream is quite easy to wade and long casts are not the norm.

Fly rodders should do well with an eight to nine foot rod, carrying a five weight line for the majority of their fishing, since only on the lower stretches does the stream exceed sixty feet in width. Many anglers switch to three and four weight outfits during the summer when flies become smaller and the water becomes thin. Long leaders of twelve feet in 6 or 7x are a must during the summer months.

The trout fisheries like the people have seen many changes. Once a brook trout mecca, Kettle Creek now attracts those in search of browns and the occasional rainbow, although "native" brookies still reside in most tributary streams. I say native with reservations because stocking of brook trout took place in the early nineteen hundreds. Brookies of fingerling size were shipped by railroad cars and placed into the stream by sportsmen. Even then brook trout did not stay in Kettle the season long. Warming water plaques the lower reaches of the stream; water temperatures well above the tolerance level of the brookie have been consistently reported since as far back as 1939. The warm water sends brookies, browns and rainbows scurrying for the tributaries, headwaters and underground springs as early as July during many years.

Kettle Creek is easily accessible from Route 144, which parallels the stream for most of its length. Route 144 may be accessed from Route 6 from the north or Route 120 from the south. Having a good map will be useful.

Lodging is available in the area although there are certainly no Holiday Inns or Hiltons. This is backwoods country and while you can expect comfortable lodging, don't look for in-room phones, cable T.V. or swimming pools. For more information concerning lodging in the area contact: Potter County Recreation Incorporated, RD#1, Galeton, Pennsylvania.

For those interested in camping, Ole Bull State Park encompasses 117 acres and has 81 campsites. You may contact the state Park by writing: HCR62, Box 9, Cross Park, PA 17729. Another choice is Kettle Creek State Park (1,626 acres), which does have good fishing on Alvin Bush Dam. It offers 72 campsites and may be reached at HCR62, Box 96, Renova, PA 17764.

Kettle is steeped in tradition, part of the reason for its repute among eastern anglers. It is not without its problems, however. We are fortunate that no industry exists here, save for the nouveau logging industry which has been careful to exercise conservation practices. Siltation from run-off of the dirt roads in the area is a problem, but to date, not a major detriment to the stream. Special regulations have helped stave off over-fishing, and even though put-and-take harvest of stocked fish is the rule in early season, Kettle holds a more than respectable head of wild trout.

The soil in the areas is classified DeKalb. It is sandstone in origin, and because it lacks the alkalinity of the state's limestoners, Kettle and its tributaries are vulnerable to acid precipitation. Certainly, acid rain is the biggest overall threat to Pennsylvania trout streams at present, and although Kettle has not been seriously impacted, all the freestones in the northern part of the state are threatened by this widespread menace.

I have fished Kettle in the bitter cold, taking trout on large muskrat nymphs and little black stones. I have been there when green drakes brought large trout to the surface. I have also been there when trout ignored the glorious drakes for sulfur spinners that were masked by the larger mayflies. I have taken trout on beatles and ants during the low flows of summer, and on one delightful afternoon, took a six and a half pound brown on a 24 cream midge attached to an 8x tippet.

I have fished her swollen waters, boiling and the color of coffee with light cream, and I have prowled her banks casting long leaders tight to the bank where trout would rise to take my terrestrials. I have lived through days when I thought I knew behind what boulder each trout resided; and then the waters dropped and the trout moved, and the fishing was like a new season on a new stream.

Dave Wolf is Media Relations Director for the Pennsylvania Fish Commission. A prolific free-lance writer, he has authored three books and has had articles published in *Fur-Fish-Game, Fly Fisher,* and many other publications. His column, "On The Water With Dave Wolf" appears regularly in *Pennsylvania Angler* magazine. Dave has presented hundreds of slide shows and casting demonstrations, and has played a leadership role in numerous outdoor organizations.

Eighteen

The Sinnemahoning
by Mike Sajna

Sometimes things, and people, are just a little to the left or right of center in the mountains. But then, that may be one of the reasons we go to them. Take one morning on north central Pennsylvania's Driftwood Branch of Sinnemahoning Creek.

It was late June. The water was low and flat and clear. The sky was bright, and the sun only occasionally eclipsed a broken sheet of lofty cirrus clouds. Conditions were hardly promising for trout, but the water was a cool enough 62 and the challenge of such a day has always excited me. Fool a few fish under these conditions and the world rings with accomplishment and satisfaction.

I was perched alongside the decayed remains of an old bridge pier on the stream's Delayed Harvest Fly Fishing Only Project behind the Cameron County Fairgrounds. I had just released my first fish, a small rainbow, and was luxuriating in the event when the bumper sticker we had seen in the bar where we had stopped for dinner the previous evening reappeared. "If You Love Something, Set It Free", it had started in best greeting card fashion. But then it added, "If It Doesn't Come Back, Hunt It Down And Kill It!" I had to laugh all over again. Such a wonderfully warped attitude must be admired. It made me think of a romance that had ended on less than amicable terms nine years earlier and miraculously rekindled itself a month ago. I wanted one of the bumper stickers for a gift.

Still smiling to myself, I shot another cast out over the pool while my thoughts shifted to a poster hanging in the same bar. It was Nixon and Agnew at the podium after being nominated for a second term. There they stood with hands clasped, arms held high in triumph, ear to ear grins on their faces and prison stripes on their backs. A popular piece of art on college campuses during the mid-1970s, I had not seen the poster for at least fifteen years. Then I remembered the bumper sticker on the Cadillac that had pulled up next to me at the convenience store where I had stopped for coffee. "He's Tan. He's Fit. He's ready", it had read. "Nixon in '88." Had I wandered into some kind of Twilight Zone, I wondered, as I sent a cast toward the trace of current coming off the pier above.

My fly had barely touched the surface when a rustling in the trees on the mountain behind me turned my head and brought me a glimpse of a white-tailed buck still in velvet, and two doe. We were still sizing each other up when a fish rose from the bottom of a deep spot a few feet away from the pier and took my fly. Instinctively, I raised my rod and, as I felt the weight of the fish, the deer bolted and two Canada geese winged down the stream directly over my head.

"Talk about being submerged in nature", a friend laughed when I described the scene later, "you must have loved it."

And I did. Especially since the brown on the end of my line measured in the neighborhood of fourteen inches, a very respectable neighborhood for such a time of year and such a piece of water. But then, that's the Driftwood Branch.

"It's nice," sighs Ken Igo, a camp owner in neighboring Potter County who never fails to stop at the Driftwood on his trips north from his home in southwestern Pennsylvania. "It's fun to fish in the early spring and early summer. When I've fished it, I've always found insect activity, whether it be caddis or mayflies. And there are some nice fish in there. They're tough, but they're in there. I caught a twenty-inch palamino one time."

The Sinnemahoning watershed drains parts of Cameron, McKean, Elk, Potter, Clinton and Clearfield counties in Pennsylvania's "Big Woods Country." The main stream is formed by the junction of Driftwood Branch and Bennett Branch at the village of Driftwood. It's later fed by the First Fork about five miles downstream and then empties into the West Branch Susquehanna River at Keating.

The Driftwood Branch is overlooked by towering mountains and unbroken forests of lighter hardwoods and dark hemlock. Preserved in large part by its location within state park and state forest land, and civilized only by hunting camps, abandoned farms and the remnants of old lumbering and

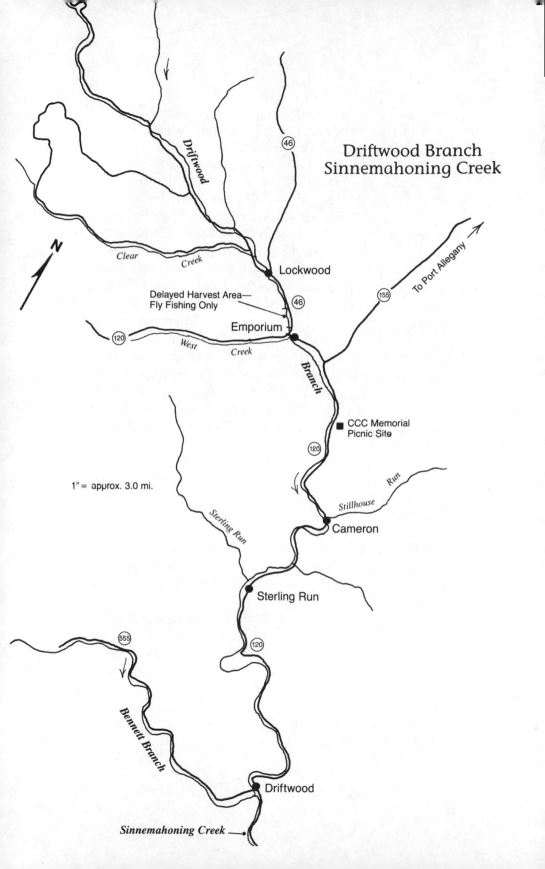

Driftwood Branch
Sinnemahoning Creek

46

To Port Allegany

155

Driftwood

Clear   Creek

Lockwood

Delayed Harvest Area—
Fly Fishing Only

46

Emporium

120

West   Creek

Branch

CCC Memorial
Picnic Site

120

1" = approx. 3.0 mi.

Stillhouse   Run

Sterling Run

Cameron

Sterling Run

555

120

Bennett Branch

Driftwood

Sinnemahoning Creek

mining towns, the Sinnemahoning watershed holds some of the most spectacular scenery to be found on major streams anywhere in the state. Views along it might even include the only elk to be found in the Northeast. Sadly, both Bennett Branch and the Main Stem Sinnemahoning are so polluted with acid mine drainage that they cannot sustain trout. Until or unless these streams are cleaned up there is, fortunately, the Driftwood Branch.

Forty miles of fine and diverse trout fishing begin with the seeping and dripping to life of the Driftwood in the far northeast corner of Elk County on the opposite side of the mountain from Straight Creek. The distance between the headwaters of the two streams can literally be measured in yards, yet their waters end up a thousand miles apart. Straight Creek drains into the East Branch Clarion River to the Clarion and then down the Allegheny, Ohio and Mississippi Rivers to the Gulf of Mexico. The Driftwood sends its flow down to the Susquehanna and then on to Chesapeake Bay and the Atlantic Ocean.

From its headwaters downstream to Rich Valley, Driftwood Branch is a small mountain stream of shallow pools and short riffles. It's well shaded by overhanging trees, loaded with backcast snagging obstacles and full of wild trout. "The stream from Rich Valley to its headwaters is really good wild trout water for about ten miles," notes Bruce Hollander, area fisheries manager for the commission's North Central Region. "There are so many wild browns and brookies that the Elk County section has been taken off the stocking list."

Based on this, an angler new to the area might expect the upper portion of Driftwood Branch to be remote, even inaccessible. But in reality, Rich Valley Road, which can be picked up off Route 46 a couple of miles north of Emporium, closely parallels the stream over practically its entire upper length. Anglers need only find a parking spot to find access to the stream.

Driftwood's stocked trout water begins at the village of Elk River on Rich Valley Road and continues for 28.3 miles downstream through the Cameron County seat of Emporium to the Village of Driftwood. Like the headwaters, the stretch from Elk River to the Village of Rich Valley is small and protected from the sun, and remains cool and hospitable to trout throughout the season. From Rich Valley to Emporium, however, the tributaries of Bobby Run, Cooks Run, Clear Creek and North Creek widen Driftwood Branch to between thirty and forty feet and open the overhead canopy so that the water begins to warm and becomes uncomfortable, even marginal for trout during the height of summer. Temperatures in this stretch often push well beyond the seventy-degree mark, prompting the fish to move to the colder water upstream or congregate around spring seeps and the mouths of cooler tributaries.

Although the movement of trout upstream to cooler water is an instinctive quest for survival and to be expected during the summer, when combined with man-made regulations it also cuts short some of the fine fishing the Driftwood Branch offers. The problem is that the stream's one mile long Delayed Harvest section lies within the lower portion of the Rich Valley to Emporium stretch. The purpose of such special regulation areas is to give anglers the opportunity to fish over a large population of trout and encourage them to practice catch-and-release. Fishing is permitted year-round, but fish cannot be taken out of the projects until June 15, a full two months after the season has opened; and then only three, half of what can be removed from the rest of the Driftwood Branch.

A large portion of the Driftwood's fish abandon the regulated stretch during the summer in search of cooler water upstream. Here, in open regulations water, they become easy marks for bait and spin fishermen. One solution might be to extend the Delayed Harvest water upstream. Whether or not that will happen, though, remains to be seen, as many fishermen continue to resent the presence of such special regulation sections.

The Delayed Harvest project is clearly marked by large, wooden signs and posters along Route 46, which follows it and provides ready access. Parking is available at scattered locations both along the road and off it, at the Cameron County Fairgrounds. Pools along the upper stream are the Township Building, Dodge Hollow, Deflectors, Hertlein, Steel Dam, Fairgrounds and Water Company Dam.

Fishing in the project must be done with artificial flies constructed of natural or synthetic materials wound on a single hook. Molded facsimiles or replicas of insects, earthworms, fish eggs, fish or any invertebrate or vertebrate are prohibited. Anglers also must use fly tackle. Regulations are posted at numerous locations along the stream.

Hatches along the Driftwood Branch can verge on the incredible, and they draw fishermen from near and far. Even anglers who have camps on other streams in northcentral Pennsylvania will leave their home waters to hit the Driftwood when hendricksons, green drakes and brown drakes appear. Mid-April to early May hatches include: early brown stonefly, blue-winged olives, blue quills, quill gordon, hendrickson, green caddis and grannom. Mid-May to early June: sulphurs, gray fox, March brown, light cahill, green drake, brown drake and blue-winged olives. Early June through late June: light cahill, little green stonefly, golden drake and slate drake.

Emporium, with a population of roughly 3,000 is the only town on the Driftwood Branch. Industry robs it of a quaint air, but anglers will find restaurants, motels, gas stations, supermarkets, sporting goods outlets and other necessities in it. There are no campgrounds in town, but Sizerville State Park lies about seven miles north on Route 155 and has a 30-site Class B campground with flush toilets and a dump station. It is open from the second Friday in April to the end of antlerless deer season in mid-December. The park also contains a swimming pool, open from Memorial Day weekend to Labor Day, plus picnic areas, nature programs and hiking trails. Anglers with family along might be interested in these facilities.

Travel by canoe was a difficult proposition for early settlers in Pennsylvania because, unlike in Canada, where the land was mostly flat, and New England, where the rivers cut through the mountains, in the Keystone State rivers and streams flow parallel to the mountains. Instead of creating passes, they leave the mountains as insurmountable barriers on each side of a waterway. Then, too, there was a near total absence of good canoe birch in the state's forests. Indians and settlers had to use dugouts or canoes made of elm bark. Craft made out of these materials were both clumsy and heavy when compared to birch bark canoes, and next to impossible to portage over the mountains.

For these reasons early travelers through the state would normally abandon their canoes near the headwaters of one stream, walk across the mountains to the next watershed and then build another dugout or elm bark canoe for the trip down that river or stream. This portage problem led to many early settlements around Pennsylvania (including Emporium) being called "Canoe Place", since they marked the beginning or end of a canoe portage.

Emporium, sitting at the confluence of the Driftwood Branch and Portage Creek, was the eastern terminus of one of the most important and unique portages in the nation's history. With only one major carry of twenty-three miles from Emporium to Port Allegheny, it is possible to travel by canoe all the way from Chesapeake Bay to the Yellowstone Country. How many individuals, if any, actually made the entire journey is impossible to say. But the route—from the Chesapeake up to the Susquehanna River, West Branch Susquehanna and Sinnemahoning Creek to Driftwood Branch and Portage Creek, then over Keating Summit to Portage Creek and down the Allegheny and Ohio Rivers to the Mississippi, and finally up the Missouri and either the Yellowstone or Madison into Yellowstone National Park—was busy enough for the Indians to develop the Big Portage Path over Keating Summit and settlers to make a living off the traffic.

"I soon had plenty of work," wrote Benjamin Burd after coming to the area in 1810, "As settlers commenced to come up the Susquehanna River to Shippen, now Emporium, with flat boats, and pack their goods across the Portage to Canoe Place, where they made canoes and floated down the Ohio River. I had a lot of work making these canoes out of white pine logs."

By the turn of the century, Emporium, which for a time was called Shippen, for Edward Shippen the original owner of the land, gained notoriety for a couple of other things besides its location. The opening of the Climax Powder Co. plant in the town in 1890 gave it the nickname "Powder City." It was at the Climax facility where dynamite used in the construction of the Panama Canal was manufactured. From the hills above the town also was taken the flagstone used in the walkway at the Tomb of the Unknown Soldier in Arlington National Cemetery.

The addition of West Creek at the upper edge of Emporium and Portage Creek at the lower edge begins to swell the Driftwood Branch, pushing it toward an average width of 100 feet for the remainder of its length. The stream from Emporium to Driftwood is too warm for trout after June. Anglers seeking trout in the lower Driftwood Branch after mid-June must concentrate on areas around cooler feeder streams and springs.

High warm temperatures and low flows are the two biggest problems the Driftwood faces as a trout fishery. July, August and September are the worst months, as they are for most large freestone trout streams in the Northeast. West Creek and Sterling Run, which enter the Driftwood roughly midway between Emporium and the Village of Driftwood, have some acid mine drainage problems, according to the Fish Commission's Hollander, but they are rapidly diluted by the large flow of the Driftwood Branch. A little sewage effluent also enters the stream in Emporium, and there is the occasional small industrial accident in the town or railroad accident along the line that follows the stream. But "Overall, Driftwood is a very clean stream," Hollander adds.

Warm temperatures and low flow also keep trout in the lower Driftwood from reproducing like those above Elk River. However, some large holdover fish can be found in its deep holes and other cool spots. And the warm water is not all bad as far as good fishing is concerned. One evening during the

"Nixon-Agnew trip," my friend Bruce VanWyngarden, the editor of *Pittsburgh Magazine* and an old bass fisherman from Missouri, hooked and landed a three pound smallmouth in the lower stream. It was the largest smallmouth he's taken in Pennsylvania outside of Lake Erie.

The size of the lower Driftwood makes it a good choice for a float fishing trip early in the season, though anybody contemplating floating it would do well to avoid weekends when portions of the stream can get crowded with fishermen who might not take kindly to a canoe drifting through their favorite hole. The trip is an easy one, holding only a scattering of Class II riffles, barely enough for a little push.

The first good put-in spot for a float fishing trip is near the mouth of the Driftwood's junction with Portage Creek below the Route 120 bridge in Emporium. From there, it is about six miles to the twin bridges around the Village of Cameron. Another short, three to four mile long float can be done by putting in at Cameron and taking out at the bridge in the Village of Sterling Run. The remaining ten miles of stream to the Village of Driftwood flows through a deep, canyon-like valley without an easy take-out point. Anglers floating it should do so with the idea of an all day trip in mind. An Emporium to Driftwood float would also make a nice overnight trip.

Pools heading downstream from Emporium include the Y, Mallorys,

Friendly Garden, German Rocks, Memorial Springs, Coke Oven, Canoe Run, Cameron Hotel and Tunnel Springs. Anglers contemplating floating the Driftwood Branch also should be aware that canoe rentals are not available in either Emporium or Driftwood.

As on some other streams in northern Pennsylvania, hatches on the Driftwood Branch seem to start first in the warmer lower reaches and work their way to the colder water upstream. The green drake, for instance, will emerge five days to a week sooner at Driftwood than Emporium. Fishermen might do best to concentrate on the lower Driftwood early in the season, gradually working upstream to cooler water as summer approaches.

While heavy hatches are something most fly fishermen eagerly seek out, they also can be confusing and frustrating at times. On the Driftwood Branch, anglers may sometimes find rising trout repeatedly ignoring what, at least according to the books, they should be taking. When that happens, one of the best things a fisherman can do is pause and look around. Although green drakes are a quick and easy mouthful for a trout there will be times when Driftwood fish will refuse them in favor of the smaller brown drake spinners that appear at about the same time. Anglers who get caught in such a situation should not be afraid to experiment a bit. Breaking the rules can occasionally mean the difference between success and failure on a stream like the Driftwood Branch.

Fishing the lower six or seven miles of the Driftwood also carries with it the possibility of glimpsing an elk. The chances are less favorable than on the Bennett Branch around the Village of Benezette, though.

Eastern woodland elk once roamed throughout Pennsylvania. By the mid 19th century, destruction of habitat and unrestricted hunting had forced what was left of the herd into a small area in Elk County. The last native Pennsylvania elk was killed in 1867 near Ridgway.

Between 1913 and 1926, the Game Commission imported a collection of elk from Yellowstone National Park in an attempt to restore the state's herd. The transplants flourished to the point that a hunting season was established and 98 of the animals were legally taken from 1923 to 1931 when a decline in the herd was noticed and the season closed. Through the 1940s and 1950s, the herd shrank to about fifty animals and was practically forgotten. From that low period, the herd gradually grew beyond the 100 mark, until an attack of brain worm hit it in the early 1970s and cut its number down below 100 once again. Today, the herd, after rebounding from the brain worm trauma, contains almost 150 animals, any one of which is a truly inspiring sight to behold in a state as heavily populated and industrialized as Pennsylvania.

Since Route 120 parallels the lower Driftwood over its entire length, access to the stream between Emporium and the Village of Driftwood is mostly a matter of finding a place to park. Then you just walk down over the bank, though that can be tough at times since the setting for the lower stream is a steep, heavily wooded and narrow valley. Amenities along Route 120 are something else that can be tough, limited to a couple of bars, restaurants and gas stations. Camping is allowed free of charge in Elk State Forest, which borders parts of the stream, but there are no facilities. A permit is required. Details may be had by contacting: District Forester, Elk State Forest, RD 1, Route 155, Emporium, PA 15834. A stamped, self-addressed envelope will speed a reply.

Bucktail State Park also lies along the lower Driftwood. Named in honor of the Bucktail Regiment, it stretches from just south of Emporium past Keating on the main Sinnemahoning and through Renovo to Lock Haven on the West Branch Susquehanna River. Facilities in the undeveloped park are limited to some picnic sites, among them a memorial to a group of Civilian Conservation Corps members who died fighting a forest fire in the area back in the 1930s.

The Bucktail Regiment was a group of Civil War volunteers who answered a call in 1861 by General Thomas Kane to "Save the Union." The regiment's name came from the bucktails they wore in their hats. From Elk, McKean and Cameron Counties, they descended the Driftwood on rafts to gather at the village of Driftwood before journeying south to Harrisburg. The Bucktail Monument in Driftwood commemorates the spot where the regiment met. As recently as the late 1970s the oak tree to which the Bucktails tied their rafts was said to be still standing along the creek. The regiment distinguished itself in numerous battles during the Civil War, including the Battle of Gettysburg, where its marksmen took part in the defense of Little Round Top.

The village of Driftwood at the lower end of the stream is hardly more than a street of old frame homes with a general store and gas station. Amenities end about there, as does Driftwood Branch. Unless, of course, an angler is heading upstream. Then forty miles of some of the best trout fishing available in northcentral Pennsylvania lie ahead.

"I know John had to catch a hundred," Igo says about a stop he made at the stream on one of his trips north with his friend John Giesey. "We fish a lot of droppers early in the season and I know he had three fish on at one time.

I was standing next to him when he did it. He said, 'Can you believe this?' It's pretty bad when you're keeping score and catch sixty or seventy fish like I did and lose."

Sometimes things are just a little off center in the mountains.

Mike Sajna is a native Pennsylvanian who has been fishing his home state's waters all of his life. He is the outdoor columnist for *Pittsburgh Magazine,* and the author of *Pennsylvania Trout and Salmon Fishing Guide* and *Buck Fever: The Deer Hunting Tradition in Pennsylvania.* His work has appeared in a wide variety of publications, including *Field & Stream, Fly Rod & Reel, Flyfishing* and *Pennsylvania Angler.*

Nineteen

Penns Creek
by Dave Johnson

The old Lewisburg and Tyrone Rail Line came through in 1872. It was an eventful year for my father, Albert W. Johnson, was born in a log cabin on the banks of Penns Creek.

Gone now, the "L & T" made this remote valley accessible, as it had not been—beckoning anglers to Tight End, where mountains cleave. Barely a trickle at first, they came, not to fish Penns, but its then rich tributaries: Laurel, Weikert, Cherry, Poe, Swift; and others—Pine, Elk and Sinking Creek—in the upper valley.

They were after brook trout, for only later came the browns. Brookies held in the feeders, migrating up and down to Penns in spring and fall. (Later the brown trout would do likewise.)

Penns Creek lies within the ridge and valley region of central Pennsylvania and rises at 1,201 feet of elevation in Penns Valley near Spring Mills. It has a drainage basin of 554 square miles, and an average gradient of 25 feet per mile in the Swift Run and Weikert stretch. The stream channel is nearly 100 feet across near Cherry Run, the mid-section of the trout water.

From its source at Penns Cave to its confluence with Pine and Elk Creek at Coburn, Penns is relatively flat—somewhat characteristic of the chalk streams of England—dropping on average eight feet per mile.

This valley through which Penns courses for nine miles is predominately agricultural, while the fourteen mile section between Coburn and Weikert is almost totally covered by forest, largely lying within the Bald Eagle State

Forest. Gently sloping contours mark the valley throughout; below Coburn steep mountains with glacier-like rock formations are characteristic.

Whitetailed deer are common throughout the area and the occasional black bear is seen. While Pennsylvania's state bird, the ruffed grouse, is sometimes flushed, the mountains here are not prime grouse habitat. Grey squirrel are abundant from Glen Iron to Coburn, while cottontail rabbits thrive in Penns Valley and below Weikert in Buffalo Valley. There are no varying hare (snowshoe rabbits). Turkey hunting is popular, as this big bird's needs are met in the mostly second-growth hardwood forest consisting largely of mixed oak, red maple and black birch. The understory is dotted with mountain laurel, the state flower, while the rugged slopes of the White Mountain Wild Area along the Catch-and-Release stretch support lush stands of rhododendron that are crowned by virgin white pine and hemlock.

The bobcat or wildcat, though seldom seen, is present. Coyotes, though rare, are documented to inhabit the hills of central Pennsylvania. There are plenty of raccoons and fox (grey and red species) some mink, and the odd beaver.

Penns Creek is brown trout water, which during a dryspell, as endured in '88, can suffer thermal stress. However, it is rare that Penns exceeds 74°, well below the upper limit for browns.

George Sholter, a Weikert native and dean of the Penns Creek masters, recalls the first browns were caught "around the turn of the century." Sholter managed a hatchery located on the little brook flowing through this hamlet (population 15). Each fall during the 30's they hand-carted 35,000 brown trout fingerlings (5-7 inches) up the tracks, as far as the "lower tunnel." This is now the Walk-in-Only section of the Catch-and-Release stretch. Closed now, the hatchery building still stands.

By the end of World War I, Penns was still the best kept secret of the locals and those with enough time and money to come here by rail. It was still excellent fishing—30 miles of prime, unpolluted pleasure.

There remained a measure of solitude until Sparse Grey Hackle (Richard Miller) tossed his line here in 1958, then wrote about it for *Sports Illustrated,* the new and immediately popular outdoor journal. (John McDonald's report on Montana's Armstrong Spring Creek appeared in the same issue.) Reaching the newsstand in time for the opening of trout fishing in Penns woods, the article inspired swarms of anxious anglers to descend upon this gem, where they might tie into "four or five huge trout, one after another—fish so big and strong that they cannot be held, but run off downstream to the end of the line

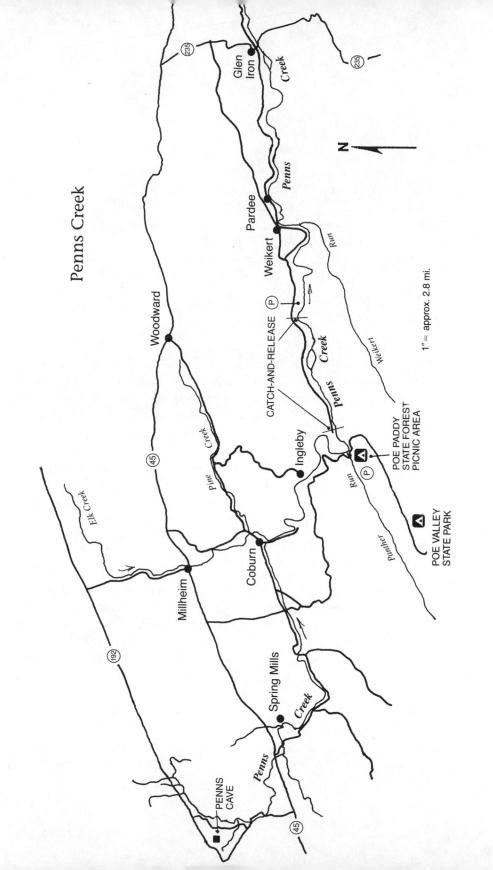

Penns Creek

and break the leader unless the fisherman has a great deal of backing line, skill and luck."

Penns Creek would never be the same!

That story was followed by many others in national publications, including *Fly Fisherman* and Trout Unlimited's *Trout,* gaining for Penns an exposure and reputation far above what anyone thought possible. By the late 60's it had gained national prominence and was mentioned alongside the legendary Catskill rivers and even the great Western waters.

Earlier it had been Cumberland Valley's limestone spring runs that drew the far-away crowds, with the Yellow Breeches likely the best known and Letort Spring Run not far behind. Among the Letort's champions were Charlie Fox, who lives aside it, and the late Vince Marinaro (*A Modern Dry Fly Code*) who had his private beat on this vintage stream.

They came and they came that spring and summer of 1958, all with their copy of *Sports Illustrated,* itching to do battle with brown and rainbow trout, "Up to seven pounds weight and possibly twice that." Wishing in no way to make light of this venerable, witty and gifted writer, nor in any manner suggest he wrote other than what he presumed to be fact, it is still my opinion that Sparse learned more from hearsay than from in-depth experience on Penns' waters.

I have fished Penns Creek for over 50 years. I fished it first at the ripe age of ten; and after 1937 whenever I could, which when school was out, was everyday, sometimes all day. (Daddy had bought a summer place along the Creek, just down from where Cherry Run joins, on land his Uncle William had inherited from his father.) My younger brothers Fred and Van came to love it too.

The truth about Penns Creek, as I've found it, and as have the many Penns Creek regulars I've met, is that it lies somewhere between its numerous, glowing accounts and the realities of modern trout fishing. Were you to believe all that has been written about it, you might think it to be not just one of the best in the East, but one of the best in the country. Make no mistake: Penns is among the better limestoners in this state and is certainly the largest. Pennsylvania Fish Commission studies in the Catch-and-Release stretch (depressed some since the '88 drought, though now recovering) showed that the stream here harbors more than 150 trout per acre. Based on this, Penns clearly rates as Blue Ribbon water.

Acid precipitation has not adversely impacted Penns Creek. With a pH reading of 8 at Weikert, buffering action is sufficient to negate any threat on that score.

Surveys show brown trout spawning as adequate. The majority of the browns are in the 287 mm (11 inch) size range. These fish exhibit good growth rates with 18 month old individuals averaging 184 mm (7 inch) in total length and 30 month old individuals averaging 279 mm (11 inch) in total length. Some larger fish are present but very few exceed 508 mm (20 inch).

The stocked (Class B) water up and down from the Catch-and-Release Project, though not quite as productive, is good enough. In fact, anglers will encounter less pressure there later in the season than on the Project section.

What's so special about Penns is these fish are chiefly wild trout recruited primarily from feeder brooks. There is also some instream spawning and this all adds up to a most impressive head of streambred natives.

Penns Creek is not, in my view, where you're likely to do battle with a seven pound trout. A five pounder would be most unusual but not impossible. Writing in *Trout Magazine* (Winter, 1982) Ron Evans, past president of Trout Unlimited's Spring Creek Chapter based in State College, noted that though some extraordinary specimens may "prowl its pools and runs, actually the number of documented 20+ inch fish caught in Penns is surprisingly small." So Penns is not really the place to go should you be after a "wallhanger."

However, the Creek does support an impressive population of 11 to 14 inch wild brown trout which are well fed, fat and sassy. And, what's so bad about that?

The best bona fide trophy I've known in my time was a majestic 25 inch beauty caught behind Little Mountain, between Weikert and Cherry Run, by the late Bill Pursley. This exceptional lunker, taken on a minnow, was never weighed, but considering the configuration of Penns Creek fish, it may well have gone six pounds.

Certainly there were other unpublicized "hogs" over the years, for the residents don't fuss much over their catch. The Kerstetter boys who work the Creek around Coburn and the upper RR tunnel took some of these. George Sholter told me that in 65 years his best trout here measured 22½ inches. And George knows a thing of two. He took this great one on a minnow below Weikert.

My red letter day, given considerable luck and credit hours, matched Sholter's. Again, it wasn't weighed. There were a couple of 21 inchers and several more edged 20 inches by "fisherman's measure." A resident 21 inch brown from Penns may be a once-in-a-lifetime prize, but it's a bragging trout on any stream.

My largest, all but one, were creeled during the famous green drake hatch. That one exception came on a minnow, when I did fish minnows.

Finest day? It was while fishing with my late brother Van, on Memorial Day weekend, below the Broadwater—now within the Catch-and-Release area. He took one 21 inches; mine went 20. Yes, it was the green drake. (Van, I felt, and not because he was a brother, was the hardest and most consistent fisherman I've known.)

Penns never was a rainbow trout stream, although Pennsylvania does have maybe a half-dozen streams that support wild rainbows. Falling Spring in Cumberland County is one. However, you will find them in the stocked sections, during the spring, since normally about one half the Fish Commission's consignments are 'bows. People do like to catch them. But a big rainbow? Not in Penns, unless it arrived via the hatchery truck.

Another fallacy regarding Penns is that it's often thought to be the bait fisherman's province. While the majority did and do fish bait, it's surprising how many switch to flies when trout start hopping.

Sunbury's Ike Siler; the Musser boys out of Lewisburg; Tater Swank, the famous fly-tier from the same town; and Samuel "Skeet" Smith—my mentor—those gentlemen knew the Creek and the value of presentation. Leading the way they used flies, sometimes exclusively. Siler tied what became locally known as Siler Specials—grey, black and brown palmer-tied wet patterns with the only variation a yellow body or tinsel.

A theory that's been kicked around here is that it is impossible to bring Penns' well-fed fish to the surface by fishing the water with big patterns when there is no natural hatch. My late Uncle Bill Steck, oftentimes said to be the "Patriarch of Penns Creek" and one of the earliest proponents of the dry fly on central Pennsylvania streams, invariably cast a brown bivisible (Hewitt's fly), one of the Wulffs, or sometimes a Royal Coachman. In 16's and 18's? Often not. Tens and twelves, and dry, for that's all he fished or knew. Part of the answer was, he worked the riffs, not the flat water, and his presentation was nearly flawless.

Another misconception revolves around float fishing. Penns Creek cannot, in the western manner, be successfully floated and fished. There's just too much shin-deep water between pools. Ditto the riffs, where much water is too low for any advantage that floating might render. A Mackenzie boat is out of the question. You can try a canoe during high water periods but you'll probably still spend most time out of the canoe.

You wade Penns, although there are good riffs and pools where casting can be done from the bank. Often it's wading in and out—walking the shoreline from one productive pool or riff to another.

Old Sparse Grey was right-on about wading Penns. Better know it can be a real buster. Not only are the currents tricky and deep, but those hidden rocks and boulders can be slick and treacherous.

Few anglers use hobnails, for in the mountains from about Ingleby to Pardee they prove a disadvantage. Most of the stones are too big and algae-covered for hobnails to grip. Better go with felt or carpet-soled boots when using hippers or waders. I waded wet for years, using nothing more than an old pair of rubber hunting boots and later on, Vietnam combat boots. Not any more, though.

The hip boot will suffice for most summer and fall fishing, but in the early spring when the Creek flows high, waders are in order. To be on the safe side, have both in the car. Some kind of wading boot is advised in Penns, for central Pennsylvania is home to the rattlesnake and copperhead. You may never encounter one, but high boots do provide insurance.

In the open water, bait fishermen far outnumber fly fishermen—certainly during the early season. After that it's a tossup.

Worms and minnows are clearly the first choice. Some use salmon eggs, feeling that "stockies" go for them, rainbows particularly. Finally, crawfish and hellgramites are good natural bait.

Today almost all bait fishermen carry spinning rods. Normally some additional weight is needed to drop the bait where the fish are—at or near bottom.

Deadly for big trout is "spinning" a minnow across and downstream around rocks and boulders, then retrieving the minnow rapidly with a little wrist action on the take-up.

From July on grasshoppers and crickets are okay if you can avoid the white chubs (fallfish) and what are known locally as "horny chubs," for the Creek has plenty of these. They love hoppers, so put in a good supply. (Fallfish grow to 16 inches and are sporty when caught on light tackle.)

THE HATCHES

Al Caucci and Bob Nastasi, authors of *Comparahatch* and *Hatches* told this writer that Penns Creek has "One of the best cross sections and populations of mayflies that one could expect to see in the limestone streams of Pennsylvania."

Al Troth *(Masters of the Nymph)* before he tracked to Dillon, Montana to be a river guide, believed it to have "The most varied insect life" he's found anywhere.

Most legendary of the bountiful hatches of mayflies is the eastern green drake *(Ephemera guttulata)* or colloquially, the shad fly, for it normally emerges after the shadbush blooms. Swarms of anglers descend on Penns hoping to deceive one of the lunker browns for which it has become known. Not so prolific as in earlier years, Penns still has, according to Caucci and Natasi, "One of the best populations of *guttulata* in the country."

Today, solitude is rare. Heaviest pressure occurs during the shad fly hatch which usually appears during late May through early June, progressing from Glen Iron to Coburn within a 10 day span. In the evening, when the spinner of this fly descends, feel lucky to have 100 feet of water to yourself. In the real hotspots, where larger fish may lie, the squeeze can be even tighter.

The best action, if it does come, usually begins at dusk. For about 45 minutes (give or take) you may, if lucky, locate a good fish and raise it, for the green drake is about the only fly to bring heavier fish to the surface (the hendrickson sometimes will).

Fish or not, the Dance-of-the-May is an unforgettable sight!

The green drake is not the only significant hatch on Penns Creek. Hen-

dricksons, numerous species of caddis (the most abundant class of flies here), sulphurs, red fox and cahills, March browns and *Isonychias* are all important.

Stoneflies come in all sizes, including the jumbo *Pteronarcys* and *Perla*. Primarily nocturnal emergers, the nymphs may remain active at any hour making those imitations an excellent choice on a daily basis.

Terrestrials should not be ignored, for they have saved the day when the going gets tough, particularly during the "dog days" of July and August. Hoppers and field crickets, the ants, including the little black and red ants and also the Carpenter ant, work when trout feed close to shore.

Other terrestrials include Japanese beetles, gypsy moth larvae, ladybird beetles, maybeetles and the 17-year locust (periodical Cicada). The latter can prove too good and might be spurned by the ethical sportsman!

THE CATCH-AND-RELEASE STRETCH

This 3.6 mile project is walk-in-only water. Now owned and managed by the Pennsylvania Fish Commission, it was Trout Unlimited (along with several landowners of whom the author takes pride in being one) who spearheaded the struggle to save this resource from put-and-take management. It was the local R.B. Winter Chapter, named for the late Raymond B. Winter from whose estate the tract was purchased, and the Penns Creek Chapter who fought the battle in the trenches.

T.U. also engineered the acquisition of the old Penn Central RR grade, which parallels the Project Area water, by the Nature Conservancy. The Conservancy then transferred it to the PA Department of Environmental Resources to be maintained as a non-motorized wilderness trail.

This special regulations area is open to artificial lures only, spinning gear or fly rods. A barbless hook rule applies. Wading is permitted, but fishing after dark is not, which assists enforcement of regulations. This section is open year-round. No trout are stocked. There is Fish Commission parking one-half mile west of Cherry Run and at Poe Paddy Camping and Picnic Area near the upper end.

General or statewide regulations apply in the remaining 27-odd miles of Penns. They are: eight trout per day, seven inches or more in length, except during the extended season from Labor Day to the end of February when the creel limit drops to three.

The season is closed from March 1 until mid-April, the opening day of the regular trout season in Pennsylvania.

All is not ideal in Camelot, however. Since Penns courses through farmland for its first eight miles, as do its tributaries, it receives considerable agricultural runoff. When downpours drench the valley, even one heavy thunderstorm, the water can color brown in a matter of hours downstream. Numerous gravel roads add to the problem. Serious trout fishing is then zapped for days.

Especially in the spring, when fishing is often best, canoe flotillas run the rapids. They usually put in at Coburn, Ingleby or Poe Paddy, often floating the entire 20 odd miles. Expect to encounter them on weekends during periods of high water.

TRAVEL INFORMATION

Reaching Penns Creek is a cinch. Locating the water you wish to fish is not so simple.

Besides the map in this book, two others are recommended: the latest *Pennsylvania Official Transportation Map* and the *Bald Eagle State Forest* map. The latter is free through the Bureau of Forestry, P.O. Box 1467, Harrisburg, PA 17120. The Bureau's map is excellent as it pinpoints all back roads and trails, contours, state parks and picnic areas, plus the streams in detail. It is a great aid for anyone fishing Penns for the first time.

In addition, there's *Trout Fishing in Pennsylvania* showing all the waterways. Write: PA Fish Commission, Publications Section, P.O. Box 1673, Harrisburg, PA 17105. Remit $1.50.

R.B. Winter State Park, 16 miles west of Lewisburg on PA Route 192 has tent and trailer campsites, as does Poe Valley State Park located about eight miles south of Millheim off PA Route 45. Motels and hotels are to be found in State College, home of Penn State football. Williamsport has ample accommodations, as does Selinsgrove on its Golden Strip along Routes 11/15. Lewisburg has several motels, plus one hotel in town.

While there's little posting along Penns, most of the property bordering the stream is private. Neither parking nor stream access is difficult, but ask permission before crossing private lands. Vandalism and improper conduct are on the increase, and are the cause of most No Trespassing and No Hunting signs you will encounter.

Dave Johnson's romance with Penns Creek stretches back more than 50 years. All of Penns is familiar ground to him, with his pet beat being that 10-mile stretch from Pardee to the "lower tunnel." He has also fished the great western rivers, as well as many other waters back east. He is currently outdoor columnist for the *Sunbury Daily Item*. Dave is a member of the Outdoor Writers Association of America and OWA Pennsylvania.

Twenty

The Youghiogheny
by Mike Sajna

At first it appeared only to be a trick of the water, an illusion of the late summer light. Then, as we rode on, I began to think it must be me, my mind reacting to a bad bit of beef, an undigested spot of mustard or, more likely, the somewhat undercooked sunny-side-up eggs I had just eaten. When we had crossed the bridge at Ohiopyle the river had been as clear as the mountain air above it, and then we stopped for breakfast and now it was as dirty as the coffee that had started our hearts. It didn't make sense.

"Tug!" I shout at my friend on the bicycle ahead of me. "Look at the river!"

He glances up from his handlebars and out at the water, but we still continue to peddle. Unable to overcome our disbelief, we keep up the pace for another hundred yards or so until enough reality sinks in to make us apply our brakes.

"What happened?" he asks.

Stunned, we stand and devise various theories for what is in front of us, the most plausible revolving around a hydroelectric plant at the dam in Confluence eleven miles upstream. It is only when we return to Ohiopyle and seek an answer from one of the rafting outfitters do we learn that the mud is the result of a rain three days earlier along the upper Casselman River in the state of Maryland.

The moral of the story, if there is such a thing, is you never know what to expect of the Youghiogheny. Of course, the same might be said about any other trout river in the world, but southwestern Pennsylvania's Yough, as it is known locally, seems to take contrariness to extremes. One day, with no hatch in sight, it will gladly surrender fifty fish to the dry fly. Then, the next day, though the weather, water temperature and everything else we are instructed to concern ourselves about are exactly the same, and there are flies everywhere, it will yield but a lone six-incher. Then a day or two later, in the middle of a bright, sweltering afternoon, it will produce one of the most beautifully colored four-pound browns imaginable. It doesn't seem to make sense. It's not the way the books and magazines say things are supposed to be. But that's the Yough.

The Youghiogheny River (pronounced Yok-a-ganee), is an Indian word meaning "A stream flowing in a contrary direction" or "In a roundabout course." Mention it in outdoor circles in the Northeast and almost certainly the first words to arise will be white water rafting, for the Yough is one of the finest and most reliable white water runs in the nation. The standing of the river in this respect is instantly evidenced by the number and variety of license plates that can be found in the parking lot above the falls in Ohiopyle on almost every weekend from early spring to mid-fall. One rafting outfitter I know even jokes that the reason the town is called Ohiopyle is because there are so many cars from Ohio in the parking lot. But then there are almost an equal number from Michigan, Maryland, Connecticut and Virginia, as well as a few from a half dozen or so other states.

Besides the exciting rapids with which Mother Nature has endowed the river, what makes the Yough so popular a white water run is the U.S. Army Corps of Engineer's flood control dam at Confluence, a few miles above the Maryland line. Controlled discharges from the dam make the river runnable 24 hours a day, 365 days a year. When other rivers in the Northeast have been turned into trickles by the summer doldrums, the Youghiogheny flows steady.

The dam at Confluence is of equal importance to fishermen. It both marks the start of the river's approximately twenty-seven miles of trout water and keeps maybe half of it cold enough to numb feet and legs to the bone even through the steamiest summer. Actually, the Yough may be most popular with fishermen during the Dog Days of August. When trout in every other stream in the area are living in suspended animation around spring seeps, the Yough's fish remain wild and full of fight.

"Most trout rivers or trout streams you can't expect to have much activity in August or September," notes Rick Lorson, area fisheries manager for the Pennsylvania Fish Commission. "But down there you expect it. Whether you're

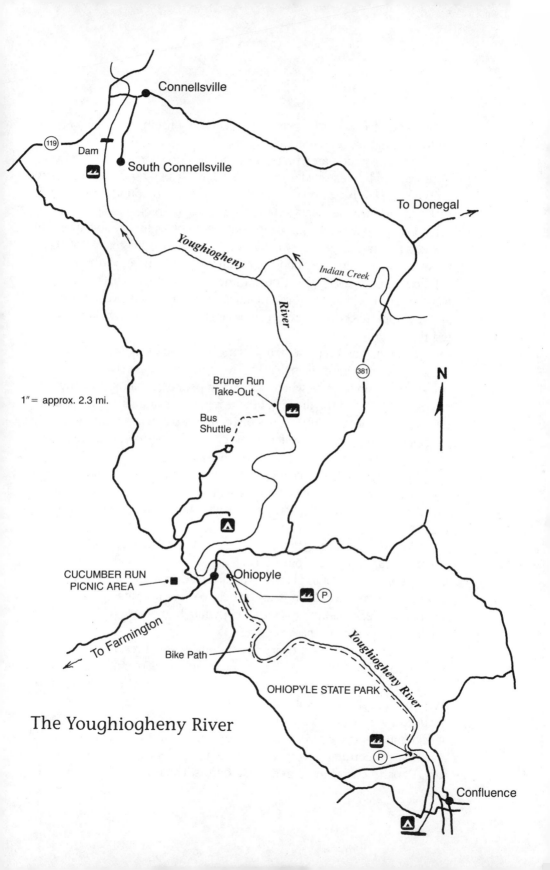

Connellsville

119

Dam

South Connellsville

To Donegal

Youghiogheny

Indian Creek

River

381

Bruner Run
Take-Out

Bus
Shuttle

1″ = approx. 2.3 mi.

N

CUCUMBER RUN
PICNIC AREA

Ohiopyle

P

To Farmington

Bike Path

Youghiogheny River

OHIOPYLE STATE PARK

P

The Youghiogheny River

Confluence

fishing with live bait, fishing with spinners or fly fishing, any one of those groups of anglers seems to have success."

Neoprene waders are a prerequisite on the upper stretches of the river's trout water, while felt soled wading shoes and a wading staff are a necessity everywhere. The bottom of the Yough is a collection of round rocks, square rocks, triangular rocks, pentagonal rocks, trapezoidal rocks, hexagonal rocks, octagonal rocks, flat rocks, just plain boulders, pebbles and some shapes only a student of fractual geometry could identify. Add a good coating of algae, powerful currents and deep pools, and extreme caution becomes the only rule to follow. Many of the Yough's trout are impossible to reach. That is the simple fact. And anglers should not be tempted to try for them. The river is full of fish and if it wants to cooperate they can be caught practically anywhere. Never test the Yough.

The recent addition of a hydroelectric facility to the dam at Confluence has caused many long time anglers here to complain that the river is "not what is used to be." In sections where stream temperatures seldom rose into the sixties, according to the diaries of those regulars, readings of over seventy degrees now occur. According to Lorson, the rise in temperature was only temporary and caused by water being drawn off the top of the reservoir, instead of the bottom, during work on the plant.

"It did not necessarily have an impact from a fish kill standpoint," Lorson says, "But it may have created a reduction in fingerling survival from the previous spring's stocking, and growth may have been affected because of that.

"Now as far as the warming goes," he continues, "that should not come into play. It's part of the stipulation of the license for the plant that if there is any warming coming into play it has to be remedied or the plant will be shut down. And there is a daily monitoring of it. We'll be keeping a close eye. We get monthly reports on that so it is pretty much in check. We don't want anything happening to that resource."

Far more dangerous and far less controllable as a threat to the Youghiogheny's trout fishery are the problems of acid rain and acid mine drainage. The Yough flows through Somerset and Fayette counties, the very heart of southwestern Pennsylvania's coal country. Although most of the mines have been out of business for decades many of them continue to discharge "yellow boy," as acid mine drainage is commonly called, into local streams and so into the main river, according to Tom Proch, an aquatic biologist with the Pennsylvania Department of Environmental Resources. The Youghiogheny's troubles come mainly from the Casselman River, which joins it at Confluence, and the monstrous, century old Shaw Mine complex outside of the Somerset County town of Meyersdale.

But the situation is improving for a combination of reasons, including treatment efforts, stricter environmental laws, a decline in the number of mining permits issued and the fact that some of the mines have been discharging yellow boy for so long, upwards of a century in the case of Shaw, that they are simply beginning to run out of the toxic water.

At the same time the effects of acid mine drainage have begun to decline, however, problems with acid rain runoff have worsened. After more than a century of being doused by rain ladened with smoke from industry to the west, the soil of the mountains around the Yough has very little buffering ability left. A decade long research project by scientists from Pennsylvania State University on Linn Run, a small stream that does not feed the Yough but lies just to the north, has shown land in the region to have the highest concentration of sulfites in the nation and one of the highest in the world.

Laurel Hill Creek, the second major tributary whose waters enter the Yough at Confluence, has a slight limestone influence and a sewage treatment plant along it that provides some buffering ability. But with less than half the flow of the Casselman River, it is not nearly large enough to fend off any surges of acid water into the main river.

Despite the fact the Youghiogheny is one of the best large trout rivers in the Northeast, it has almost no natural reproduction of trout. Lorson says he has found this to be true for both the river and its tributaries. The Yough's trout population is sustained by a fingerling stocking program that dates back to 1973 when the Fish Commission released some 160,000 browns into the river. Now, both browns and rainbows are planted.

While the Youghiogheny may not sustain a naturally reproducing population of trout, it does contain an abundant food supply to support the stocked fingerlings. Caddisflies are the dominant aquatic insect, but the river also contains a decent number of mayflies, as well as a scattering of stoneflies. Kick samples by Lorson and other Fish Commission personnel have revealed populations of black caddis, gray caddis, brown caddis, olive caddis, cinnamon caddis, *Isonychias,* blue-winged olives, March browns, blue duns, light cahills, yellow drakes, *Caenis,* sulphurs and midges. Stonefly shucks dot rocks in various locations too. Lorson does not believe the river holds many stoneflies, but a stonefly nymph fished through the riffles can be deadly.

Non-insect foods include very large and healthy populations of minnows

As is true on so many rivers, the people who float the Yough are often casual or non-fishermen. The serious anglers here fish from the bank or wade.

and crayfish, which Youghiogheny trout attack ravenously. Every fish I have ever seen taken from the river had crayfish or crayfish remains in its stomach, an observation shared by other anglers.

Trout fishing on the Youghiogheny is open year-round. Bait and lure fishermen can find success almost anytime, even during the relatively high water periods of early spring. Fly fishermen, on the other hand, generally need to wait for lower water before they start to take trout with any degree of regularity. Russ Mason, a friend who has been fishing and keeping notes on the river since the beginning, maintains it is useless to approach the Yough's trout water with fly tackle until it is down to the two feet, two-inch level. He points out that two inches of water does not mean much on the wide lower river, but the Yough around Confluence and Ohiopyle flows through a steep, narrow gorge. Compressed and speeded up by the terrain, two extra inches on the upper river can add up to a torrent impossible to fish with flies.

Although it seems impossible to say how the Yough will receive a fisherman from one day to the next, there are a few things you can do to improve your chances. During the day, fish the fast pocket water and riffles, especially if caddis are emerging. As evening approaches move to the flats and wait for insect activity and rising trout. And don't quit too early. Feeding activity on the Youghiogheny often does not commence until after dark. Staying on the river until sundown may be tougher than it sounds, though, as access to almost all of it is limited and requires either a hike, a bike ride or a float trip.

Actually, compared to many northeastern trout streams, the Youghiogheny along its trout water is a wilderness river. Confluence, population about 1,000, and Ohiopyle, population just over 100, are the only towns within the twenty-seven-mile stretch. Try finding that anywhere else in southwestern Pennsylvania.

Confluence, at the head of the river's trout water, is a backwater old lumber, mining and railroad town of mostly plain two-story frame homes and a few essential businesses built around a rather pleasant town square park. Christopher Gist, a friend of George Washington and one of the most noted explorers of western Pennsylvania, crossed the river, which he called "South Fork," on November 24, 1751 when he was working as an agent for the Ohio Company of Virginia. He called the site on which Confluence now stands "Three Forks" and then "Turkey-foot" because he thought the junction of the Youghiogheny, Casselman River and Laurel Hill Creek resembled a turkey's foot, an observation that aerial photographs have since shown to be surprisingly accurate. Turkeyfoot remains a name tourist literature still occasionally employs.

George Washington visited the site in 1754 and wrote: "Tarried there some time to examine the place, which we found very suitable for the erection of a fort, not only because it was gravelly, but also because it was at the mouth of the three branches; and in some places there was a good tough bottom on which to build." Like Pittsburgh, Confluence would arise at the meeting place of rivers, but unlike that famous city it never saw a fort. The site had no strategic importance in the great game Britain and France were playing for western Pennsylvania and the riches of the Ohio Country in the 1750s.

The first white settlers soon followed Gist and Washington, but were forced to evacuate the area in 1763 when Pontiac's Rebellion touched off a series of Indian raids on frontier settlements. The town was never attacked, but the possibility was too great for settlers to remain in the area. About ten families returned in 1765 and 1766, despite warnings from the colonial government to stay off Indian lands.

The Army Corps of Engineers' dam at Confluence is the third highest dam in Pennsylvania and backs the river up for approximately 17 miles. Construction on it began in 1939 and it was completed in 1943. The Corps suspended work on most such civilian projects after Pearl Harbor, but decided to complete the Youghiogheny Dam after study revealed that flood waters striking the partially built structure could cause as much damage to industry downstream around McKeesport as an enemy air raid.

Youghiogheny Reservoir today is one of the most popular recreation sites in southwestern Pennsylvania. Three campgrounds are maintained around it by the Corps of Engineers, including one at the dam outflow that trout anglers should find handy. The Class A campground is suitable for both tents and recreational vehicles. It is open all year and managed on a first-come, first-served basis. Information may be had by contacting the Resource Manager, Youghiogheny Lake, RD 1, Box 17, Confluence, PA 15424.

Fingerling stockings may be the main source of the Yough's trout, but the first mile of the river, from the dam to the mouth of the Casselman River, also is stocked by the Fish Commission with adult fish. From the dam to Ramcat Falls, about two miles downstream, the river is wide and mostly flat with only an occasional riffle. Access to the entire stretch is readily available off a paved road that parallels the river on its western side from the bridge at Confluence.

Below Ramcat Falls the valley through which the Youghiogheny flows narrows from a one mile width at Confluence to only 150 yards, and then the river's first rapids appears. Ramcat also marks the end of road access to the Middle Yough, as the stretch is called since it marks the exact middle of the river. For the next nine miles to Ohiopyle, the Youghiogheny is reachable only off a beautiful bicycle path or by canoe. "We also found other places where the water was rapid but not so deep, " Washington writes of the area in a description that continues to hold true, "And the current smoother, we easily passed over them, but afterwards we found little or scarce any bottom. There were mountains on both sides of the river. We went down the river about ten miles."

The Youghiogheny cuts through two major mountains: Laurel Hill below Ramcat and Chestnut Ridge below Ohiopyle. Except for the lower half of Chestnut Gap, Laurel Hill Gap is the widest and most open, offering a succession of incredibly beautiful views of mountains towering a thousand feet and more above the riverbed. The rapids are gentle, not usually more than sharp Class II in even high water, and easily handled by anglers with just basic canoeing abilities.

Not too long ago the river between Confluence and Ohiopyle was the

sole domain of a few kayakers and anglers willing to hike the old railroad grade on which the bike path was built. The purchase of the grade by the Western Pennsylvania Conservancy and construction of the path, along with a push by rafting outfitters in Ohiopyle to exploit more of the river, has ended that splendid isolation. Close to 50,000 people now float the section annually. Where once a fisherman could stand in the river and hear only the rush of water over rock, he is now just as likely to hear the laughter and squeals of canoeists and cyclists. But the distraction does not seem to have ruined the fishing.

Both the bike path and take-out point for canoeists lie a short distance above the bridge at Ohiopyle. Below the bridge lies Ohiopyle Falls, the place where George Washington wrote, "It became so rapid as to oblige us to come ashore." Downstream at the falls he ended his journey, as well as his plans for using the Yough as a means to transport troops for an attack on the French in Fort Duquesne (otherwise known as Forks of the Ohio, or, later, Pittsburgh).

Ohiopyle, like Confluence, is a town a person would have to want to visit to be there, for no main road runs through it. Or even near it. The town was settled in 1770, making it one of the last communities established in the region. Philadelphia and Baltimore, less than 250 miles to the east, were already over 100 years old at the time. The reason Ohiopyle was settled so late is evident on every trip into town. Mountains surround everything. Roads leading in burn up the brakes, roads leading out often require downshifting into second gear.

Nevertheless, people have been coming to enjoy a day along the river and its falls for over a century. Excursion trains once made regular runs to the town from Pittsburgh. Over one million people a year visit Ohiopyle State Park today. They come to camp, fish, picnic, sightsee and, especially, raft. The commercially rafted section of the river from just below the falls to Bruner Run, a distance of about seven miles, would be completely overrun by people if it were not for the fact park officials limit traffic on it to 960 commercial spots and 960 private spots per day.

Ohiopyle, meaning "water whitened by froth," caters to its visitors far more than does Confluence. In addition to rafting outfitters and the expanded services they offer, it holds a visitor's center, restaurants, changing rooms, observation decks for viewing the river, a huge parking lot, a youth hostel and loads of other amenities. Only a minimal amount of tackle, especially fly tackle, is available, however.

For anglers interested in camping in the area, Ohiopyle State Park has a

223-site Class A campground with hot showers, flush toilets, a dump station, a contact station to secure permits and park information and four playgrounds. The campground is open year-round. Due to all the rafters, however, reservations are required. They are accepted throughout the year by contacting: Ohiopyle State Park, Department of Environmental Resources, P.O. Box 105, Ohiopyle, PA 15470.

Limited accommodations also are available at the Ohiopyle Youth Hostel. Reservations are suggested. Details may be had by writing the Pittsburgh Council, American Youth Hostel Inc., 6300 Fifth Avenue, Pittsburgh, PA 15232.

Both canoes and bicycles for use on the Middle Yough are available for rent from outfitters in Confluence and Ohiopyle. A fishing guide service also operates out of Confluence. Further information may be had by contacting: Laurel Highlands Tourist Promotion Agency, 120 E. Main Street, Ligonier, PA 15658.

Float fishing out of a raft is possible along the Youghiogheny's whitewater section, but the succession of rapids running up to Class IV stop all but a few people. Most angling is from the bank and access is off hiking trails or two railroad grades, one abandoned, the other active. Since the hiking trails are rather convoluted and numerous, the best approach is to stop at the park headquarters, visitors center or campground and acquire a free map.

The river from Ohiopyle downstream is called the Lower Yough. Like the middle river, it flows through a gorgeous, steep-walled gorge dressed in mountain laurel, hemlock, wildflowers and numerous varieties of hardwoods. Twelve major rapids dot the stretch, but most of them are near the beginning and end of the run. Though the stretch is heavily used, most rafting trips are finished by mid-afternoon, leaving the angler alone on the river as shadows lengthen.

Bruner Run to South Connellsville is the last portion of the Youghiogheny's trout water, and its nine miles are among the most isolated and least used on the river. While a road does touch it about a third of the way along the run, no hiking trails or bike paths follow it (though plans are in the works to extend the bike path along it). Floating is difficult because of the more than 30-mile shuffle involved, and the fact that a collection of Class II and III rapids lie near the start. These are tough for novice canoeists or rafters to handle without a portage. Then, too, floaters must contact the park office a day or two in advance to make arrangements for the gate to be opened at Bruner Run. Otherwise, it is an arduous 1.5-mile walk with a canoe or raft from the parking lot to the water.

The first part of the Bruner Run to South Connellsville stretch of the Yough is much the same as the river above, with plenty of beautiful views of the surrounding mountains, steep rock walls and lush forests. Near Indian Creek, which adds another shot of yellow boy to the river from the mining activity along it, the Yough begins to widen and warm. The water becomes somewhat marginal for trout, but still holds some nice fish, though in smaller numbers. More smallmouth bass begin to appear.

Mike Sajna is a native Pennsylvanian who has been fishing his home state's waters all of his life. He is the outdoor columnist for *Pittsburgh Magazine*, and the author of *Pennsylvania Trout and Salmon Fishing Guide* and *Buck Fever: The Deer Hunting Tradition in Pennsylvania*. His work has appeared in a wide variety of publications, including *Field & Stream*, *Fly Rod & Reel*, *Flyfishing* and *Pennsylvania Angler*.